A Decade with LESA

The Evolution of Land Evaluation and Site Assessment

This book is based on selected papers presented at the first national LESA conference organized by John Keller.

A Decade with LESA

The Evolution of Land Evaluation and Site Assessment

Edited by Frederick R. Steiner, James R. Pease, and Robert E. Coughlin

Published by the
Soil and Water Conservation Society

Manufactured in the United States of America

Library of Congress Catalog Card No. 93-35710

ISBN 0-935734-30-9

Library of Congress Cataloging-in-Publication Data

A Decade with LESA: The Evolution of Land Evaluation and Site Assessment / edited by Frederick R. Steiner, James R. Pease, and Robert E. Coughlin.
p. cm.
Based on selected papers presented at the first national LESA conference, held in Kansas City, Mo., Mar. 26-28, 1992.
Includes bibliographical references and index.
ISBN 0-935734-30-9 (pbk.)
1. Land use, Rural--United States--Evaluation--Congresses. 2. Land capability for agriculture--United States--Evaluation--Congresses. 3. Land use, Rural--United States--Planning. I. Steiner, Frederick R. II. Pease, James R. (James Robert) III. Coughlin, Robert E.
HD256.D43 1994
333.76'15'0973--dc20 93-35710

Contents

Preface

This book is based on the first national LESA conference held March 26-28, 1992, in Kansas City, Missouri. The meeting was organized to assess the first 10 years of experience with the U.S. Soil Conservation Service's land evaluation and site assessment system. John W. Keller, professor of planning at Kansas State University, coordinated arrangements for the conference and deserves special credit for the time, energy, and thought devoted to the organization of facilities and speakers. We are grateful to him as well as to the conference hosts—the Department of Community and Regional Planning, Kansas State University, and the Small Town and Rural Planning Division of the American Planning Association. We also appreciate the assistance of the conference organizing committee—Norm Berg, David Dyer, Nancy Bushwick Malloy, Neil Sampson, Max Schnepf, Lynn Sprague, Lloyd Wright, and Warren Zitzmann, who assisted us in organizing the format and content of the program for the conference.

The conference and this book were made possible through cooperative agreements between the U.S. Soil Conservation Service and Arizona State University, Oregon State University, the University of Pennsylvania, and Kansas State University (Agreements 68-3A75-0-162, 68-3A75-1-48, and 68-3A75-2-3). Other sponsors of the conference included the Soil and Water Conservation Society, the National Association of Conservation Districts, the American Farmland Trust, and American Forests (formerly the American Forestry Association).

Several graduate students from the cooperating universities participated in the research for some of the chapters in this book. They included John Leach, Lyssa Papazian, Joyce Pressley, Christine Shaw, and Adam Sussman. Sasha Valdez administered many of the budgetary details with the cooperative agreement. Stefani Angstadt-Leto coordinated much of the correspondence with authors and reviewers and typed large sections of the manuscript.

We appreciate the time many individuals took reviewing papers for this book. Their comments were most helpful. The reviewers included: Richard Bowen, Kenneth Brooks, William Budd, Tom Daniels, Michael DeMers, Carol Ferguson, Ralph Grossi, Christopher Hamilton, Nancy Bushwick Malloy, Lee Nellis, Jim Riggle, and Gene Yagow. Jim Riggle and Jim Cubie were helpful liaisons with the office of Senator Patrick Leahy. Max Schnepf of the Soil and Water Conservation Society played a key supportive role in initiating and encouraging the publication of this book. We also appreciate the assistance of Doug Snyder, Anne Kindl, and Joann Schissel of the Soil and Water Conservation Society who crafted our manuscript into a book.

Throughout the effort of organizing the conference and preparing this book, crucial guidance and support has been provided by Lloyd E. Wright of the U.S. Soil Conservation Service. He is the principal originator of LESA and has been an influential advocate for the protection of farmland within SCS and other federal agencies.

Frederick R. Steiner
Arizona State University
James R. Pease
Oregon State University
Robert E. Coughlin
University of Pennsylvania

Foreword

Patrick J. Leahy

In my home state of Vermont, farmland protection is serious business. That was not always the case, though, and in many ways we Vermonters learned our lessons the hard way. While our land area is now about three-fourths forested, there was a time when early settlers cleared and tried to grow crops or graze livestock on nearly all the land, including steep hills and fragile soils. The resulting ravages of soil erosion and crop failures demonstrated the importance of our prime valley farmlands.

With that experience as a backdrop, I have long been an outspoken advocate of the need for active efforts to protect agricultural lands. I supported passage of the Farmland Protection Policy Act at the federal level in 1981, believing it would reinforce the growing number of state and local initiatives on this important issue. Shortly thereafter the Soil Conservation Service in USDA developed the land evaluation and site assessment system, LESA as it became known, to evaluate federal agency projects that threaten to convert farmland.

More than a decade later LESA programs are serving the cause of farmland protection in states and local communities across the country. The articles and essays contained in this book offer thoughtful and historical perspectives on this valuable decision-making tool. I am grateful that USDA sponsored the 1992 conference in Kansas City that produced this volume, and I hope readers will apply the lessons conveyed by the authors herein.

Introduction

Soil Conservation Service photo

Introduction

Frederick R. Steiner

In 1981, the U.S. Soil Conservation Service launched a new system to make objective ratings of the agricultural suitability of land against demands for other uses. The land evaluation and site assessment (LESA) system is designed to help elected officials, citizens, farmers, soil conservationists, and planners rate a tract's soil potential for agriculture, as well as social and economic factors, such as location, access to market, and adjacent land use.

Soon after it was designed, LESA became a procedural tool at the federal level for identifying and taking into account the adverse effects of federal programs on farmland protection, and to ensure that federal programs, to the extent practical, are compatible with state, local, and private programs and policies to protect farmland. These requirements are spelled out in the Farmland Protection Policy Act of 1981 (Public Law 97-98) and its subsequent amendments.

Many state and local governments also use LESA. The rating system is often modified to reflect local conditions. Once a state or local government has adopted a LESA system, it may become part of that government's land use planning program. One incentive for the adoption of a local LESA system is that federal agencies must use a certified local LESA system in project reviews. The Soil Conservation Service (SCS) state conservationist is responsible for certification according to national criteria. Local adaptation might allow the state or locality more control when federal projects are proposed because impacts would be evaluated according to criteria generated by the state or community.

Why Was LESA Designed?

It seemed to SCS and local government officials in the late 1970s and early 1980s that standard soil surveys did not provide enough information to meet public policy needs regarding issues of farmland conversion and farmland protection. Thus, the soil science aspects of land evaluation were merged with the social and economic criteria of site assessment to create a comprehensive planning tool (*3*).

The land evaluation (LE) portion of the system is a process of rating soils for a given area from best to poorest for a specific agricultural use. A relative value is determined for each soil type. The LE may use one or a combination of various existing rating systems, such as the land capability classifications, important farmlands classifications, soil productivity ratings, or soil potential ratings. Factors included in the site assessment (SA) portion of a LESA system can include parcel size, relationship with nearby land uses, land-use regulations, farm-use taxation status, impacts of proposed use compatibility with local comprehensive or general plans, and proximity to urban areas (*3*). LE and SA factors for a particular parcel are given scores (sometimes weighted), which, when totaled, indicate to local officials the parcel's relative agricultural value.

A local LESA system is often designed by a committee of farmers, extension agents, citizens, planners, scientists, and elected officials, with advice from SCS. Only the jurisdiction can determine what importance to attach to LESA in determining future uses of agricultural land; in a few cases, evaluations are binding. In most cases, LESA scores are part of the background information to aid in the decision-making process.

Need for Research

SCS is required by Congress to submit an annual report on farmland protection activity, including the use of LESA. A census of LESA systems, however, had not been completed since 1987 (*2*). That survey reported at least 46 local governments in 19 states were actively using LESA (*2*). Twenty of the active programs were in Illinois. The state with the next most LESA systems was Virginia with four. Not only had no count of LESA systems been undertaken since 1987, there had been little critical analysis of LESA.

As a result, a project was proposed to SCS to inventory and analyze existing LESA systems and to make recommendations for improving LESA. The research addressed the needs for more information about state and local LESA systems by posing the following questions:

- How many state, metropolitan, county, and local units of government are using the LESA system? Besides farmland, what other resource lands are being rated by a LESA type system? What is the geographic distribution?
- What are the characteristics of the existing LESA systems? What factors and weights are employed?
- How is LESA used as part of local, regional, and state resource lands protection programs?
- What are the strengths and weaknesses of existing LESA systems and the ways they are used?
- How could LESA systems be improved to more reliably rate resource lands? How could they be used more effectively in implementing federal, state, and local policy for the protection of resource lands?

In order to answer those questions, a three-phase research program was developed. In phase 1, a nationwide inventory of existing state, regional, county, and municipal LESA programs was conducted (*1*). In phase 2, the technical reliability of existing LESA systems was evaluated. In phase 3, improvements for the design of LESA systems were recommended.

The Reliability of LESA

The technical reliability of existing LESA systems was evaluated through specific case studies (see chapters 7 and 8). LESA was further assessed during a national LESA conference held March 26-28, 1992, in Kansas City, Missouri. The conference brought together LESA practitioners from throughout the United States and attracted participants from Canada and England. The presenters at the conference represented many types of organizations, including SCS, state and local agencies, business, and non-profit groups. Soil scientists, planners, geographers, engineers, economists, landscape architects, and others participated. Selected papers from the conference were reviewed and revised and are published here as chapters in this book.

In chapter 1, Ralph Grossi of the American Farmland Trust, provides an overview of farmland protection in the U.S. He notes that ultimately land use is a local issue in spite of all the federal and state agency land protection efforts (though federal policy has enormous influence). LESA can be an important component of local land use decision making.

The next three chapters constitute the first part of the book and address the history and status of LESA. Chapters 2 and 3 present a federal perspective of LESA—first Lloyd Wright of SCS describes the development and status of LESA and then Galen Bridge, also of SCS, assesses how well LESA is helping implement the federal Farmland Protection Policy Act.

In chapter 4, the results of a nationwide survey of state and local LESA systems are summarized (*1*). The study identified 212 local and state governments in 31 states as current, former, or future users of LESA. Of these, 138 local governments are currently using LESA. Most local LESA systems have been adopted by counties. These local systems are mainly found in metropolitan areas or other locations where there are strong development pressures.

The next five chapters form the second part of the book—an evaluation of LESA systems. In chapter 5, Herbert Huddleston of Oregon State University, addresses agriproductivity and thresholds for decision making in LESA systems. Based on experience in Oregon, he argues that the focus of a LESA rating system should be on a single kind of land use for maximum effectiveness. In the sixth and seventh chapters, James R. Pease and Adam Sussman, also of Oregon State University, describe a five-point approach to evaluate LESA models, and discuss how LESA models can be benchmarked using the Delphi expert opinion panel method. They use an Oregon case study to apply the procedures and discuss the results.

Robert E. Coughlin, senior fellow at the University of Pennsylvania, discusses sensitivity, ambiguity, and redundancy in LESA systems in chapter 8. He addresses four specific questions. First, how sensitive are LESA scores to the many weights that are built into the system? Second, to what extent do ambiguities in interpreting LESA scores actually result from the fact that final scores are made up of a variety of mixes of LE and SA characteristics? Third, to what extent do LESA models contain redundant factors, which add to the complexity of rating but bring little additional independent information into the evaluation? Fourth, to what extent do people knowledgeable about farmland and farmland protection experts find that local LESA system scores are reasonable and consistent with the judgments they would make as experts?

LESA application in Hawaii is the focus of chapter 9. Therein Carol Ferguson and Richard Bowen of the University of Hawaii discuss the political context, the Hawaii LESA model, and make recommendations for LESA improvements. Hawaii was one of the first state governments to embrace LESA and remains the only state to have developed an area-wide system for all agricultural land within its jurisdiction. The experience in Hawaii indicates that a changing policy environment over time requires continuous adaptation of a LESA system to support decision making about land use.

Six more chapters forming the third part of the book address applications of LESA. James Riggle traces the development of LESA as part of the Illinois Farmland Protection Program in chapter 10. He describes the Illinois program as a management decision-making system. Illinois has adopted a course of action designed to minimize the amount and quality of agricultural land converted directly or indirectly by government agencies, and to do so for the lowest administrative costs.

Lancaster County, Pennsylvania, is the topic of chapter 11. Thomas Daniels analyzes how the LESA system has been used as part of a purchase of development rights program. He describes how LESA can be used as an analytical tool to rank applications for the sale of development rights and implement different farmland protection strategies.

In chapter 12, planning consultant Lee Nellis describes how LESA has been linked to local land-use planning in Idaho. He describes constraints to rural land-use planning and how LESA can be used as an analytical tool. Nellis contends that rural communities can use LESA in their efforts to maintain a rural identity and a viable agricultural economy. He uses examples from planning efforts of two eastern Idaho counties to explain where development of a LESA system fits into the local land-use planning process; to show how a LESA system may be used as one basis for the implementation of a local comprehensive plan; and to suggest that development of a LESA system should be standard practice in planning for any community where agricultural lands are an important economic asset or an essential element in the character of the local landscape.

Chapters 13, 14, and 15 address the linkage of LESA with geographic information systems (GIS). In chapter 13, Christopher Hamilton describes the use of GIS in a forestry LESA study in Vermont. Then Gene Yagow and Vernon Shanholtz of Virginia Polytechnic Institute and State University analyze how the utility of LESA may be extended through a GIS template. Michael DeMers of New Mexico State University discusses the requirements for GIS LESA modeling in chapter 15.

In conclusion, Nancy Bushwick Malloy of the National Center for Food and Agricultural Policy and Joyce Pressley of the University of Illinois, probe the weaknesses of LESA and make recommendations for its improvement. Their comments are based on workshops conducted at the 1992 national LESA conference. They note that the next decade may bring much more widespread use of LESA. The application of LESA systems may be enhanced by application of results, better training for those developing the system, and by technical progress made with GIS advances.

The Refinement of LESA

As this book goes to print, the LESA handbook is being revised. The national LESA handbook (*3*) was issued in 1983 in order to guide state and local governments interested in formulating and implementing LESA systems. At the time, few LESA systems had been prepared and the jurisdictions that had adopted them had little experience in actually using them. Since then, the use of LESA has become much more widespread.

At the first national LESA conference, workshops were conducted to explore the adequacy of the SCS LESA handbook (*3*) and to make recommendations on any changes that should be made to it. The conferees recommended that the handbook be rewritten as soon as possible. The new handbook should be much easier to use than the existing handbook. In addition, it should embody the lessons learned during the decade since the original handbook was issued.

The revision of the LESA handbook is now well underway. The new handbook as well as this book should help those interested in LESA learn from the experience of others. With such a foundation, LESA will continue to evolve. As states and local governments continue to adapt LESA, refinements can be based on the knowledge gained from critical review and analysis.

References

1. Steiner, F., J. R. Pease, R. E. Coughlin, J. C. Leach, J. A. Pressley, A. P. Sussman, and C. Shaw. 1991. *Agricultural Land Evaluation and Site Assessment: Status of State and Local Programs.* The Herberger Center, College of Architecture and Environmental Design, Arizona State University, Tempe.
2. Steiner, F., R. Dunford, and N. Dosdall. 1987. *The Use of the Agricultural Land Evaluation and Site Assessment System in the United States.* Landscape and Urban Planning 14:183-199.
3. U.S. Department of Agriculture-Soil Conservation Service. 1983. *National Agricultural Land Evaluation and Site Assessment Handbook.* Washington, D.C.

SECTION I

LESA: History and Status

1

Farmland Preservation: A Decade Later

Ralph Grossi

In the Fall of 1981, many of us celebrated the passage of the federal Farmland Protection Policy Act (FPPA)—landmark legislation that would provide a powerful new tool in the protection of this nation's most productive farmland. Today, a dozen years later, we still await full implementation of the FPPA! The Reagan and Bush administrations showed little interest in, and sometimes hostility to, farmland protection. And so, the law has been bureaucratically buried until early in the Clinton administration. We should not dwell on past frustrations, however, but should instead focus on the promise of one of the very useful farmland protection tools available to governments—the land evaluation and site assessment (LESA) system.

The development of the LESA system was a response to a woeful lack of analytical tools for local and state governments on which to base land-use decisions and was inspired by the 1981 National Agricultural Lands Study (NALS). The NALS also was the inspiration for American Farmland Trust, established to assure that farmland protection had a strong advocate in the private sector. There has been a lot of debate since the release of NALS about how much farmland the United States is losing to urbanization. The NALS suggested three million acres per year. The Soil Conservation Service is now estimating more than two million acres lost per year (*2*).

Whether it is one, two, or three million acres that are being lost from agriculture, the point is we are wasting a valuable, irreplaceable resource. And it is valuable. Let us not get hung up over precise numbers. The loss of even two million acres per year assumes greater significance when considering that the loss includes some of the best land this country has available to produce food and fiber. That is not a surprise, but it is an alarm bell. Most cities across the heartland and on the coastal plains and valleys were settled as agricultural communities. Our ancestors settled where the best farmland was, and it is that land that is lost first. Let me give you an example from my home state. The Central Valley of California is one of the most productive regions in the world. The Highway 99 corridor through the Valley is where the best, most inherently productive land is located. This land requires the least irrigation, water transfer, horsepower, fertilizer, and chemicals per unit of production. It is in the midst of this land that the cities of Sacramento, Stockton, Modesto, Fresno, and Bakersfield grew up—and continue to grow. The County of Fresno, for instance, already has 55,000 acres of productive farmland inside its sphere of influence (land designated for future urbanization) and it continues to annex more land to control its future use (*1*).

Over the long term the urbanization of this highly productive land is causing agriculture to shift away from the most inherently productive land on to less productive and more environmentally sensitive lands. The issue of farmland protection is much more than just a concern about acres. It is a case of building into the food production and distribution system liabilities that will haunt our children and grandchildren. Not only is this nation having to rely increasingly on long distance transportation for its food supply but the land that is relied upon to replace urbanized farmland is often associated with environmental conflict.

Again, the Central Valley is a case in point. The continuing loss of prime land on one side of the San Joaquin Valley has been masked by expanded production on the west. But farming on the west side requires massive water transfers—an increasingly precious resource in California—and the environmental costs of farming this relatively poor land are only now becoming evident. The selenium problem at Kesterson National Wildlife Refuge is just one example.

This nation has always had abundant food production, but part of the reason is that we've always had a new frontier available to us. When we used up the land in the Northeast, we simply moved south and west, down through the Ohio Valley; out across the Plains and on to the West Coast. When we ran out of new geographical frontiers we relied on mechanical, chemical, and technological frontiers to enhance production. But, there is reason to believe that those rapid productivity gains of the last 50 years are tapering off. National average yields in corn production in 1991 were about equal to what they were 10 years ago—the first decade in this century when we have not had a continuing upward trend in productivity (*3*). Is the apparent leveling of the yield curve a temporary occurrence? Or, is it an indicator that technology is running up against the natural limits of the land? In any case, it seems risky to count on continuing technological advances for future food production. Biotechnology holds great promise. A new generation of genetics, chemical, and other production enhancers may just be around the corner, but can we take the chance?

It is therefore prudent to protect the land, especially our best land, as insurance. Why build into our food system the kinds of risks and costs, including the external costs, associated with farming land that is less productive? One caution about the food supply issue: this nation is developing a heavy reliance on imported food and fiber. At current trends, in less than 15 years, we will be net importers of food and fiber. Ten years ago the food and fiber export surplus was $23 billion. Now it is $11 billion (*3*)—much of the reduction due to an increased reliance on Central and South America for fresh fruits and vegetables. To some extent, that can be connected to the rapid urban expansion onto the coastal farmland of California and Florida where most of the high value winter vegetables and citrus crops are grown. I am not suggesting that we shouldn't have free trade, but these are issues that should be debated in the public policy arena. Free trade of food isn't quite the same as free trade of cars and computers in the eyes of most of the public. For one thing, unlike factories, it is unlikely that we could ever "rebuild" those unique coastal farmlands once they are covered with concrete.

The reasons for increased interest in farmland protection today are not always connected to food at all. Quality of life seems to be of greater importance to the American public, especially the suburbanites who are now a majority, and farmland protection is one of the tools to ensure that their open spaces remain intact. The *Compact Cities* report in 1980 documented the real linkage between development patterns and other issues such as energy consumption (*4*). Since then, we have been reminded all too often of the related problems of air pollution, inner city deterioration, and the frustrations resulting from the increasing distance between a person's job and home. The fallout from poorly planned, sprawling development is now evident also in the fiscal crises facing local and state governments, as "bedroom" communities struggle to provide public services to a widely scattered population.

The constituency for farmland protection today is as likely to be built around open space, recreation, wildlife habitats, and the image of the family farm as it is a concern about food production. The suburbanites who make up this constituency represent a potentially powerful coalition to address this issue to the benefit of all. Our challenge is to make sure that they understand that while they are trying to preserve the land, there are real people out there trying to make a living from it. That balance between the recognition of the societal values associated with land preservation and the economic reality of the farmer is a real concern at AFT. As we develop protection programs, we have to make sure that there is some kind of connection and balance between the two.

Ten Years of Progress

The past decade has seen both success and setbacks in farmland protection. The 1981 FPPA, as amended in 1985 and 1990, was intended to be the centerpiece of farmland protection. It calls on the federal government not only to curb spending that wastes farmland but also to respect the hundreds of state and local programs that are trying to protect it. The failure of the Reagan and Bush administrations to enforce it was a major disappointment. In 1990, the Farms for the Future Act, a chapter of the Farm Bill, established the first federal cost-sharing for the purchase of agricultural conservation easements, or purchase of development rights (PDR), on a state matching basis, though the appropriation was very modest. Together, these laws represent a needed shift of farm programs toward the objective of protecting rather than destroying the nation's farmland.

It is at the state level where most of the farmland protection activity has been undertaken. There are now 12 states with direct compensatory programs like PDR or transfer of development rights (TDR) that protect farmland while respecting property rights and contributing to the local economy. There are about 200,000 acres that have been protected under PDR programs in the United States as of today. Nearly half of that is in one state, Maryland. The rest is scattered, mostly in the Northeast. The most aggressive new program is in Pennsylvania where the voters initially passed a $100 million bond issue in 1987. In 1991 the legislature passed a cigarette tax that will generate about $20 million per year for farmland protection. Delaware is the most recent state to add a PDR program, which passed in 1991, but is not yet funded.

Funding for compensatory programs is always a big issue. Critics often cite the high up-front cost as a reason to dismiss tools such as PDR, usually without having carefully researched the issue. Here are a few important points about purchasing conservation easements to keep in mind:

- Many farmers in a given area will continue to farm and will not seek compensation from development rights.
- The cost of a conservation easement program can be spread out over many years. Even the most aggressive compensatory programs are purchasing easements on less than five percent of farms per year.
- The saving in avoided costs of future public services to that property may alone be greater than the initial cost.
- The permanence of conservation easements is reassuring to the taxpayers who are footing the bill.
- The option to sell an easement is an important "carrot" to accompany the "stick" of zoning in gaining farmer support for comprehensive programs.

Historically, PDR programs have been funded either by direct appropriation, sale of bonds, or special dedicated tax revenue. Future efforts will probably continue using these methods of financing with the probable addition of more creative techniques like special taxation districts (such as California's Mello-Roos authority) and limited development clusters—creating a market for land protection. The case for compensatory programs continues to grow stronger. As the fiscal impacts of sprawling development become painfully evident all across the country, growth control that includes farmland protection is gaining momentum. Farmland pays more in property taxes than it demands in public services—cows don't go to school.

Ultimately land use is a local issue in most of the United States. In spite of all the federal and state agencies' land protection efforts, most land-use decisions are made at the local level (though federal policy has enormous influence over them). Even the statewide PDR programs are often at county option. In Pennsylvania, each county must establish its own program to qualify for state funding. In King County, Washington, voters taxed themselves to spend $50 million to protect farmland around Seattle. The Marin County, California, program that I was involved with is a public/private partnership with a local land trust. The Marin Agricultural Land Trust (MALT) has raised money through a variety of techniques to buy easements, but it was the sale of general obligation bonds through the county government that has been critical to its success. Marin County may have the most successful of the private county programs in the United States. They now have 23,000 acres under easement that have been purchased or donated to the local land trust. But they, too, will run out of money shortly if they don't find another source of revenue.

There are also statewide land trusts like the Vermont Land Trust that work very well with state programs. And in Maryland, the Maryland Environmental Trust (MET) is the private counterpart to the state and county PDR programs. The MET works with landowners who are motivated to donate easements over their land for the tax benefits that can reduce both income and estate tax liabilities, helping to keep the land in the family through generational transfers.

Our own organization has provided assistance to many local land trusts by providing technical assistance and occasionally a little financial help with real estate transactions. But AFT is really a policy organization. We see our job as helping to establish farmland protection programs and making sure that the programs are comprehensive. We will not recommend a program that is simply a PDR program. There has to be more to it than that, including a sound regulatory framework. "Regulatory" sounds terrible these days but successful farmland protection programs must include a balance of compensatory and regulatory land conservation techniques. This is especially true for county programs. Agricultural districts, agricultural protection zoning, right-to-farm laws, and direct marketing opportunities are critical components of a successful program. As noted earlier, PDR programs are an important "carrot" that help attain the support of the farm community for agricultural zoning. This is critical because PDR alone is simply not going to get the job done. To ensure that the regulatory aspects of a farmland protection program are equitable and consistent, systems like LESA are very useful.

LESA is a land use-planning tool for agriculture. I want to emphasize *for agriculture* because what we have very little of in this country is planning for agriculture. In most communities around the country, the community-wide planning process involves planning for everything else: for residential development, open space, low and moderate income housing, highway transportation, and public services. Agriculture usually gets what's left over! Agriculture needs to be elevated to the same priority as other land uses in the planning process. The LESA system helps do that.

References

1. American Farmland Trust. 1989. *Risks, Challenges, and Opportunities; Agriculture, Resources and Growth in a Changing Central Valley.* Washington, D.C.
2. Andreucetti, E. 1992. Personal interview. U.S. Department of Agriculture, Soil Conservation Service.
3. O'Connell, P. 1991. Personal interview. U.S. Department of Agriculture, Cooperative State Research Service. Washington, D.C.
4. Subcommittee on the City, Committee on Banking, Finance and Urban Affairs, U.S. House of Representatives. 1980. *Compact Cities: Energy Saving Strategies for the Eighties.* July, 1980. Washington, D.C.

Soil Conservation Service photo

2 The Development and Status of LESA

Lloyd E. Wright

The agricultural land evaluation and site assessment (LESA) system was created by the Soil Conservation Service (SCS) in 1981 as a tool for local, state, and federal officials to determine which lands at a specific location should be given the highest level of protection from conversion to non-agricultural uses (*6*). LESA identifies the best land in the most valuable agricultural regions, allowing local governments to direct development to non-productive or less productive lands and areas that will have the least impact on agriculture.

LESA was designed in 1981, at a time when there were great concerns with the high rate of farmland conversion.

The National Agricultural Lands Study (NALS), completed in 1981, found that three million acres (later estimates revised that amount to 2.2 to 2.5 million acres) of farmland were being converted to nonagricultural uses each year (*1*), much of which was the most productive farmland.

The *Compact Cities: Energy Saving Strategy for the Eighties* report concluded that even if the United States has a surplus of farmland, there is "strong justification for development and implementation of programs to retain farmland" (*4*) in order to maintain quality of life and use land and other resources effectively and efficiently.

Many local and state governments were designing programs and policies to protect farmland. Some officials were developing programs to protect all prime farmland without regard to location, while others proposed to protect only prime farmland, with no provisions for other lands that were important to agriculture. LESA was created as a tool to assist local officials in identifying farmland for protection by taking into account not only soil quality but other factors that affect agricultural practices and then classifying farmland on a relative scale for decision making.

History of the LESA System

I created the LESA system initially as a land classification system for Orange County, New York, in 1971. A number of counties with agricultural districts used this land classification system on an ad hoc basis to determine agricultural land value for tax purposes.

In developing the land classification system, I used the National Cooperative Soil Survey to determine the characteristics of the soil as they related to agricultural use and productivity. Once I had determined the relative degrees of quality of the land for agricultural productivity, dollar values were assigned, and taxes were assessed according to each parcel's relative agricultural value.

In 1979 I spent one year on assignment to the New York State Department of Agriculture and Markets, at which time land classification became the official tool to determine the class of land for agricultural value assessment for the entire state.

In 1980 I moved to Washington, D.C., to join the Land Use Division in SCS headquarters. That same year SCS adopted the concept of the land classification system from New York, in response to the demand from district conservationists, county extension agents, and state and local government planners, who wanted to have technically defensible criteria with which to evaluate land, and determine under what conditions agricultural lands should be protected from conversion to other uses.

In 1981 the land use staff in the SCS national headquarters bridged the gap between the land classification system and the LESA system. First, the name of the system was changed from land classification to land evaluation. Second, the site assessment criteria were designed from the information presented in the NALS and the *Compact Cities* report (*4*). The NALS reports recommended methods of protecting farmland from conversion; the *Compact Cities* report documented the ravages of urban sprawl, from the decay of the central cities to the destruction of the nation's best farmland, and made recommendations on actions the government could take in order to prevent such sprawl. The staff used recommendations from the reports to develop criteria that could be used in addition to the land evaluation criteria to assess parcels of land relative to one another to determine which would be the least destructive to agriculture assuming that one site had to be developed.

The site assessment criteria identified numerous social, political, geographic, and economic factors that would also affect land-use decision making, such as: which lands were near urban centers and which lands were not; which lands had significant agricultural investments and which did not; and which lands were serviced by significant agricultural infrastructure and which were not. By adding the site assessment portion of LESA, SCS produced a tool which, when used properly, would help federal agencies to ensure that they did not fund projects that would augment urban sprawl.

To assist in documenting the prime farmland lists and to assure consistency (a primary criterion for defensibility), two computer programs were designed for the LESA system. One is located at Iowa State University, which computes prime farmland, and the second is on the Corps of Engineers computer system in Champaign, Illinois, which computes the land evaluation portion of LESA.

LESA Pilot Program. Once developed, SCS began testing the LESA system by implementing pilot programs in 12 counties in six states. In each county, an SCS district conservationist teamed up with the county planner and other local officials to create a locally focused site assessment system to accompany the local soils and agricultural productivity data in the land evaluation part of the system.

The pilot states were to represent different types of land use and land capability from around the nation. For example, in DeKalb County, Illinois, (one of the twelve pilots) 97 percent of the land was prime farmland in 1980, whereas in Whitman County, Washington, less than 10 percent of the land was prime, not because the soils were not fertile, but because they were highly erodible. The pilot testing was designed so that if the test was successful, the LESA system would illustrate that both areas should be protected from conversion to nonagricultural uses at their respective local levels, even though the characteristics might have differed significantly between the two regions as a whole.

The states, counties, and SCS staff involved in the LESA pilot testing program are listed in Table 1.

Table 1. The states, counties, and SCS staff involved in the LESA pilot program.

State	County	State Leadership	District Conservationist
Florida	Palm Beach	Robert Johnson	Donald Vandergrift
	Lake	Robert Johnson	Mark Burgess
	Orange	Robert Johnson	Richmond Hoffman
Illinois	DeKalb	Duane Johnson	Robert Gotkowski
	McHenry	Duane Johnson	Edward Weilbacker
Maryland	Howard	Thorton Secor	James (Jack) Helm
Pennsylvania	Dauphin	Robert Heidecker	Warren Archibald
	Chester	Robert Heidecker	Elbert Wells
	Lancaster	Robert Heidecker	Warren Achibald
Virginia	Clarke	Willis Miller and Richard Googins	Mark Davis
Washington	Clark	Warren Lee	James Crane
	Whitman	Warren Lee	R. Dennis Roe

Other significant contributors to the development of the LESA system include:

Steve Aradas, the McHenry County, Illinois, director of planning, led the development of site assessment factors in Illinois. Aradas and his staff determined these factors by doing significant background work on the local economy, policy, and land use. Their research involved the review of the county comprehensive plans, zoning ordinances, state farmland protection policy, information on county land-use trends (including the number of vacant lots, existing and planned sewer systems, and water and transport facilities), and case files on pending law suits involving zoning ordinances.

Sue Pfluger was the DeKalb County, Illinois, planning director. Pfluger also worked very closely with the county, the SCS district conservationists, and the Land Use Division at SCS headquarters to develop site assessment criteria.

Frederick Steiner was a professor at Washington State University. Steiner provided leadership in designing the LESA system and in conducting the pilot test in Whitman County, Washington. He also helped evaluate the test results and made recommendations on the final design of the system.

Warren Zitzmann was the community planning officer for the Land Use Division at SCS headquarters. Zitzmann assisted others in the division in the development and testing of the LESA system. His knowledge of the planning field aided in establishing the site assessment factors.

Ron Darden also played a part in developing a viable LESA system. Darden, as chief of the Land Management Section of the Division of Natural Resources for the Illinois Department of Agriculture, was involved in the pilot testing of the system in Illinois, and in promoting the system throughout the United States.

LESA Develops

At the end of the pilot LESA program in 1981, participants in the program attended a conference in Washington, D.C., to share information and their experiences, and make recommendations on the development of the LESA system.

In 1982, LESA was completed and presented to the states. The SCS land use staff, assisted by Ron Darden, Duane Johnson, and Richard Googins, visited SCS offices in all 50 states to train them to develop and use their own LESA systems to meet local needs. From the data collected at the conference and in the field, the *Agricultural Land Evaluation and Site Assessment Handbook* was written to serve as the guidelines for implementation of the LESA system in the rest of the nation. The handbook was distributed in 1983.

The year 1984 was important for the recognition of the LESA system and its authors. The site assessment criteria were included in the Federal Farmland Protection Policy Act rule to help federal agencies determine which agricultural land should be protected from development. This meant that for the first time, federal agencies had formal guidelines to enable them to make decisions about how their funds would contribute to land use on and around agricultural lands.

What is LESA?

LESA is a two-part system, with the land evaluation part usually being designed by SCS and local Soil and Water Conservation Districts (S&WCDs). Soil limitations and important farmland ratings are considered when evaluating the land. A land evaluation committee should include the district conservationist, a cooperative extension representative, S&WCD directors, farmers, planners, local agricultural officials, and others who have knowledge of the land resources in the area.

The site assessment part of LESA is usually designed by local officials, or a site assessment committee appointed locally. Site assessment factors include parcel size and on-farm investment, as well as characteristics external to the parcel of land itself, for example, the type of land use nearby and adjacent to the site, whether zoning ordinances are in place, and the existence of other farmland protection measures, to name a few. The site assessment committee or work group could include local planners, citizen members of the county or township planning commission, S&WCD directors, a cooperative extension representative, building industry representatives, recreational representatives, public interest groups, concerned citizens, and other government officials with interest in farmland protection.

Objectives of the System

The system was designed to be flexible enough to accommodate differences among states, counties, or areas. A system can be designed for areas with 95 percent prime farmland, as well as for counties with only five percent prime farmland. Systems can be designed for areas in the shadows of cities as well as for areas with only small towns and villages.

LESA systems are designed based on existing knowledge of the area, local soils surveys, land use plans, policies, and programs. It is important to note that LESA can be applied consistently, on a case-by-case basis. The numerical values a site receives can be compared with other parcels, and a relative protection scale can be established.

LESA can be used as part of a program to do the following:

- Determine lands to be included in transfer or purchase of development rights.
- Implement the federal Farmland Protection Policy Act (FPPA).
- Choose the farm units to be included in agricultural land protection programs.
- Determine minimum parcel size for farm subdivisions in agricultural districts.
- Plan sewer, water, and transportation projects or the creation of agricultural districts.
- Determine the need for an agricultural land protection program and the type of program to be used.
- Assess and review environmental impacts.
- Develop guidelines under which agricultural land conversion to nonagricultural uses should be permitted (*5*).

Land Evaluation Part of LESA

Land evaluation procedures for use in LESA have been developed for cropland and forest land. In evaluating land for crop production, soils are rated by one or all of three systems: land capability classification, important farmland identification, and either soil productivity or soil potential ratings.

Land Capability Classification. Land capability classification is a U.S. Department of Agriculture (USDA) system for classifying soils according to potential for field crops or pasture. Eight classes and four subclasses indicate the limitations of each type of soil. This system is the most widely used land-rating scheme in farmland protection. "The soils are classed according to their limitations when they are used for field crops, the risk of damage when they are used, and the way they respond to treatment" (*5*).

Important Farmland Identification. Important farmland identification is a USDA rating system that places land in one of four groups: prime farmland, unique farmland, land of statewide importance, and land of local importance. Prime Farmland is land that has the best combination of physical and chemical characteristics for producing food, feed, forage, fiber, and oilseed crops and is also available for these uses. It has the soil quality, growing season, and moisture supply needed to economically produce sustained high yields of crops when treated and managed, including water management, according to acceptable farming methods (*5*).

Unique Farmland is land other than prime farmland that is used for the production of specific high-value food and fiber crops. Examples of such crops are citrus, tree nuts, olives, cranberries, fruit, and vegetables (*5*).

Additional Farmland of Statewide Importance is land, in addition to prime and unique farmlands, that is of statewide importance for the production of food, feed, fiber, forage, and oilseed crops. Criteria for defining and delineating this land are to be determined in the appropriate state agency or agencies (*5*).

Additional Farmland of Local Importance: Where appropriate, these lands are to be identified by the local agency or agencies concerned (*5*).

Soil Productivity. Soil productivity is perhaps more an economic than a soil science concept. It is the capacity of a soil to produce a specified plant or sequence of plants under a physically defined set of management practices. Modern soil surveys predict, for locally grown crops, yields that are possible under specified high-level management. Differences in yields of a specific crop on different soils provide a measure of comparison among the soils (*5*).

Soil Potential. Soil potential ratings are classes that indicate the relative quality of a soil, compared with other soils in the area, for a particular crop. Considered are predicted yields, the relative cost of applying modern technology to minimize the effect of any soil limitation, and the adverse effects of continuing limitations, if any, on social, economic, or environmental values (*5*).

The land evaluation process may take, for example, 150 soils in a given county and evaluate them according to the following criteria:

- Land capability classification.
- Whether they qualify as important farmland.
- Soil productivity or soil potential.

Ten groups of soils with relative values between 0 and 100 may be derived from these procedures or soils may be arranged on a 0-100 scale, without grouping.

Site Assessment Part of LESA

The site assessment part of LESA is designed to rate those factors other than the soils and overall agricultural productivity of the land. Site assessment involves the human influence on the land, such as the proximity of the land to urban centers and the amount of on-farm investments.

The site assessment part of LESA is designed by the state or local unit of government that will use the system. Leadership for development of the system usually is provided by state or local planners. The types of factors that may be included in site assessment include the following:

1. Percentage of land in urban use within a few miles of the proposed site, as well as the percent of land in urban use adjacent to the site, and the distance of the site from an urban area.

2. The percentage of the site that has been farmed in the past few years.

3. The extent to which the site is protected by state and local farmland protection policies and programs.

4. The size of the farm containing the site, as compared to the average farm size in the county.

5. The extent to which the conversion of the proposed site causes the conversion of other farmland to non-farm uses.

6. The extent to which agricultural support services exist in the area, and whether the conversion of the proposed site would reduce the demand for such services.

7. The extent to which on-farm investments have been made and maintained.

8. The extent to which the proposed land use is compatible with agricultural uses in the area.

The maximum scores for each factor are assigned according to the importance of the factor. The scores for the FPPA factors are given below (*3*).

Scoring for FPPA Factors

Factor	Points
1. Area in non-urban	15
2. Perimeter in non-urban use	10
3. Percent of site being farmed	20
4. Protection provided by state and local governments	20
5. Distance from urban built-up area	15
6. Distance to urban support services	15
7. Size of present farm unit compared to county average	10
8. Creation of non-farmable farmland	10

9.	Availability of farm support services	5
10.	On-farm investment	20
11.	Effects of conversion on farm support services	10
12.	Compatibility with existing agricultural use	10
Total:		160

Once the LESA system was designed, it was tested in 12 counties within six states, including Washington, Maryland, Pennsylvania, Illinois, Virginia, and Florida. The results of the test were used to issue a LESA handbook in 1983. That handbook has not been revised, meaning that much of what we have learned in the last ten years has not been provided to the public. In fact, services provided to support LESA over the past decade have been minimal (*6*).

Since 1981, LESA systems have been developed in many state and local units of government as a tool to protect farmland. Data from these systems are reported in a recent status report (*3*).

The study found that, "LESA's role in agricultural policy continues to be advisory. LESA provides background information only in 45 jurisdictions, and is regarded as an important part of the decision in 39 jurisdictions. Decisions made with LESA are binding in only five of the 212 jurisdictions surveyed" (*3*).

In addition to the state and local LESA systems, LESA criteria are used to implement the FPPA. More than 1,000 counties have used the land evaluation (LE) part of the FPPA system.

One of the concerns raised by users of LESA and FPPA relates to the need for additional guidelines for rating the site assessment factors in FPPA. The guidelines for LESA recorded in the FPPA are short and without details (*2*). For example:

> How much land is in non-urban use within a radius of 1.0 mile from where the project is intended? The maximum score is 15 points.

More than 90 percent:	15 points
90-20 percent:	14 to 1 points
Less than 20 percent:	0 points

This factor is designed to evaluate the extent to which the area within one mile of the proposed site is non-urban. A definition of non-urban is needed. Guides as to whether the measurement should be made from the outer edge or from the center of the proposed site are needed. Without the specific instructions, people will interpret the guidelines very differently. Consequently, the numerical results may not be consistent, and parcels of land may not receive an adequate score to warrant protection from conversion to nonagricultural uses.

Conclusion

The SCS soil survey has been called "one of the most comprehensive and standardized sources of information about the natural environment in the United States." Not only does LESA use technical information, such as the SCS soil survey, about the environment, it also employs information pertinent to human needs, such as location in relation to urban centers, adjacent land uses, and zoning. Although there is criticism of certain technical aspects of LESA, there is no question as to the benefits of a system that provides a mechanism by which people can gather as much information as possible about a site and its surroundings before taking any actions to change the existing land use. LESA is a valuable, quantitative tool to aid decision makers in protecting our valuable farmlands.

References

1. Gray, R. 1981. *National Agricultural Lands Study Final Report 1981.* Superintendent of Documents, U.S. Government Printing Office, Washington, D.C.
2. Office of the Federal Register. 1990. *The Farmland Protection Policy Act, part 658.* Code of Federal Regulations-Agriculture, Parts 400 to 699, January 1, 1990. National Archives and Records Administration, Washington D.C.
3. Steiner, F., J. R. Pease, R. E. Coughlin, J. C. Leach, J. Pressley, A. Sussman, and C. Shaw. 1991. *Agricultural Land Evaluation and Site Assessment: Status of State and Local Programs.* The Herberger Center, Arizona State University, Tempe, Arizona.
4. Subcommittee on the City, Committee on Banking, Finance, and Urban Affairs, House of Representatives, 96th Congress, second session 1980. *Compact Cities: Energy Saving Strategies for the Eighties* (Committee Print 96-15). U.S. Government Printing Office, Washington, D.C.
5. U.S. Department of Agriculture-Soil Conservation Service. 1983. *National Land Evaluation and Site Assessment Handbook.* Washington, D.C.
6. Wright, L. E., W. Zitzmann, K. Young, and R. Googins. 1983. *LESA— Agricultural Land Evaluation and Site Assessment.* Journal of Soil and Water Conservation 38(2):82-86.

Soil Conservation Service photo

3 LESA in the Farmland Protection Policy Act: How Well is it Working?

Galen Bridge

The success of the Farmland Protection Policy Act (FPPA) and the land evaluation and site assessment (LESA) system can be determined by reviewing the history of the FPPA policy, the development of its implementing rules, and the legal challenges and amendments to strengthen the law. FPPA is a national policy requiring federal agencies to assess the impact of their programs on farmland, so that farmland is not unnecessarily converted to nonagricultural uses. Since the 1970s there have been growing concerns with the conversion of prime farmland, and the resulting urban sprawl. The National Agricultural Land Study (NALS) of 1980-81 found that millions of acres of farmland (some studies suggest three million, while other later studies indicate 2.2 to 2.5 million acres) were being converted each year (*3*).

In 1981 Congress produced the report *Compact Cities: Energy Saving Strategies for the Eighties* (*5*). The report identified the need for Congress to implement programs and policies to protect farmland and combat urban sprawl and the needless waste of energy and resources that accompanies sprawling development. The burden of paying for the services associated with urban sprawl is on rural counties with limited fiscal resources. The *Compact Cities* report indicated that much of the conversion of farmland was the result of projects funded by federal assistance (*5*). With this concern in mind, on December 22, 1981, Congress produced the 1981 Farm Bill, Public Law 97-98, containing the subtitle Farmland Protection Policy Act (*4*). The bill was signed into law by President Ronald Reagan. The purpose of FPPA is to minimize the extent to which federal programs contribute to the unnecessary and irreversible conversion of farmland to nonagricultural uses, and to assure that federal programs are administered in a manner that, to the extent practicable, are compatible with state, units of local government, and private programs and policies to protect farmland (*4*).

The U.S. Department of Agriculture (USDA), in cooperation with other departments, agencies, independent commissions, and other units of federal government, was directed to develop criteria for identifying the effects of federal programs on the conversion of farmland to nonagricultural uses.

The criteria are to be used to identify and take into account the adverse effects of federal programs on the preservation of farmland, consider alternative actions, as appropriate, that could lessen such adverse effects, and assure that such federal programs, to the extent practicable, are compatible with state, units of local government, and private programs and policies to protect farmland.

Background of Development of FPPA Criteria

The FPPA was signed into law in December 1981. Immediately afterwards, USDA began developing criteria to implement the law. In August of 1982, then USDA Secretary John Block sent a letter transmitting a draft of the criteria to be used in administering the Farmland Protection Policy Act to heads of twelve major federal agencies, including the departments of commerce, energy, housing and urban development, transportation, army, and the interior. The agencies were invited to submit comments on the proposed criteria to USDA by September 30, 1982.

Many federal agencies outside of USDA responded to the first draft of the "criteria" for implementation of the FPPA and requested that "criteria" be interpreted as "standards" for determining quantitative or qualitative values, and not procedures.

On March 9, 1983, two years after the farm bill was written, USDA sent the first draft FPPA rule to the Office of Management and Budget (OMB) and other federal agencies for general comment. Response to the draft rule by OMB and others noted that the draft rule provided procedures for evaluating federal program alternatives and not criteria as required by the act. It was recommended by OMB and others that the LESA system be used as criteria in FPPA.

On July 12, 1983, a proposed rule with criteria based on the national LESA system was published in the *Federal Register.* The proposed rule made use of the land evaluation criteria, with 100 points as provided by the Soil Conservation Service (SCS) in its LESA handbook, as well as 16 proposed site assessment factors, with 10 points each or 160 points total score.

USDA received 149 responses to the July 12, 1983 proposed rule. Eighteen of the comments were from federal agencies. Comments were made on all parts of the rule with a large number of comments on the LESA criteria. It was recommended that four of the 16 criteria be dropped, and that the maximum points for assessment factors should reflect the degree of importance of the factor.

LESA Criteria in FPPA

The FPPA criteria assist federal agencies to consider protection of the best farmland in the strongest agricultural areas. The development of the FPPA criteria was designed to do two things: first, to identify those projects that had a combination of farmland value and site factors that would require additional consideration under FPPA, and second, to compare alternative sites for the project if a particular site reflected a high enough value for agricultural use.

The maximum score from the FPPA criteria is 260 points, 100 maximum points from the land evaluation part of the criteria, and 160 points from the site assessment part of the criteria (*4*). The number of points assigned to each item of the criteria increases as the condition changes from one that supports urban development to a condition that supports agriculture. Under the land evaluation component, land that is not suitable for production of an agricultural crop will be rated "0". The number assigned for each soil type will increase as the land becomes more suitable for production of agricultural crops, and the best agricultural soil type in the area is rated 100 points (*4*).

The site assessment part of the criteria is rated in the same manner as the land evaluation part. Sites located in the center of an urban area that is planned and zoned for urban use—with existing urban support services, no agricultural support services, and no off-site impact to agricultural areas next to the site—will be rated "0" points. As sites are evaluated that are further from urban areas, that are not planned or zoned for urban use, and that do not have urban support services, but do have agricultural support services where the conversion of the site to nonagricultural use would have a negative impact on other agricultural land in the area, the total score is increased so that the most rural farmlands in large farms that are in agricultural districts are rated 160 points. If such a site also has the best agricultural soil type for the area, the total score would be 260 points. For any proposed site that scored 160 or more, federal agencies would be required to consider alternative sites (*6, 8*).

Site Assessment Criteria

The twelve FPPA site assessment factors and maximum scores are as follows:

1. Amount of land in non-urban use within a one mile radius of the project. The maximum point score is 15.
2. Percent of the perimeter of the site bordering land in non-urban use. The maximum point score is 10.
3. Amount of the site which has been farmed for more than five of the last 10 years. The maximum point score is 20.
4. Whether the site is subject to state, unit of local government, or private policies or programs to protect farmland. The maximum point score is 20.
5. Proximity of the site to an urban built up area. The maximum point score is 15.
6. Proximity of site to local facilities and services which promote non-agricultural use, for example, sewer and water lines. The maximum point score is 15.
7. Size of farm unit containing site in relation to the average size farm unit in the county. The maximum point score is 10.
8. Percent of land which will become non-farmable as a result of the implementation of the proposed project. The maximum point score is 10.
9. Amount of farm support services available. The maximum point score is 5.
10. Amount of on-farm investment in place. The maximum point score is 20.

11. Whether farm support services would suffer as a result of the conversion of the proposed project. The maximum point score is 10.
12. Whether the proposed use of the site is compatible or incompatible with agriculture. The maximum point score is 10 (*4*).

"Final" Rule and Amendments Published

The final rule to implement the FPPA was published on July 5, 1984. The LESA system was used as the criteria within the FPPA. This final FPPA rule limited the application of FPPA by instructing federal agencies not to withhold funds based on LESA. The rule provided a definition of prime farmland based on zoning that exempted much of the prime farmland from FPPA (*2*). One report was provided to Congress and the rule noted that additional reports would be made (*2*).

1985 Amendments

Congress amended FPPA in the 1985 Food Security Act to (*1*) require an annual report to Congress by USDA regarding federal efforts towards farmland protection, and (*2*) allow the governor of a state with a farmland protection policy or program to bring court action against a federal agency to enforce FPPA requirements. A final rule to implement this amendment has not been published, and no state has yet taken legal action to enforce the FPPA requirements.

Proposed Rule to Implement Amendments

Proposed rules to implement the 1985 amendments to FPPA were published January 14, 1987. Final rules to implement the amendments were approved by the secretary of agriculture on January 30, 1990, nine years after the initial passage of FPPA by Congress and its signing by the president, and four years after Congress made the amendments. In addition to providing for the two 1985 FPPA amendments, the final rules revised the definition of prime farmland by removing zoning and comprehensive plan criteria and replacing it with the LESA rating. This rule also provided a policy change allowing federal agencies to withhold or provide assistance based on FPPA, consistent with its published guidelines. The latter change was the basis of considerable policy-level discussion and a primary reason for delay in promulgating final rules.

On July 2, 1990, OMB concluded that the 1990 January draft final rule of FPPA to implement the amendments from the 1985 Food Security Act repeated sections of the act and was being published three years after the proposed rule. The draft final rule was returned to the USDA for reconsideration.

OMB raised concerns with both the present rule as well as the draft amendments. OMB expressed concerns that the existing rule and the draft amendments create a complex administrative system that places special burdens on other federal agencies.

1992 Proposed Rule

In response to the need to fully implement FPPA, which had passed Congress and been signed by the president, USDA proposed another rule. The 1992 proposed rule would have removed all definitions and exemptions as well as sections on technical assistance, and statements requiring federal agencies to review their policies. Federal agencies would use the 1981 act as amended in 1985 to make decisions on withholding funds and review of policy. The 1992 proposed rule was rejected by OMB.

Using LESA to Implement FPPA

The FPPA requires that federal agencies submit an AD-1006 form (called a "Farmland Conversion Impact Rating Form") to the appropriate SCS local field office when a federally sponsored program or project contributes either directly or indirectly to the conversion of important farmland to nonagricultural uses (see form in Figure 1). This form is not a request for permission to convert farmland; it serves chiefly to gather, evaluate, and report information related to the impacts of a proposed conversion on important farmland. The form has been used since 1986 to make required reports to Congress on FPPA. Federal agencies also are expected to inform SCS on progress in review of their policies and programs to protect farmland. Some of the information that the forms collectively provide includes the following:

- The total number of AD-1006 request forms received by SCS from other federal agencies in 1991 was (*7*)
  - 1 State had none
  - 24 States had 1-20 forms
  - 13 States had 21-50 forms
  - 6 States had 51-100 forms
  - 5 States had 101 to 200 forms
  - 1 State had more than 100 forms

U.S. Department of Agriculture

FARMLAND CONVERSION IMPACT RATING

PART I *(To be completed by Federal Agency)*	Date Of Land Evaluation Request
Name Of Project	Federal Agency Involved
Proposed Land Use	County And State
PART II *(To be completed by SCS)*	Date Request Received By SCS

Does the site contain prime, unique, statewide or local important farmland? *(If no, the FPPA does not apply – do not complete additional parts of this form).*	Yes ☐ No ☐	Acres Irrigated	Average Farm Size
Major Crop(s)	Farmable Land In Govt. Jurisdiction Acres: %	Amount Of Farmland As Defined in FPPA Acres: %	
Name Of Land Evaluation System Used	Name Of Local Site Assessment System	Date Land Evaluation Returned By SCS	

PART III *(To be completed by Federal Agency)*	Maximum Points	Alternative Site Rating: Site A	Site B	Site C	Site D
A. Total Acres To Be Converted Directly					
B. Total Acres To Be Converted Indirectly					
C. Total Acres In Site					
PART IV *(To be completed by SCS)* Land Evaluation Information					
A. Total Acres Prime And Unique Farmland					
B. Total Acres Statewide And Local Important Farmland					
C. Percentage Of Farmland In County Or Local Govt. Unit To Be Converted					
D. Percentage Of Farmland In Govt. Jurisdiction With Same Or Higher Relative Value					
PART V *(To be completed by SCS)* Land Evaluation Criterion Relative Value Of Farmland To Be Converted *(Scale of 0 to 100 Points)*					
PART VI *(To be completed by Federal Agency)* Site Assessment Criteria *(These criteria are explained in 7 CFR 658.5(b)*	Maximum Points				
1. Area In Nonurban Use					
2. Perimeter In Nonurban Use					
3. Percent Of Site Being Farmed					
4. Protection Provided By State And Local Government					
5. Distance From Urban Builtup Area					
6. Distance To Urban Support Services					
7. Size Of Present Farm Unit Compared To Average					
8. Creation Of Nonfarmable Farmland					
9. Availability Of Farm Support Services					
10. On-Farm Investments					
11. Effects Of Conversion On Farm Support Services					
12. Compatibility With Existing Agricultural Use					
TOTAL SITE ASSESSMENT POINTS	160				
PART VII *(To be completed by Federal Agency)*					
Relative Value Of Farmland *(From Part V)*	100				
Total Site Assessment *(From Part VI above or a local site assessment)*	160				
TOTAL POINTS *(Total of above 2 lines)*	260				

Site Selected:	Date Of Selection	Was A Local Site Assessment Used? Yes ☐ No ☐

Reason For Selection:

(See Instructions on reverse side) Form AD-1006 (10-83)

Figure 1. Farmland conversion impact rating form.

- The number of federally assisted projects evaluated is tracked by the number of AD-1006 forms that federal agencies submit to each state SCS office each year. Some of the agencies tallied include the SCS, Farmers Home Administration (FmHA), the Federal Highway Administration, the Department of Housing and Urban Development, the Environmental Protection Agency, the Federal Aviation Administration, the Rural Electrification Administration, the Economic Development Administration, the Corps of Engineers, among others. Some agencies submit significantly more forms than others. For example, a review of the average number of forms submitted over a five year period from 1987 to 1991 showed FmHA to have the highest average with 994 per year and Department of Energy to have the lowest average of 14 per year.

  The number of forms submitted in 1986, the first year of the report, was 2,036. The number of forms submitted in 1992 was 2,566, an increase of 530 forms. This growth was due primarily to the fact that the number of AD-1006 forms submitted by FmHA alone doubled. However, for most of the agencies, the number of AD-1006 forms submitted fluctuated up and down from year to year.

  The overall increase in the number of forms submitted could indicate a greater acceptance and utilization of the FPPA policy over time. The possibility should not be overlooked, however, that more projects were converting farmland in 1991 than in 1987 (Figure 2).

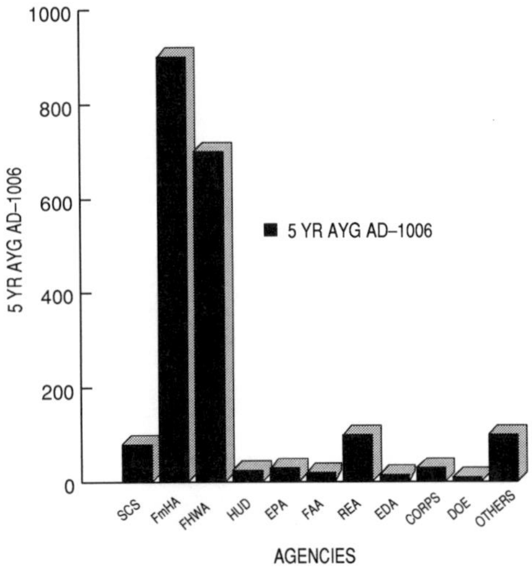

Figure 2. Average number of AD-106 forms submitted by federal agencies (five-year averages).

- The AD-1006 data compiled in each state also make it possible to determine both the number of AD-1006 forms submitted to each SCS field office per year and the use of LESA systems in each state each year. As is evident in Figure 3, there is not a strong correlation between the number of AD-1006 forms submitted per state in 1991 and the number of local LESA systems per state in the same year. The compiled data suggest that, just because a state has widespread use of the LESA system, does not mean that the state follows the FPPA strictly, and vice versa. Some states that have submitted many AD-1006 forms make little or no use of the LESA system.

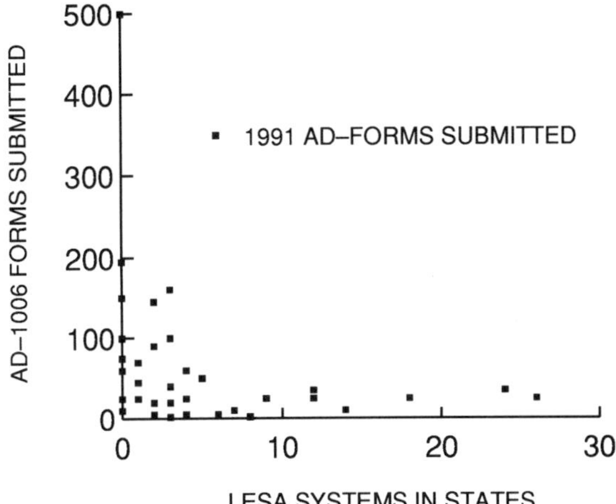

Figure 3. Number of AD-1006 forms submitted to SCS from states vs. number of LESA systems adopted in states for 1991.

It was hoped that those states using the LESA system would have strong participation in the FPPA process, since the site assessment factors in LESA are used within FPPA; however, this is not the case. There is no conclusive evidence as to why one state submits more forms than another, because there are many factors involved—the amount of prime farmland in the state, existing development pressures, and whether or not agencies are submitting the forms when conversions occur. At this time, the last factor probably has the greatest effect upon the number of completed AD-1006 forms.

Impacts

With this background in mind, there have been major problems with the implementation of FPPA and the use of LESA as criteria in the rules, including the following:

1. many federal agencies have not evaluated proposed conversions;
2. the lack of training has presented some concerns in scoring projects with the site assessment criteria; and
3. lack of detail in criteria has caused problems with the accuracy and consistency of the site assessment scoring data.

Requirement

By law in FPPA, federal agencies must use the LESA criteria to identify each federal project that would convert farmland to nonagricultural uses. The FPPA states specifically in section 1542(b) of the Code of Federal Regulations the following:

Departments, agencies, independent commissions, and other units of the federal government shall use the criteria established under FPPA:

- to identify and take into account the adverse effects of federal programs on the preservation of farmland;
- to consider alternative actions, as appropriate, that could lessen such adverse effects; and
- to assure that such federal programs, to the extent practicable, are compatible with state and local government, and private programs and policies to protect farmland (*4*).

FPPA Report for 1991

Details on the type of land being converted and the extent to which federal agencies have reviewed their policies and programs to protect farmland will not be available until a final rule is published that will enable USDA to collect the needed information.

Concerns with Criteria

FmHA, SCS, and other federal agency field staff have voiced concerns about the accuracy of the site assessment criteria. Numerical ratings may differ from person to person and agency to agency as a result of vague and incomplete instructions in the factors and from undefined words, resulting in poor and inconsistent ratings. Inconsistent and inaccurate ratings are significant, because they could make the difference in whether farmland is designated to be preserved or converted to nonagricultural uses. The FPPA specifically relies upon the scores from the site assessment criteria in order to determine which lands deserve the highest protection from conversion. The act states as follows (*4*):

1. Sites with the highest combined scores be regarded as most suitable for protection under these criteria and sites with the lowest scores, as least suitable.
2. Sites receiving a total score of less than 160 be given a minimum level of consideration for protection and no additional sites need be evaluated.
3. Sites receiving scores totaling 160 or more points be given increasingly higher levels of consideration for protection.
4. When making decisions on proposed actions for sites receiving scores totaling 160 or more, agency personnel should consider the following:
   - Use of land that is not farmland or use of existing structures.
   - Alternative sites, locations, and designs that would serve the proposed purpose, but convert either fewer acres of farmland or other farmland that has a lower relative value.
   - Special siting requirements of the proposed project and the extent to which an alternative site fails to satisfy the special siting requirements as well as the originally selected site.

Conclusion

The Farmland Protection Policy Act, with its use of the LESA criteria, was designed to protect the nation's best farmland. As the population increases and the amount of farmland steadily decreases, it is more and more important to protect these valuable lands from conversion to nonagricultural uses, so that it is possible to continue to produce enough food, forage, and fiber to meet the country's growing needs. FPPA can help protect the nation's farmland, especially from conversion by federally sponsored projects. However, more than 10 years after the FPPA was signed, the rules to fully implement the act have not been published. In addition, some agencies have not taken the act seriously, nor implemented the policy effectively. The relatively low number of AD-1006 forms completed in some states, and especially by some agencies, indicate this lack of support for, and adherence to the FPPA policy. The LESA criteria are adequate to enable agencies to assess alternatives under FPPA, but additional guidelines and training are necessary.

References

1. Coughlin, R. E., and J. C. Keene (Senior authors and editors). 1981. *National Agricultural Lands Study - The Protection of Farmland: A Reference Guidebook for State and Local Governments.* A report to the National Agricultural Lands Study from the Regional Science Research Institute, Amherst, Massachusetts.
2. The Food Security Act of 1985. Public Law 99-198, Title 12 as amended by Public Law 100-624 (Food, Agriculture, Conservation, and Trade Act of 1990).
3. Gray, R. 1981. *National Agricultural Lands Study Final Report 1981.* Superintendent of Documents, U.S. Government Printing Office, Washington D.C.
4. Office of the Federal Register National Archives and Records Administration. 1990. *The Farmland Protection Policy Act, part 658. Code of Federal Regulations-Agriculture, Parts 400 to 699.* January 1, 1990.
5. U.S. Congress, Subcommittee on the City, Committee on Banking, Finance, and Urban Affairs, House of Representatives, 96th Congress, second session, July 1980. *Compact Cities: Energy Saving Strategies for the Eighties* (Committee Print 96-15). U.S. Government Printing Office, Washington, D.C.
6. U.S. Department of Agriculture-Soil Conservation Service. 1983. *National Land Evaluation and Site Assessment Handbook.* Washington, D.C.
7. U.S. Department of Agriculture-Soil Conservation Service. Unpublished. FPPA Reports to Congress 1986-1991. Washington, D.C.
8. Wright., L. E., W. Zitzmann, K. Young, and R. Googins. 1983. *LESA- Agricultural Land Evaluation and Site Assessment.* Journal of Soil and Water Conservation 38(2):82-86.

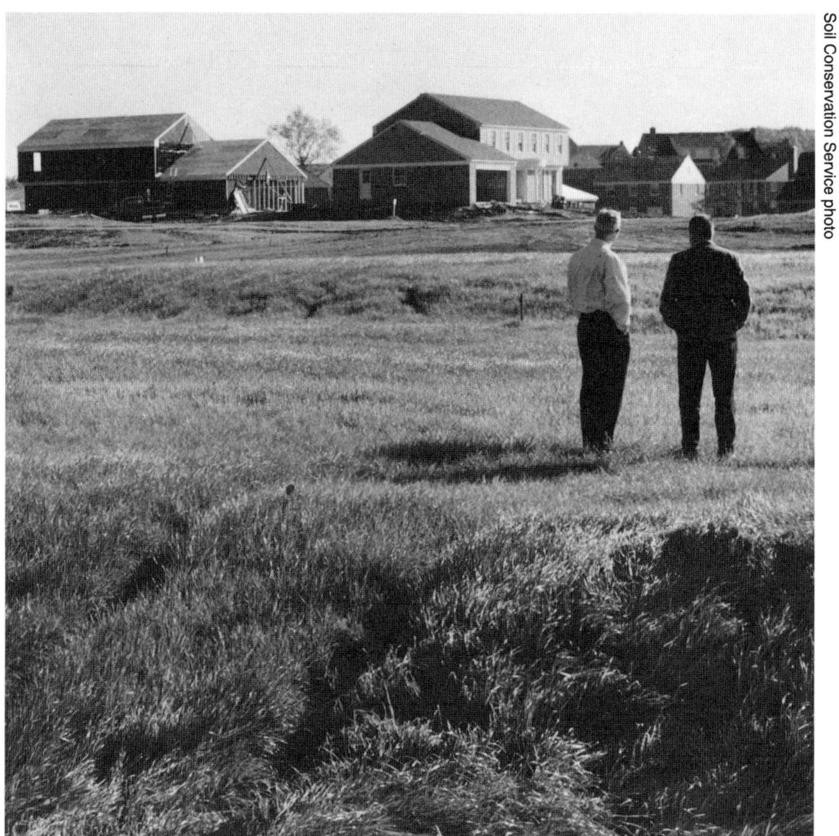

Soil Conservation Service photo

4 State and Local LESA Systems: Status and Evaluation

James R. Pease, Robert E. Coughlin, Frederick R. Steiner, Adam P. Sussman, Lyssa Papazian, Joyce Ann Pressley, and John C. Leach

The land evaluation and site assessment (LESA) system was designed by the USDA Soil Conservation Service "to determine the quality of land for agricultural uses and to assess sites or land areas for their agricultural economic viability" (*10*). The 1984 rules implementing the federal Farmland Protection Policy Act of 1981 gave LESA prominence by requiring its use by federal agencies, but many local governments have also used LESA. A limited inventory of LESA use by local governments was conducted in 1985 and published in 1987 (*6*), but the first comprehensive study was conducted in 1990-1991 (5).

The comprehensive study used a mailed survey questionnaire to document the extent to which local governments have adopted LESA systems throughout the United States, the process by which each jurisdiction formulated its LESA system, the land use questions addressed with LESA, and the degree of reliability ascribed to LESA scores. Through analysis of materials supplied by local governments, the study also documented the factors and weights used in the LESA systems.

Several methods were used to identify LESA systems, including telephone and written contacts with state SCS and planning offices, notices in newsletters and journals, computer literature searches, review of journal abstracts, and referrals from respondents. In states where few or no LESA systems were initially identified, such as California, contacts were made directly with local governments. While it is possible that a few LESA users, or former users, were not identified, the researchers are confident that the respondents represented nearly all active LESA users in 1991.

Extent of Adoption

The study identified 212 local and state governments in 31 states as active or former users of LESA (Figures 1 and 2 and Table 1). Of these 212 jurisdictions, 138 local and eight state governments are currently using a LESA system. LESA use is much more common in east coast states (70 percent of users) than in midwestern (except Illinois) and western states.

States with the most local systems include Connecticut, Georgia, Illinois, New Jersey, Pennsylvania, Vermont, and West Virginia. A large proportion of local LESA systems are found in metropolitan areas or other locations where there are strong development pressures. Most local LESA systems are in states that have adopted policies and undertaken programs to protect farmland.

Ten states have developed LESA systems or adaptations of LESA systems. Most of these systems are used only by state agencies (Connecticut, Hawaii, Massachusetts, Michigan, New Jersey, and West Virginia), but in Illinois, Pennsylvania, and Vermont they are also used as models for local governments that develop their own systems. In Delaware, state planners worked with three counties to tailor a system for each of them.

The use of LESA by local jurisdictions increased sharply between 1983 and 1985, leveled off during 1985-1989, and then accelerated again in 1989-1990 (Figure 3). The recent acceleration can be traced largely to state programs that call for the use of a LESA system. For example, Pennsylvania's program for purchase of agricultural conservation easements required LESA evaluation of farmland for setting purchase priorities, and

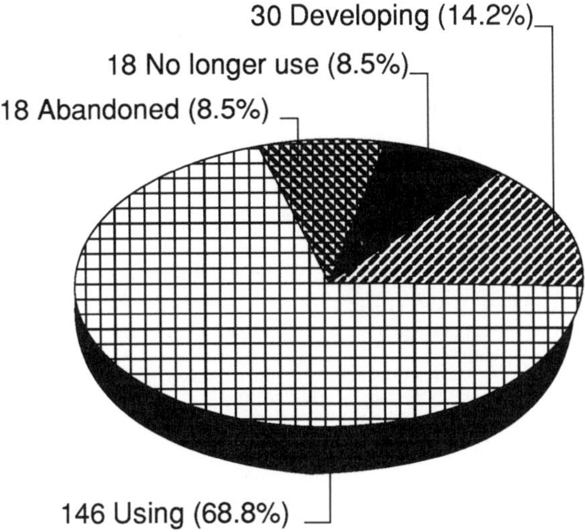

Figure 1. Status of LESA programs in 212 state and local jurisdictions.

Vermont's Land Use Act of 1988 required the use of LESA to determine farm and forest land-use designations by local governments. The number of jurisdictions using LESA is likely to increase significantly in the near future. Thirty jurisdictions reported that they were currently developing a LESA system, eight of which are in Vermont and four in Pennsylvania. Nevertheless, many counties with significant agricultural areas have not yet begun a LESA system.

In addition to the 138 local governments currently using a LESA system, 18 jurisdictions have developed LESA systems but no longer use them for various reasons. For example, Kenai Borough, Alaska, used LESA for a public land disposal program. Once the program was completed, LESA was no longer needed. Planners in Tillamook County, Oregon, used LESA to identify farmland for exclusive farm use (EFU) zones. Once zoned, they relied on the ordinance to sustain farm protection policies. Others found LESA too time-consuming, some found that their version of LESA did not give reliable results, and some replaced it with a state-designated scoring system.

Eighteen jurisdictions started to develop LESA systems but abandoned the idea before implementing a system. Several of those found the system too complicated or time consuming; some noted a lack of interest or support by landowners or planning bodies; one noted that development of LESA ended with a personnel change in the position of town zoning administrator.

Table 1. Jurisdictions with LESA experience.

Alaska
Kenai Peninsula Borough
Connecticut
State of Connecticut
Town of Bloomfield
Town of East Windsor
Fairfield County
Harford County
Middlesex County
Town of Suffield
Windham County
Town of Windsor
Delaware
State of Delaware
New Castle County
Kent County
Sussex County
Florida
Highlands County
Marion County
Pasco County
Georgia
Barrow County
Coffee County
Crisp County
Dooley County
Hall County
Houston County
Lee County
Macon County
Morgan County
Richmond County
Tift County
Turner County
Hawaii
State of Hawaii
Idaho
Bonneville County
Latah County
Illinois
State of Illinois
Boone County
Brown County
Champaign County
DeKalb County
Ford County
Fulton County
Grundy County
Henry County
Jackson County
Kane County
Kankakee County
Lee County
McHenry County
McLean County
Mercer County
Monroe County
Peoria County
Pike County
Putnam County
Rock Island County
St. Clair County
Sangamon County
Schuyler County
Stephenson County
Whiteside County
Will County
Iowa
Black Hawk County
Johnson County
Muscatine County
Story County
Kansas
Douglas County
Kentucky
Clark County
Hardin County
Maine
Aroostook County
Dover-Foxcroft
Knox County
Waldo County
Maryland
Baltimore County
Cecil County
Harford County
Howard County
Massachusetts
State of Massachusetts
Barnstable County
Essex County
Hampshire County
Middlesex County
Suffolk County
Worcester County (northeast part)
Michigan
State of Michigan
Minnesota
Carver County
Holding Township
La Cresent Township
Ramsey County
Stearns County
Montana
Flathead County
Nevada
Douglas County and Carson City
New Hampshire
Belknap County
Cheshire County
Grafton County
New Jersey
State of New Jersey
Burlington County
Camden County
Cumberland County
Hunterdon County
Middlesex County
Monmouth County
Morris County
Ocean County
Salem County
Somerset County
Sussex County
Warren County
New York
Cortland County
Erie County
Monroe County
Town of Penfield
Town of Perinton
Town of Rush
North Carolina
Forsyth County
Gaston County
Henderson County
Stanly County
Wake County
Ohio
Medina County
Oklahoma
Rogers County
Oregon
Baker County
Clatsop County
Columbia County
Josephine County
Lane County
Linn County
Marion County
Tillamook County
Washington County
Pennsylvania
State of Pennsylvania
Adams County
Berks County
Bradford County
Bucks County
Carbon County
Centre County
Chester County
Dauphin County
Lancaster County
Lehigh County
Lycoming County
Mercer County
Monroe County
Montgomery County
Northampton County
Snyder County
Westmoreland County
York County
South Carolina
Aiken County
Charleston County
Vermont
State of Vermont
Bennington
Brattleboro
Caledonia County
Chittenden County
Town of Dorset
Town of Dummerston
Town of East Montpelier
Essex County
Franklin County
Grand Isle County
Town of Granville
Town of Hancock
Town of Hartland
Lamoille County
Town of Newbury
Orange County
Town of Pawlet
Town of Pecham
Town of Putney
Town of Randolph
Town of Rockingham
Rutland County
Town of Stowe
Town of Thetford
Town of Westminister
Town of Weston
Windham County
Windsor County (North)
Windsor County (South)
Virginia
Clarke County
Culpeper County
Hanover County
Washington
Clark County
Douglas County
Island County
Stevens County
Walla Walla County
Whitman County
West Virginia
State of West Virginia
Berkeley County
Brooke County
Calhoun County
Gilmer County
Grant County
Hampshire County
Hancock County
Hardy County
Jackson County
Kanawha County
Marshall County
Mason County
Mineral County
Morgan County
Ohio County
Pendleton County
Pleasants County
Putnam County
Ritchie County
Roane County
Tyler County
Wetzel County
Wirt County
Wood County

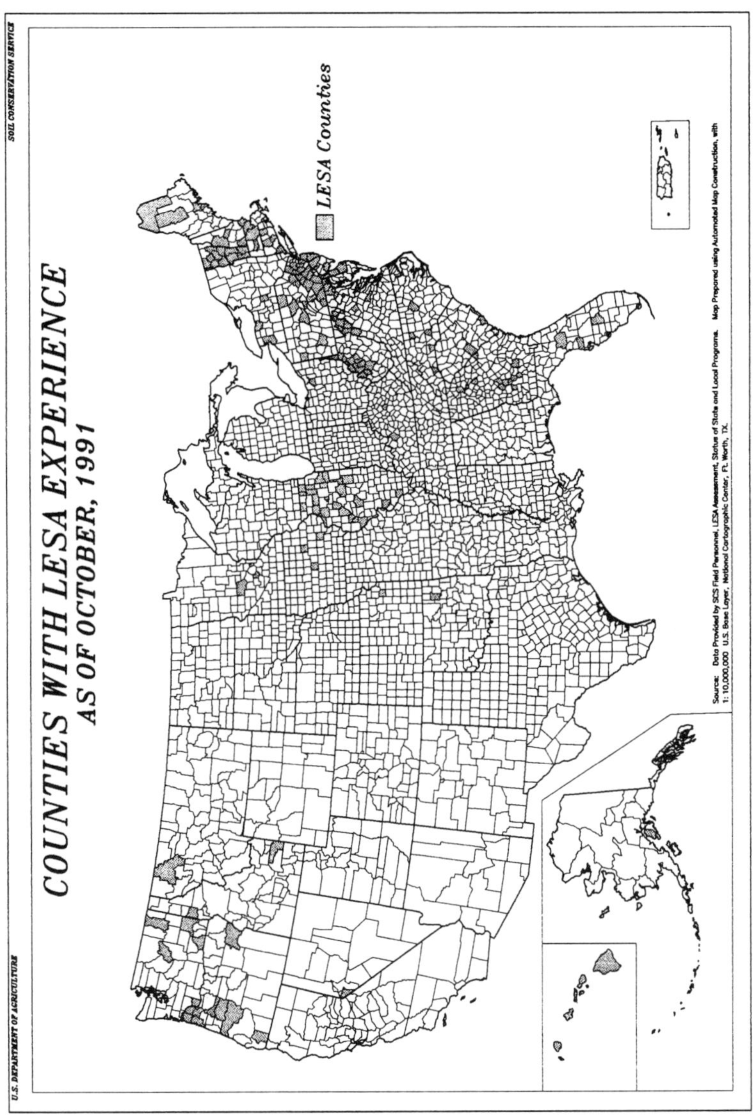

Figure 2. Counties with LESA experience.

Process of Formulation

Although about 26 percent of the jurisdictions simply adopted the federal SCS LESA system (see chapters 2 and 3 for explanation of the federal model), the large majority, 74 percent, adapted their own versions of LESA. Most of these adapted a full LESA system, but 10 percent of them limited their adapted systems to the land evaluation (LE) portion. Local adaptation of the LESA system is attractive to local jurisdictions, because once a local jurisdiction develops its own version of LESA and SCS approves it, then SCS is required to use the local version in reviewing federal projects.

The choice and weighting of land evaluation (LE) and site assessment (SA) factors were usually carried out by local committees in order to make full use of local knowledge and to assure local acceptance (Figure 4). In preparing the LE component, committee representation was usually broad-based (59 percent of jurisdictions), but seven percent of the jurisdictions relied on more restricted committees made up of planning commission members or local officials. One-third of the jurisdictions, however, relied on the SCS alone to make LE determinations.

SCS personnel were the most commonly found members of LE committees—79 percent of the jurisdictions reported that their committee included an SCS representative. County or town planners were found on 50 percent of the committees, followed by state university extension service staff, 44 percent; local farmers, 36 percent; local citizens, 32 percent; local public officials, 32 percent; non-SCS soil scientists, 12 percent; and other unspecified persons, 32 percent.

Broad-based committees were relied on more heavily to choose and weight SA factors. They were used by 78 percent of the jurisdictions, while six percent used smaller committees made up only of planning and other local officials. Only 16 percent relied solely on SCS for SA formulation.

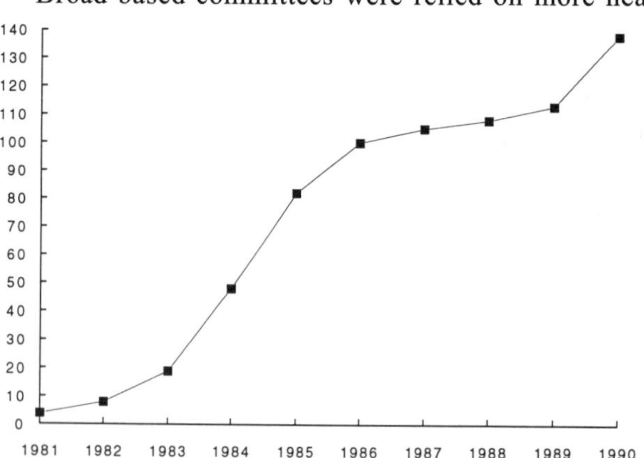

Figure 3. Local jurisdictions with LESA systems, by

County or town planners were most commonly found on SA committees—67 percent of the jurisdictions reported that their SA committee included a planner. SCS personnel were found on 54 percent of SA committees. Less commonly found were local farmers, 50 percent; local citizens, 47 percent; county or town officials, 44 percent; state university extension service staff, 38 percent; non-SCS soil scientists, 11 percent; and other unspecified persons, 30 percent. SA committees tended to be larger than LE committees, so more groups were likely to be included on them.

Applying LESA for Decision Making

LESA has been used to provide information for a variety of purposes. Deciding whether to permit or deny requests for zoning permits or zone changes was the most common, cited by 40 percent of respondents. About half of the jurisdictions that applied LESA for this purpose used it as background information only. Forty-four percent, however, considered LESA an important part of the zoning decision, and five percent treated the LESA score as binding on the decision.

Linn County, Oregon, is an example of a jurisdiction that uses LESA as background for zoning decisions. It uses LESA not only to rate the subject parcel (i.e., the one requested to be converted) but also to rate surrounding

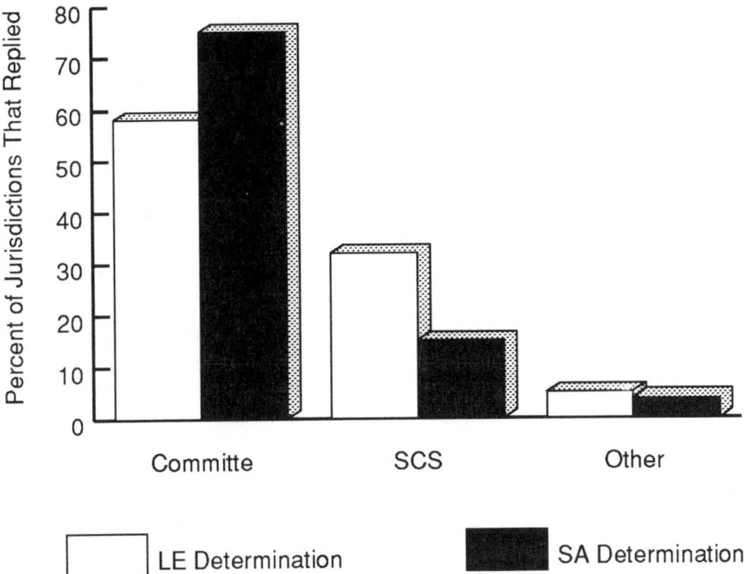

Figure 4. Methods of determining LE and SA factors.

parcels before and after development to determine how their agricultural suitability would be affected by the proposal. This type of analysis addresses the creeping effect of land-use conversions on subsequent LESA scores.

Twenty-five percent of the respondents used LESA to help determine what land to include in agricultural zones. Another 20 percent used LESA in delineating agricultural districts, which are non-zoning districts established through voluntary cooperation of farmers to protect agricultural practices within the district.

The demands of state and federal programs tended to determine other applications: 29 percent reported using LESA for environmental impact assessments and 23 percent used it for ranking farms for purchase of development rights. Less common uses included lending to property owners by a federal agency, acquisition and disposal of land by federal agencies, and property tax assessment.

LESA is often used for several purposes by the same jurisdiction. For example, the township of Putney, Vermont, uses LESA for environmental impact assessment, purchase of development rights, and designation of agricultural zones. By contrast, Howard County, Maryland, reports using LESA only for mapping and zoning board of adjustment decisions. In Bennington, Vermont, LESA was used only for deciding on connections to the municipal sewer system.

Some variation by region was noted. The use of LESA for zoning designations, rezoning, and zoning permit decisions was especially strong in the West and Midwest. The use of LESA for environmental impact assessment, agricultural districting, acquisitions of land, property tax assessment, and lending by federal agencies is less common in the West and Midwest than in eastern states. Purchase of development rights and property tax assessment applications are exclusive to eastern and southern states. Figure 5 illustrates this regional variation.

Geographic information systems (GIS) for LESA applications have been used in Hawaii, Illinois, Kansas, Oregon, Vermont, and probably in some other states as well. Forestry LESA systems have been developed in Lane and Columbia counties in Oregon and in various townships in Vermont. Since the completion of the survey, a riparian evaluation and site assessment has been developed for a watershed in Yavapai County, Arizona. Profiles of some of these applications are given in the LESA status report (*5*).

Degree of Reliability Ascribed to LESA

A most important question was whether LESA scores gave the right answers; that is, whether they were consistent with the judgements of knowledgeable local people. Eleven percent of the jurisdictions responded that their LESA system always distinguished reliably between land that should remain in agriculture and land that could be converted to other uses; 68 percent responded "most of the time." Thus, taken together, 79 percent of the jurisdictions appeared to be satisfied with LESA results. One respondent noted that "prior to adoption, our county tested LESA on 100 sites. Since adoption, LESA has been used to rate over 110 sites. LESA has become an integral part of our county's land-use planning and zoning program and has been largely successful."

Some 19 percent, however, reported that LESA scores were reliable "not very often" and about two percent reported that the scores "never" were reliable—a total of 21 percent who had generally negative opinions of their LESA ratings. The survey did not gather information on why they found LESA to be less than reliable. From comments made by LESA respondents, lack of reliability or effectiveness in the decision-making process could be attributed to technical problems with the particular LESA system, staffing inadequacies, or to local political factors. Technical problems could be related to choice of factors or weighting, difficulties in using LESA for a specific application, or simply the failure of a generalized model to capture the complexities of all factors affecting a site.

Several respondents noted that the local political climate made effective use of LESA scores difficult. One respondent commented about a land conversion application that "although the LESA score is always taken into consideration, many times land is converted despite a high LESA score if the

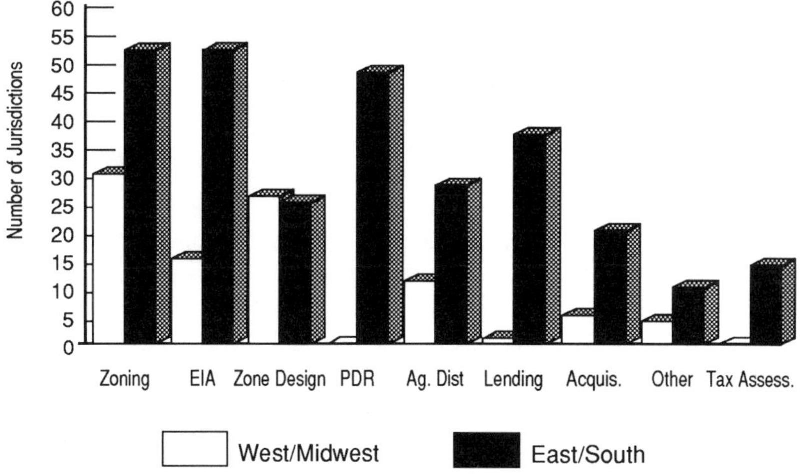

Figure 5. Types of LESA applications by region.

'right' people are in favor of the change." In a county using LESA for purchase of development rights, the comment was made that "many times only marginal land is selected over land with much greater agricultural/natural potential, simply because the local board is more familiar with one farm/landowner than another." The pressure to make decisions on political grounds can be countered only if the LESA ratings are widely recognized to be accurate and reliable.

In other instances, the LESA scores fell in a middle "grey" range (e.g., 176-225 points), which failed to give clear guidance to decision makers. In this case, the factors and weights may be inadequate to clearly differentiate parcels.

Factors and Weights

The LESA model is made up of a number of LE factors and a number of SA factors. Each factor is weighted and LE and SA are also weighted. The general characteristics of the factors and the relative magnitudes of the weights assigned were analyzed for 70 jurisdictions that provided worksheets and other documentation of their LESA models.

Most local LESA systems assigned 100 points to LE and 200 to SA, resulting in a total maximum LESA score of 300. This ratio is the one recommended in the 1983 SCS LESA handbook (*9*). However, as research in Hawaii, Oregon, and Pennsylvania determined (see chapters 7, 8, and 9), the LE to SA weight ratio is very significant in determining the overall score; the 33:67 ratio may need to be adjusted for soil conditions and/or planning goals in different jurisdictions and even sub-areas within jurisdictions. In jurisdictions with diverse soils, LE may need to be given greater weight. In jurisdictions with homogeneous soils, SA may be more significant in differentiating the relative importance of farm parcels.

Of 70 LESA systems analyzed, 50 percent used only one LE factor (usually the soils potential rating), and 50 percent used a combination of land capability, soils productivity, and important farmland rating systems. Soil potential ratings include the costs of land improvements, such as drainage or irrigation, needed to produce a yield at a given level. Yield, land improvement costs, and unit prices provide the basis for rating one or more indicator crops. Net values are then arrayed and scaled to obtain an LE score. While often preferred because it incorporates costs of overcoming soils limitations, soils potential ratings require a local group to develop criteria, select one or more indicator crops, and rate each soil in the jurisdiction. Soil capability, soil productivity, and important farmland ratings, in contrast, are readily available from SCS for many jurisdictions.

When a combination of soil rating systems is used, it may be found that, on a relative scale, all are essentially measuring the same things. This may be so even in areas with many diverse soil types. For example, Ferguson and Bowen (*1*) found in Hawaii that five different measures of LE were highly correlated.

In comparison to LE, many more factors were found in the SA part of LESA; about 40 different factors were found to be in use in various combinations. Well over half of the jurisdictions used between 10 and 20 factors in the SA component, but one used only three and one used 31 factors. Questions of whether some of these factors were redundant, and therefore possibly distorting the final LESA scores, are discussed in other chapters (see chapters 6, 8, and 9).

The various SA factors found in the 70 systems were classified into four groups: (a) factors that describe the economic viability of farming, accounting for 27 percent of the factors; (b) factors that describe the degree of development pressure, accounting for 29 percent of the factors; (c) factors that describe policies and regulations that favor the continuation of farming and the existence of important environmental, historic, and scenic features, accounting for 32 percent of the factors; and (d) other miscellaneous considerations, accounting for 12 percent of the factors (see Table 2).

The medians and ranges for maximum point scores of the four groups are shown graphically in Figure 6 for the eastern U.S. LESA systems. The graph also shows the inter-quartile ranges. To make comparability possible, the researchers transformed all systems summarized in Figure 6 to a maximum LESA score of 100. It is clear from the data that the systems vary greatly in weights assigned to each of the four groups of SA factors. There is relatively little variation in the

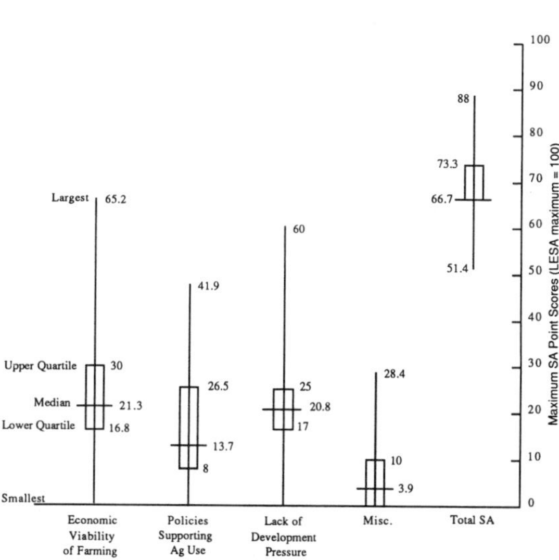

Figure 6. Maximum point scores for groups of SA factors for LESA systems in the eastern U.S.

weight assigned to SA as a whole, however. The original prescription of a 33:67 LE to SA ratio predominates to the extent that 44 percent of eastern jurisdictions use it, including both the jurisdiction at the lower quartile and the jurisdiction at the median. More detailed data are given by state in Table 2.

In an analysis of 25 LESA systems in western and midwestern states, only about 10 percent of jurisdictions weighted SA less than 50 percent of total LESA scores. Most of the 25 jurisdictions used the 33:67 ratio. The factors used in SA are listed in Table 3. As indicated in Table 4, 76 percent of jurisdictions use at least one non-quantifiable, or subjective factor, which would make it difficult to obtain consistent results. Non-agricultural factors, such as distance to sewer lines, are used by 84 percent of the jurisdictions (Table 5). Problems with the use of non-quantifiable and non-agricultural factors are discussed by Huddleston et al. (*2*) and in other chapters of this book (see chapters 5, 6, and 9).

Because of wide differences in goals and, therefore, choice of SA factors, scaling, and weights, it is not usually appropriate to compare scores across jurisdictions. In some cases, factor scaling and weighting is inverted for a specific application. In Lancaster County, Pennsylvania, for example, proximity to urban centers increases the LESA score, while in most other jurisdictions it decreases the score. The policy basis for Lancaster County's scaling of the proximity factors is discussed in chapters 8 and 11.

Conclusions

More and more local governments are using LESA. The trend has been accelerated by state programs that call for its use and by the fact that users generally find LESA a reliable method of distinguishing between land that should remain in agriculture and land that could be converted to other uses. Many jurisdictions that have significant agricultural areas, however, have not started a LESA program.

The LESA systems adapted by local governments generally all have the same format but differ considerably in the choice and number of factors and in their weighting, especially those relating to site assessment. This variability is a reflection of the local flexibility intended in the development of LESA systems; it may also indicate the lack of an adequate research base for assigning site assessment factors and weights. This point is discussed further by Huddleston et al. (*2*) and in several chapters in this book (see chapters 6, 7, 8, and 9).

In addition to agricultural land applications, the LESA concept is being applied to forest lands and riparian zones. The concept also lends itself to adaptation to other resources, such as wildlife habitat, wetlands, aquifers, as

Table 2. Characteristics of LESA systems in eastern United States (weights adjusted to total of 100 and averaged by state).

STATE	CONNECTICUT		DELAWARE		FLORIDA	
# Programs (only complete info.)	4.0		3.0		2.0	
General info. (Avg. adjusted)	**#Factors**	**Score**	**#Factors**	**Score**	**#Factors**	**Score**
#Standard LE-SA	4.0		3.0		1.0	
LE total	2.0	32.9	1.0	33.3	1.0	30.0
SA total	17.5	67.1	9.7	66.6	10.0	70.0
LESA total	19.5	100.0	10.7	100.0	11.0	100.0
Qualitative total	12.5	43.9	3.7	28.1	4.0	40.0
LE factors (Avg. adjusted)	**#Factors**	**Weight**	**#Factors**	**Weight**	**#Factors**	**Weight**
Main soil factor		32.9		33.3		30.0
Other LE factors						
LE total	2.0	32.9	1.0	33.3	1.0	30.0
SA factors (Avg. adjusted)	**#Factors**	**Weight**	**#Factors**	**Weight**	**#Factors**	**Weight**
A. Econ. viability of farming						
Size of parcel and ag. use	2.8	10.1			2.0	20.0
# of yrs. farmed, longevity and ownership	1.0	3.3	1.0	7.5		
Proximity to agric. svcs.			1.0	4.2		
Annual farm product sales						
Farm infrastructure investment and maint.	1.0	4.8	1.0	10.5		
Stewardship and mgt.						
Subtotal	4.5	17.4	2.0	16.9	1.0	10.0
B. Policies supporting ag. use						
On or adjacent to land zoned for agric.			1.0	5.8		
Agricultural use consistent w/planning	1.0	3.6	1.0	3.9		
Proximity to farms under permanent easement						
Participation in preserv. programs and proximity to agricultural districts						
Environmental, historic, and scenic features	1.5	5.6			3.0	30.0
Subtotal	2.3	8.3	2.0	9.7	1.5	15.0
C. Lack of pressure						
Proximity to other ag. land	1.8	8.9	1.7	16.6	1.0	10.0
Distance from development or urban ctr.	1.8	5.1	1.0	4.2		
Distance from utilities, public trans. or maj. hwy.	1.8	7.5	1.0	4.4	12.0	60.0
Physical features that favor development	1.0	4.0	1.0	6.7	1.0	10.0
Circumstances that favor development						
Subtotal	6.0	24.6	4.3	30.5	7.0	40.0
D. Miscellaneous						
Impact on area of conversn. to non-farm use	2.5	7.7	1.0	7.8	1.0	10.0
Other factors	2.3	9.2	1.0	5.0		
Subtotal	4.8	17.0	1.3	9.4	0.5	5.0
SA total	17.5	67.1	9.7	66.6	10.0	70.0
LESA total	19.5	100.0	10.7	100.0	11.0	100.0

Table 2 (continued). Characteristics of LESA systems in eastern United States (weights adjusted to total of 100 and averaged by state).

STATE	GEORGIA		NEW HAMPSHIRE		NEW JERSEY	
# Programs						
(only complete info.)	2.0		2.0		5.0	
General info.	**#Factors**	**Score**	**#Factors**	**Score**	**#Factors**	**Score**
(Avg. adjusted)						
#Standard LE-SA	2.0		2.0		3.0	
LE total	1.0	33.9	1.0	35.9	1.4	35.3
SA total	29.5	66.2	14.0	64.1	12.0	64.8
LESA total	30.5	100.0	15.0	100.0	13.4	100.0
Qualitative total	13.0	26.9	10.5	49.8	5.3	31.3
LE factors	**#Factors**	**Weight**	**#Factors**	**Weight**	**#Factors**	**Weight**
(Avg. adjusted)						
Main soil factor		33.9		35.9		31.1
Other LE factors					34.8	20.8
LE total	1.0	33.9	1.0	35.9	1.4	35.3
SA factors	**#Factors**	**Weight**	**#Factors**	**Weight**	**#Factors**	**Weight**
(Avg. adjusted)						
A. Econ. viability of farming						
Size of parcel and ag. use	4.0	12.0	1.0	6.9	1.6	13.3
# of yrs. farmed, longevity and ownership	1.0	2.8	1.0	5.1		
Proximity to agric. svcs.			1.0	3.8		
Annual farm product sales						
Farm infrastructure investment and maint.	1.0	1.6	1.0	4.4	1.0	8.4
Stewardship and mgt.	1.0	3.0			2.0	11.4
Subtotal	6.0	17.2	3.5	16.7	3.2	23.5
B. Policies supporting ag. use						
On or adjacent to land zoned for agric.	1.0	1.8			1.0	4.2
Agricultural use consistent w/planning	1.5	2.8	1.0	5.4	2.3	8.4
Proximity to farms under permanent easement						
Participation in preserv. programs and proximity to agricultural districts	1.0	1.4	1.0	8.3	3.7	19.5
Environmental, historic, and scenic features	6.0	11.5			1.3	2.9
Subtotal	9.5	17.3	1.0	6.9	4.8	20.1
C. Lack of pressure						
Proximity to other ag. land	2.0	5.7	2.0	6.7	1.3	7.6
Distance from development or urban ctr.	2.0	5.0	1.0	3.2	1.0	5.9
Distance from utilities, public trans. or maj. hwy.	4.5	7.2	1.0	3.4	1.7	6.9
Physical features that favor development	2.0	2.8	2.0	6.7	1.0	4.9
Circumstances that favor development					1.0	4.3
Subtotal	8.5	16.8	4.0	13.3	3.2	16.2
D. Miscellaneous						
Impact on area of conversn. to non-farm use	3.5	9.5	4.0	22.4	1.0	6.7
Other factors	2.0	5.4	1.5	4.9	1.5	9.1
Subtotal	5.5	14.9	5.5	27.3	0.8	5.0
SA total	29.5	66.2	14.0	64.1	12.0	64.8
LESA total	30.5	100.0	15.0	100.0	13.4	100.0

Table 2 (concluded). Characteristics of LESA systems in eastern United States (weights adjusted to total of 100 and averaged by state).

STATE	NORTH CAROLINA		PENNSYLVANIA		VERMONT	
# Programs (only complete info.)	3.0		12.0		12.0	
General info. (Avg. adjusted)	**#Factors**	**Score**	**#Factors**	**Score**	**#Factors**	**Score**
#Standard LE-SA	3.0		7.0		12.0	
LE total	2.3	39.0	1.8	24.1	1.2	33.8
SA total	12.3	61.0	1.8	24.1	11.8	66.2
LESA total	14.7	100.0	14.4	75.9	12.9	100.0
Qualitative total	4.0	19.8	16.3	100.0	4.7	13.3
LE factors (Avg. adjusted)	**#Factors**	**Weight**	**#Factors**	**Weight**	**#Factors**	**Weight**
Main soil factor		39.0				33.8
Other LE factors			1.0	3.6		
LE total	2.3	39.0	1.8	24.1	1.2	33.8
SA factors (Avg. adjusted)	**#Factors**	**Weight**	**#Factors**	**Weight**	**#Factors**	**Weight**
A. Econ. viability of farming						
Size of parcel and ag. use	1.7	9.1	1.8	9.8	1.9	19.0
# of yrs. farmed, longevity and ownership	1.0	4.0	1.0	3.1	1.3	10.7
Proximity to agric. svcs.						
Annual farm product sales			1.1	4.0		
Farm infrastructure investment and maint.			1.1	4.0		
Stewardship and mgt.	1.0	9.7	1.1	4.3	1.0	5.6
Subtotal	3.7	28.1	5.0	24.7	3.0	27.5
B. Policies supporting ag. use						
On or adjacent to land zoned for agric.	1.0	4.0	1.0	6.1	2.0	13.3
Agricultural use consistent w/planning	2.0	7.7	1.3	6.2		
Proximity to farms under permanent easement			1.0	7.4	1.0	0.7
Participation in preserv. programs and proximity to agricultural districts	1.0	4.0	1.8	11.0	1.0	3.3
Environmental, historic, and scenic features	1.0	3.0	1.3	5.2	4.7	10.6
Subtotal	2.7	9.9	5.2	29.2	4.5	11.4
C. Lack of pressure						
Proximity to other ag. land	2.0	11.3	1.6	10.1	2.2	16.4
Distance from development or urban ctr.	1.0	3.8	1.4	10.2	1.0	6.7
Distance from utilities, public trans. or maj. hwy.	1.5	6.1	1.5	7.1	2.0	9.5
Physical features that favor development			1.4	7.3	1.0	3.2
Circumstances that favor development	1.0	6.0	1.0	3.0		
Subtotal	3.0	14.4	3.7	20.4	3.5	23.4
D. Miscellaneous						
Impact on area of conversn. to non-farm use	2.0	5.7	1.0	2.4		
Other factors	2.3	6.8	1.2	3.5	1.8	9.3
Subtotal	3.0	8.7	0.6	1.7	0.8	3.9
SA total	12.3	61.0	14.4	75.9	11.8	66.2
LESA total	14.7	100.0	16.3	100.0	12.9	100.0

Table 3. Site assessment (SA) criteria by number of jurisdictions for 25 jurisdictions in western and midwestern states.

SA Criteria	Number (%) of Jurisdictions
% Area of surrounding land in agricultural use (.25 to 1.5 mi.)	22 (88%)
Distance from central sewer	21 (84%)
Compatibility with comprehensive plan	20 (80%)
Distance from urban center	20 (80%)
Level of public service (road access)	20 (80%)
Size of the parcel	19 (76%)
Distance to central water	15 (60%)
Availability of other suitable sites	13 (52%)
Compatibility with surrounding and adjacent zoning	13 (52%)
On-site waste disposal suitability	12 (48%)
% area of land adjacent to parcel in agricultural use	12 (48%)
% of land site in agricultural use	12 (48%)
% perimeter conflict	11 (44%)
Soil limitations for proposed use	8 (32%)
Agricultural support services	6 (24%)
% of site feasible to farm	6 (24%)
Distance from fire protection	6 (24%)
Increased government financial burden	5 (20%)
Consistent with municipal plan	4 (16%)
Flood potential	3 (12%)
Longevity credits	3 (12%)
Distance to/availability of elementary school space	3 (12%)
On-farm investment	3 (12%)
Type of agriculture	3 (12%)
Committed to development	2 (8%)
Slope/topography	2 (8%)
Row crop suitability	2 (8%)
Distance from electrical extension	2 (8%)
Conflicting residences within 1/4 mile	2 (8%)
Availability of public transit	2 (8%)
Reliable water supply	2 (8%)
Disrupt storm runoff	2 (8%)
Interference with irrigation	1 (4%)
Environmental constraints	1 (4%)
Productive quality of adjacent land	1 (4%)
Urban investment	1 (1%)
Configuration/shape of parcel	1 (4%)
% of site needed for development	1 (4%)
% of site prime farmland	1 (4%)
Compatibility with sewer plan	1 (4%)

Table 4. Subjective (non-measurable) site assessment (SA) criteria by number of jurisdictions in western and midwestern states.

SA Criteria	Number (%) of Jurisdictions
Compatible with surrounding areas	19 (76%)
Environmental impacts	15 (60%)
Historical/cultural and recreational impacts	12 (48%)
Need for additional urban land	3 (12%)
Configuration/shape of the parcel	1 (4%)
Potential traffic conflicts	1 (4%)
Impacts on water quality	1 (4%)
Impacts on mineral extraction	1 (4%)

Table 5. Site assessment (SA) criteria not focused on agricultural productivity by number of jurisdictions in western and midwestern states.

SA Criteria	Number (%) of Jurisdictions
Distance from central sewer	21 (84%)
Compatibility with comprehensive plan	20 (80%)
Distance from urban center	20 (80%)
Level of public service (road access)	20 (80%)
Distance to central water	15 (60%)
Availability of other suitable sites	13 (52%)
On-site waste disposal suitabiltiy	12 (48%)
Soil limitations for proposed use	8 (32%)
Distance from fire protection	6 (24%)
Increased governmental financial burden	5 (20%)
Consistent with municipal plan	4 (16%)
Distance to/availability of elementary school space	3 (12%)
Distance from electrical extension	2 (8%)
Availability of public transit	2 (8%)
Productive quality of adjacent land	1 (4%)
% of site needed for development	1 (4%)
Potential traffic conflicts	1 (4%)
Environmental constraints	1 (4%)
Compatibility with sewer plan	1(4%)
Impacts on mineral extraction	1 (4%)

well as to other uses, such as aggregate mining sites and homesite suitability.

In some states and local jurisdictions, geographic information systems are being employed to make it easier to use LESA ratings for land-use policy applications. While GIS allows rapid calculation of LESA scores, it is a significant investment to prepare the database and software programs, justified only in jurisdictions that have an existing GIS and that make frequent use of LESA applications. Several chapters in this book discuss considerations in linking LESA to a GIS (see chapters 13, 14, and 15).

Whether there are discernible patterns in the uses made of LESA is difficult to assess. Of the 212 LESA questionnaire respondents, 140 reported having a farmland protection policy. The most common implementation techniques were purchase of development rights, 71 jurisdictions; agricultural districts, 56 jurisdictions; farmland zoning, 52 jurisdictions; and other methods, 38 jurisdictions. In certain states with a "progressive" reputation for land use programs, such as Minnesota, Oregon, Vermont, and Washington, LESA is being used in some local counties and townships. Yet, only in Vermont can it be considered widespread (28 jurisdictions and recognition in state law). LESA is regarded as an important planning tool by an agricultural state such as Illinois (26 counties and recognition by the state). However, other states with important agricultural sectors, such as California, Nebraska, and South Dakota, did not use LESA when the survey was conducted. However, in 1993 the California legislature did mandate the use of LESA. No LESA users were found in Alabama, Louisiana, Mississippi, or Tennessee.

Where there is a convergence of good quality farmland or open space value with development pressures, as in Kane and Will counties near Chicago, Illinois, in Bucks, Chester, and Montgomery counties near Philadelphia, Pennsylvania, and in several Vermont townships, LESA appears to be a frequently used and important tool to aid in decision making. There are, of course, other areas of important farmlands and increasing development pressure, as in California's Central Valley and irrigated croplands in or near Phoenix, Arizona, where LESA is not in use. However, some California counties do use other farmland rating systems. For example, Tulare County developed a parcel evaluation checklist to rate 15 agricultural factors and derive a point total for its Rural Valley Plan in 1975. The local use of LESA in California is likely to increase because of the 1993 state legislation coupled with more local interest.

The concept of land classification and evaluation is, of course, not new with the LESA system (*3, 4, 7, 8*). Rating of resource lands pre-dates LESA and is done currently in some states independent of LESA. What is unique in the LESA system is a common terminology, set of concepts, and rating scale. With lessons learned during the past decade, LESA systems can be improved to provide a more consistent and reliable tool to aid in policy formulation and decision making.

References

1. Ferguson, C., and R. Bowen. 1991. *Statistical Evaluation of an Agricultural Land Suitability Model.* Environmental Management 15(5):689-700.
2. Huddleston, J., J. Pease, W. Forrest, H. Hickerson, and R. Langridge. 1987. *Use of Agricultural Land Evaluation and Site Assessment in Linn County, Oregon.* Environmental Management 11(3):389-405.
3. Pease, J., and P. Jackson. 1979. *Exclusive Farm Use Zone Development Ordinance.* Extension Service, Oregon State University, Corvallis.
4. Rathburn, A. 1978. *Determination of the Suitability of Land for Grazing.* Cooperative Extension Service, University of Idaho, Moscow.
5. Steiner, F., J. Pease, R. Coughlin, J. Leach, C. Shaw, A. Sussman, and J. Pressley. 1991. *Agricultural Land Evaluation and Site Assessment: Status of State and Local Programs.* The Herberger Center, College of Architecture and Environmental Design, Arizona State University, Tempe.
6. Steiner, F., R. Dunford, and N. Dodsall. 1987. *The Use of the Agricultural Land Evaluation and Site Assessment System in the United States.* Landscape and Urban Planning 14:183-199.
7. Stockham, J. 1975. *Cropland Classification System for Jackson County.* Jackson County Department of Planning and Development, Medford, Oregon.
8. Tulare County Planning Department. 1975. *Rural Valley Lands Plan.* Visalia, California.
9. U.S. Department of Agriculture-Soil Conservation Service. 1983. *National Agricultural Land Evaluation and Site Assessment Handbook.*Washington, D.C.
10. Wright, L., W. Zitzmann, K. Young, and R. Googins. 1983. *LESA Agricultural Land Evaluation and Site Assessment.* Journal of Soil and Water Conservation 38(2):82-86.

This paper is based on work completed on a cooperative project funded by the U.S. Soil Conservation Service, Cooperative Agreements 68-3A75-0-162 and 68-3A75-1-48.

SECTION II

Evaluation of LESA Systems

Soil Conservation Service photo

5 Importance of the LESA Objective in Selecting LE Methods and Setting Thresholds for Decision Making

J. Herbert Huddleston

xperience with several land evaluation and site assessment (LESA) models in Oregon has shown that a careful consideration and statement of objective is extremely important in developing an appropriate LESA model (*8*). LESA certainly can be a useful tool, when used in the classical way, for evaluating the relative quality of tracts of land for agricultural use. But the LESA approach also can be used to evaluate land quality for specific crops such as wheat, corn, cotton, or rice, and to evaluate the relative quality of land for forestry. Furthermore, the same concepts and principles behind agricultural and forestry LESA models can be used to develop LESA ratings of the relative quality of tracts of land for rural residences, subdivision development, commercial or industrial development, power plant siting, and many other non-agricultural uses of land.

For maximum effectiveness as an aid in land-use planning and decision making, however, the LESA model's objective must be narrowly focused on a single kind of land use such as agriculture, or forestry, or subdivision development, or industrial use. A corollary of this principle is that the objective should not try to accomplish evaluation of tracts of land for two or more of these or any other kinds of land use in the same LESA model.

Many of the LESA applications in Oregon deal with making choices between resource uses of land, such as agriculture or forestry, and non-resource uses, such as rural residential or industrial/commercial. In these situations it is not appropriate to use models in which there is a mix of factors, some relevant to agricultural land use, others relevant to rural residential land use (*5*), because the interpretations of the results of such models are not clear. The problem is more in the site assessment (SA) part of the model than in the land evaluation (LE) part, for it is usually the case that the best soils for resource use also are the best soils for non-resource use. But site assessment for agriculture should involve only factors that directly affect agricultural use of the land, such as parcel size and shape, location with respect to markets and agricultural services, and conflicts arising from vandalism and complaints about noise, dust, odors, and farm chemicals that may be associated with adjacent or nearby residential land uses. Factors such as proximity to schools, availability of fire protection services, quality of the road system, and location of the nearest sewer line should not be included in an agricultural LESA model. These factors do not directly affect agricultural production, but represent suitability for non-agricultural development.

To include such factors in an agricultural LESA model obfuscates the interpretation of the results, for if planning decisions were based on either the total LESA score or the separate LE and SA scores, one could never be sure whether a low SA score was the result of truly poor agricultural suitability, or represented mediocre agricultural land and mediocre development suitability, or implied that excellent development suitability rendered even the best agricultural land useless for continued agricultural production.

It is far better to keep each LESA model narrowly focussed on a single kind of land use, and, if necessary, to develop separate LESA models for each different kind of competing land use. In this way the results of each evaluation are much cleaner and more interpretable, and they can more easily be used by planners to make comparisons of relative quality for each different kind of land use.

This principle of focusing the objective on a single type of land use affects all aspects of LESA model development and use. Two of those aspects—the selection of an appropriate method for land evaluation and the setting of thresholds for interpreting the results of a LESA rating—are discussed in this chapter.

Selecting an Appropriate LE Method

Soil scientists are well aware of the problems that may arise in using an interpretation of soil survey information developed for one use to try to make an interpretation for some other use. Land capability classes (*6*), for example, were developed specifically to rate the risk of damage to a soil under cultivation, and these classes often do not work well as substitutes for ratings of soil productivity. This problem must be kept in mind when deciding on a proper method of evaluating soil resource quality for the land use under consideration.

The LESA handbook (*11*) suggests four possible measures of soil resource quality: land capability class, prime farmland classification, soil productivity ratings, and soil potential ratings. Information on land capability and prime farmland is readily available in most local offices of the USDA Soil Conservation Service. Information on soil productivity as measured by estimated crop yields is available in soil surveys and in the SCS's national soils database. Empirical soil productivity ratings, however, have been developed only in a few states such as California (*10*), Iowa (*1*), and Oregon (*3*), and they are not universally available in all parts of the U.S. Soil potential ratings are even less widely available, having been developed only for a few specific applications in local areas. Thus, one criterion for selecting an appropriate LE method may be the availability of soil quality information. Stated another way, one must decide whether methods based on readily available information are adequate, or whether the extra time and effort needed to construct soil productivity or potential ratings will produce a substantially better LESA model. Again, the objective of the LESA model is very important in making this determination.

Land capability classes might be an appropriate choice for land evaluation if the objective of the LESA model was to rate the relative quality of parcels of land in terms of enhancing or sustaining their long-term productivity. But if the objective is to rate the relative agricultural productivity of parcels of land, capability classes alone would be an inappropriate choice. Capability and productivity are two distinctly different aspects of soil behavior, and they are not necessarily highly correlated. The data in Figures 1 and 2 illustrate the relationship. In Figure 1, data from the Washington County

(Oregon) soil survey (*2*) show a very low correlation between wheat yield and capability. Yields vary widely within capability classes, and one could obtain a yield of 80 bushels on soils in each of several different capability classes. In Figure 2, data from the Linn County soil survey (*7*) show a somewhat better relationship between yield of perennial rye grass seed and capability class, but the correlation (r = 0.67) is still quite low, and there is substantial variability in yield within most capability classes. Although there may be other crops in other areas for which the correlation is much better, the principle stands that land capability classes should not be used as surrogates for soil productivity unless there is indeed a very high correlation between these two different measures of land resource quality.

Prime farmland ratings, by themselves, are unlikely to provide a satisfactory measure of land evaluation for a LESA model. One reason is that there is a maximum of five classes into which soils can be placed: prime, unique, important statewide, important locally, and other land. This method provides no way to distinguish among the many soils that would qualify as prime farmland, or those in the important farmland class, or even those that fall outside of the prime farmland classification. A second reason is that the definition of prime farmland may exclude some soils that are extremely valuable agricultural soils. In several counties of north central Oregon, for example, winter wheat production is the staple of the agricultural and county economy.

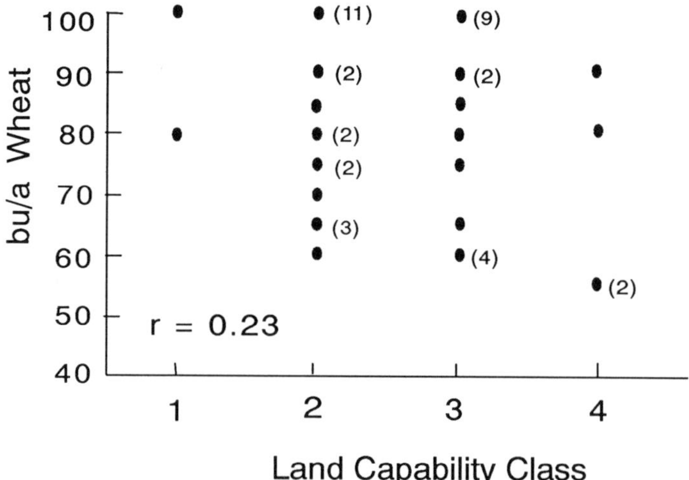

Figure 1. Relationship between wheat yield and capability class in Washington County, Oregon. Numbers in parentheses indicate the number of soil survey map units having that specific combination of yield and capability class.

There are some excellent soils for producing wheat, but even the best soils fail to be prime because wheat is produced under a wheat-fallow rotation, and the requirement that the moisture supply be adequate to produce a crop in six years out of 10 is not met. Consequently these soils and these counties would be downgraded relative to other counties in the state if LE were based solely on the prime farmland criterion, when in fact the agricultural value of these soils may exceed the value of soils classified as prime elsewhere.

Either crop yield data or information on estimated crop yields in published soil survey reports are appropriate measures of land resource quality if the LESA objective is to rate agricultural productivity. There are a couple of caveats, however. First, the data must express productivity at equivalent points in time and under equivalent levels of technology. It would be incorrect to compare a soil yielding 90 bushels of corn in a 1988 survey with a soil yielding 90 bushels of corn in a 1963 survey. One way around this problem is to express the yields in each county as a percentage of the maximum in each county, then rate soils in terms of the percent of the maximum attainable.

A second problem has to do with missing data. Estimated crop yields tabulated in soil surveys are usually given only for soils on which a specific crop is grown. A soil may not be used to grow a particular crop either because soil properties are unfavorable for the growth of that crop or because the soil, though well enough suited, provides even better yields and returns

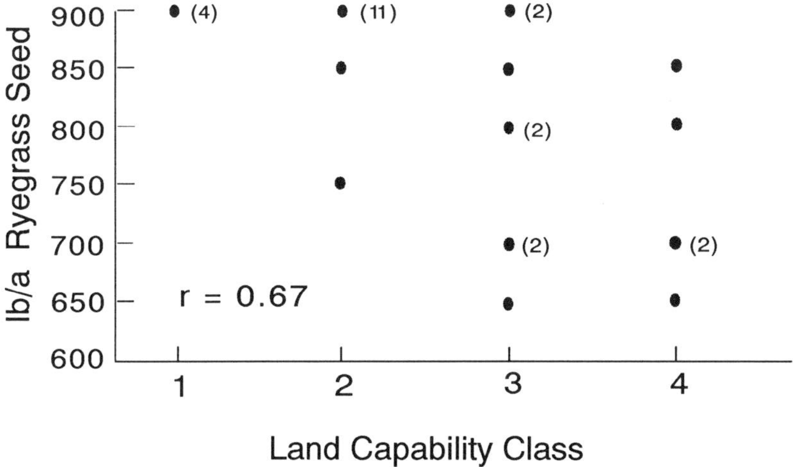

Figure 2. Relationship between perennial ryegrass seed yield and capability class in Linn County, Oregon. Numbers in parentheses indicate the number of soil survey map units having that specific combination of yield and capability class.

for another crop. In either case, missing data mandate either estimating crop yields or using some other empirically derived decision guides to provide for comprehensive LE ratings in a LESA model.

A third problem relates back to the objective itself. If the objective is to rate land for the production of a specific agricultural crop, say soybeans or cotton, then crop yield data might be the most suitable LE measure. But if the objective is to rate land for overall agricultural suitability, as is often the case in land-use planning situations that deal with choices between preservation and development of agricultural land, LE ratings based on a single crop may be misleading. This is particularly true in areas suited to a wide diversity of agricultural enterprises. Some crops may be sensitive to soil differences, others may be quite insensitive. In this case LE ratings based on crop yields require averaging yield potentials over several indicator crops representing the major kinds of agricultural enterprises in the area.

An alternative to crop yield data for evaluating soil productivity is the soil productivity rating. The difference is subtle, but important. With crop yield data, one can deduce that, because crop yields are higher on soil "A" than on soil "B", soil "A" is a more productive soil. The limitations to this approach have been discussed in the preceding paragraphs. Soil productivity ratings differ from crop yield ratings because they are derived empirically from an assessment of soil properties known to affect crop growth and yield. Soil depth, texture, organic matter content, water holding capacity, and drainage class are some of the key properties used. Numerical ratings are assigned to the values of each property such that the more favorable that property, the higher the number. Property values are then combined to yield an overall, empirical rating for soil productivity that does not depend on the availability of crop yield data. For a comprehensive review of the development and use of soil productivity ratings in the United States, see Huddleston (*4*).

Two distinct advantages of the soil productivity rating method for evaluating land suitability for agriculture are that, first, there is no problem with missing data, so that every soil in a soil survey can be evaluated, not just those for which crop yield data are available, and second, the relative quality of soils can be expressed on a continuous numerical scale, often from 0 to 100.

There are some disadvantages, however. The most serious is that productivity ratings do not always account for differences in management inputs needed to realize the level of productivity attributed to a soil. It is quite possible for two soils to have the same level of productivity, but one of those soils may require substantially more inputs of fertilizer, drainage, weed control, or erosion control than the other. For the LESA objective, it would seem that the soil requiring the greater amount of inputs to achieve the same level of productivity should have the lower LE rating.

A second disadvantage of soil productivity ratings is that the time required to develop them is substantial. The experience and expertise of a professional soil scientist is required, and for maximum effectiveness, the soil scientist should work with a local advisory committee to develop ratings that are accepted by all. The extra time and effort may be worthwhile, however, if the local advisory committee agrees that, for their LESA objective, soil productivity ratings are the best measure of soil resource quality.

The LESA handbook (*11*) suggests that information from land capability classes, prime farmland ratings, and measures of soil productivity should be integrated to create approximately 10 classes of relative suitability. Each soil can then be placed in one of the 10 classes. For some users this may be an appropriate method, particularly if the objective is to evaluate general agricultural suitability, which is in fact how the handbook was written to be used. It is certainly true that a Class I soil with high yields and a high productivity index is better than a Class VI soil with very low yields. Less clear, however, is whether a Class II soil with low yields should be rated equal to, better than, or worse than a Class IV soil with high yields. The handbook (*11*) does offer some guidelines for establishing class limits, but the development of precise criteria are left to the creativity of the person or group doing the LESA rating. This flexibility is one of the appealing attributes of the LESA process.

Another possible disadvantage of the combined rating process described in the LESA handbook (*11*) is that it creates a small number of discrete groups rather than a continuous scale of rating points. For some objectives this may be an adequate method, but for those who want to make comparisons of one soil with another, or to specify thresholds for distinguishing between different grades of land resource quality, ratings on a continuous scale are likely to be a preferred method. Continuous scale ratings, such as soil productivity ratings or soil potential ratings (discussed below), are developed simply by assigning the best soil for a specified use a value of 100 and expressing the value of all other soils as a percentage of the best soil.

So far we have discussed only LESA models for agricultural uses. What if the objective is to evaluate land resource quality for forestry, or grazing, or rural residential uses, or light industry, or recreation, or wetlands, or wildlife habitat? These kinds of applications are particularly important in view of the principle of narrowly focusing the LESA objective. The principles embodied in the concept of a LESA model for rating agricultural land quality are equally applicable to evaluations of soil quality and site suitability for any of these other kinds of land uses. And because many land-use planners are faced with the need to make choices among competing land uses, separately developed LESA models can provide them with objective, community-based tools that can help them make these difficult decisions.

For non-agricultural LESA applications, however, none of the LE methods previously discussed are appropriate. Although it is generally true that the best soils for agricultural crops are also the best soils for other, non-agricultural uses, there is no evidence that ratings based on crop potentials can serve adequately as surrogates for non-agricultural uses of land.

The solution to this problem, and indeed the best LE method for many agricultural uses of land, lies with the soil potential rating (SPR). Soil potential ratings, as defined by the Soil Conservation Service (*13*), are ratings that indicate the relative quality of a soil for a particular use compared to other soils in the area, considering yield or performance level for that use, the relative cost of management needed to minimize the effects of any soil restrictions, and the adverse effects of any continuing limitations on social, economic, or environmental values.

Soil potential ratings differ from soil productivity ratings in that the latter measure yield only. SPRs, however, account for both the level of yield, output, or performance that it is possible to obtain and the extent to which management practices are needed to overcome soil limitations in order to achieve the level of performance that is possible. Thus, by accounting for both inputs and outputs, the soil potential rating more accurately reflects the true value of a soil for a specified land use, and because potentials are expressed on continuous numerical scales, the potential of one soil relative to another is easier to assess than when LE ratings are forced into a finite number of groups or classes.

Measures of inputs and outputs for agricultural SPRs are based on the costs of the management practices needed to produce a crop and on the prices received upon the sale of the crop. Equivalent measures for non-agricultural SPRs are more indirect or empirical than for agricultural ones, but the SPR method does permit the calculation of legitimate ratings of relative soil resource quality for any kind of land use.

Development of SPRs is rooted in a committee process that draws upon the knowledge and experience of both soil scientists and local citizens familiar with the soils and land management practices in an area. The committee is responsible for specifying yields or other performance indicators for each soil, listing all of the appropriate management practices and establishing their costs or other measures of input, compiling all pertinent sources of data, and providing reasonable estimates for either inputs or outputs in cases where data are lacking.

Huddleston et al. (*5*) describe one procedure for developing SPRs for agriculture. First one or more crops are selected as representative of the kinds of agricultural enterprises in the area. Then for a given crop, such as winter wheat, expected yields are specified for each soil, and those yields, when multiplied by a dollar value per bushel, form the measure of performance. The committee decided on a list of management practices, including seedbed preparation, seeding, fertilizing, weed control, drainage, irrigation, and harvesting, and assigned costs to each practice. To the extent that costs varied by soil type, the sum total of management costs differed from soil to soil. By subtracting all management costs from the sale value of the crop, a net return was calculated. The soil having the maximum net return was assigned an arbitrary SPR of 100, and all other soil SPRs were calculated according to the ratio of their net return to the maximum net return. Where there were negative numbers in the set of net returns, the absolute value of the most negative return was added to all returns, and the ratio calculations performed on these adjusted returns. SPRs for agriculture can be calculated either by simple averaging of SPRs derived from all of the selected index crops or by weighting the average with the crop that provides the maximum net return on each soil.

SPR calculations for forestry (*9*) follow similar logic, except the crop is on a much longer rotation (60 years) and the management practices are very different. Yields in thousands of board feet of timber were specified for each soil using a computer model, and those yields, multiplied by a dollar value per thousand board feet, provided a performance index. Management practices associated with site preparation, planting, thinning, final harvest, and road building were specified, and variable costs allocated to each practice depending on the influence of soil factors such as slope, stoniness, erodibility, depth to bedrock, and hardness of bedrock. Net returns and final soil potential ratings were calculated in the same way as for agricultural SPRs.

Development of soil potential ratings for non-agricultural uses requires setting standards of performance that can be indexed, followed by indexing each management practice needed to correct limitations caused by one or more soil properties (*13*). In Stafford County, Virginia (*12*), ratings of soil potential for dwellings with basements used a value of $10,000 for the performance standard of a soil that had no limitations and required no corrective measures. This value was set equal to an SPR of 100. For all other soils, costs of corrective measures needed to overcome limitations associated with high water tables, slope, shrink-swell clays, and depth to bedrock were estimated, and each $100 increment of cost was allocated an index value of 1 point. Thus, if the sum of all costs of corrective measures came to $1,300, 13 points would be subtracted from the maximum index value of 100, giving an SPR of 87. Each map unit in the soil survey of Stafford County was evaluated in this way. There were no corrections for negative numbers, and the final list of SPRs ranged from -32 to 100.

There are two major disadvantages of the soil potential rating method: the time required to develop the ratings and the need to deal with lack of information. Because SPR development is necessarily a committee process, it simply takes a lot of time to organize the committee and set not one but several meetings at which all of the issues can be discussed and decisions made. During the course of their deliberations, the committee is likely to discover that data are lacking for one or more of the management inputs, or for measures of performance on one or more soils. They then must either perform the studies necessary to obtain the data, contact other experts who may be able to provide the data, or develop estimates that they can all agree on in lieu of primary data. To accomplish all this adds to the time required, which may be as much as several months.

The advantages of the soil potential method are substantial and are due in no small way to the nature of the disadvantages. One of the greatest strengths of the soil potential method is the committee process by which the ratings are developed. The committee structure provides a way to ensure that all parties interested in land-use decisions can have a part in creating the tools to assist in the making of those decisions. Broad representation on the committee increases the likelihood that all of the important management factors are considered and improves the odds of getting good estimates for missing data. Perhaps most important, development by a local committee may do more than anything else to establish local credibility and lead to the development of a product that will be adopted and used by local jurisdictions.

To summarize, any of the measures of land evaluation may be appropriate if they are indeed the best measures to meet the specific objective of the LESA model being developed. In general, however, the soil potential rating method, though perhaps the most tedious and time-consuming to develop, may be the method of choice because it is the most comprehensive, the most flexible, can be applied to any kind of land use, and, by virtue of its committee involvement, is likely to provide the most credible and acceptable results.

The final word on selecting an LE method is flexibility. The instructions in the LESA handbook (*11*), the methods discussed in published papers, indeed the methods discussed in this chapter should be taken as suggestions rather than as fixed rules for LE development. Individuals and committees working on LE ratings should above all apply good, sound principles of soil science, but within that they should be allowed maximum flexibility to exercise their creativity and ingenuity to modify existing methods and try new approaches to devise a system for evaluating soil resource quality that is tailored to the specific objective of their LESA model.

Setting Thresholds for Making Decisions

LESA models are designed to help users make decisions, and this requires some interpretation of the numbers generated for LE, SA, the component factors within LE and SA, and the overall total. As with LE methods, the criteria developed to make these interpretations depend on the nature of the LESA objective. If the objective mandates that any single factor could control the interpretation, threshold criteria must be written accordingly, but if the objective depends more heavily on interactions among several factors, criteria must be formulated in different ways.

The LESA model developed in Linn County, Oregon (*5*), was designed strictly to rate the quality of land for agricultural use. The objective was to provide land-use planners with a tool to help them identify three general grades of land resource quality: first, land resources sufficiently valuable for agriculture that they should be protected for that use, second, lands that were of lower quality and could be considered for other, non-agricultural uses, and third, lands that had essentially no agricultural value.

Table 1 gives the framework of the LESA model developed to meet this objective, along with the results of its application to two specific parcels of land. Soil potential ratings were used as a measure of LE, and two separate factors, conflict assessment and parcel size, were used for SA. The conflict factor was subdivided into two components, conflict associated with perimeter land uses and conflict associated with nearby but not adjacent land uses. LE and SA were weighted equally, each being allocated 150 points. Within SA, conflict and parcel size were weighted equally at 75 points each, but perimeter conflict (45 points) was weighted a little more heavily than nearby conflict (30 points).

In developing threshold criteria to distinguish among the three grades of agricultural land, the local advisory committee felt very strongly that any sin-

Table 1. Structure of the agricultural LESA model, with examples, developed in Linn County, Oregon (*5*).

Factor	Thresholds	Parcel A	Parcel B
LE			
SPR	150	149	134
SA			
Conflict			
1) Perimeter	45	45	31
2) Nearby	30	27	0
Parcel Size	75	52	30
TOTAL	300	273	195

Threshold Criteria:

Good Agricultural Land
SPR > 80 and conflict > 52 and size > 45 and total > 200.

Lower Quality Agricultural Land
SPR 50-80 or conflict 18-52 or size 10-45 or total 100-200

Nonagricultural land
SPR < 50 or conflict < 18 or size < 10 or total < 100

gle factor should be allowed to control the classification, with a minimum of compensation of one factor for another. Thus, in order for a parcel to qualify for the highest class of resource quality, the soil rating (LE score) had to be above a specified minimum of 80 points **and** the conflict score in the SA rating had to be above a specified minimum of 52 points **and** the parcel size score in the SA rating had to be above a specified minimum of 45 points. Any individual factor score falling below its threshold value caused the parcel to be rated in a lower class. Similar types of thresholds (50 for soils, 18 for conflict, 10 for size) were established to separate the middle class of resource quality from the low class.

In this model, factor compensation entered into threshold determinations only with respect to a fourth criterion based on the total LESA score. This was done by setting a minimum threshold for the total score that exceeded the sum of the threshold minimums for each of the three component factors. In specific terms, the upper thresholds for soils (80), conflict (52), and size (45) add up to 177 points, but the threshold value for the total LESA score was set at 200 points to make sure that at least one of the principal factors was better than the minimum value. Stated another way, the local committee wanted land rated in the highest class to have resource qualities that were somewhat better than the absolute minimums in each factor.

Parcel A in Table 1 exemplifies a parcel of excellent agricultural land. Soils are ideal for agricultural production, as indicated by an SPR of 149 out of a possible 150 points. Land uses adjacent to the parcel are all fully compatible, as indicated by a perimeter conflict score of 45 out of a possible 45 points. Even in the nearby area most of the land uses are fully compatible (27 of 30 possible). The total score for conflict is 72 points, which is well above the threshold of 52 points. The parcel is smaller than ideal, but it is still large enough to operate efficiently and economically, so the rating of 52 points exceeds the threshold minimum of 45 points. The total LESA score of 273 also is well above the 200-point threshold. Thus there are no limiting factors, and the parcel should be maintained in the land resource base for agricultural production.

Parcel B in Table 1 exemplifies a parcel of lower quality agricultural land. The soils are good enough (134 out of 150 points), but there are a few conflicting land uses adjacent to this parcel (31 out of 45 points), and the presence of a rural subdivision in the immediate vicinity reduces the nearby conflict score to zero. Thus the total conflict score of 31 points is below the threshold of 52 points. Further, the parcel size is below the optimum threshold (30 out of 45 points), and the total score (195) is a little below the threshold minimum of 200 points. This parcel, therefore, fails the high quality classification on three counts: conflict, size, and total. It should be designated as agricultural land of lower quality.

Other LESA applications may wish to allow much more compensation among factors in the setting of thresholds. The simplest way to do so is to set thresholds only on the total LESA score. This is appropriate if it makes no difference how the total score is derived, or if it does not matter that one or more components may have very low scores, as long as other factors have high enough scores to compensate. Users need to understand, however, that there may be many different combinations of factor scores, all of which could lead to a total score exceeding the interpretation threshold. By placing all of the interpretation on one number, i.e. the total score, much of the power of the LESA model to identify potential limiting factors is likely to be lost.

A different method for specifying thresholds using compensating factors was developed in conjunction with an unpublished agricultural LESA model for Lane County, Oregon. The LESA model itself was very similar to the Linn County model given in Table 1. The interpretation objective, however, was to classify agricultural land into two groups, the better lands being labeled primary, and the poorer lands being labeled secondary. In this case the local advisory committee wanted excellent soils to be able to compensate for limitations associated with conflict or parcel size, and vice versa. The threshold criterion used to accomplish this was quite simple: primary land had to have an LE score of 78 or more and a total LESA score of 200 or more.

This criterion mandates that primary land must have some minimum level of soil resource quality, but it allows the conflict score to vary according to the quality of the soil. In this way marginal soils can qualify as primary only if they are in large parcels virtually free of conflict, whereas the very good soils can tolerate much higher levels of conflict on smaller parcels.

A slight variation of this criterion was used to distinguish between primary land and secondary land in a LESA model for forestry (*9*). The structure of the model itself was very similar to the agricultural LESA models described above and in Table 1, except that LE was allocated only 35 percent of the total points, and SA conflicts were weighted at 40 percent of the total instead of 25 percent. Given a 300-point total, scores were distributed as follows: Soils, 105; Parcel size, 75; Adjacent land use, 75; Surrounding land use, 45.

In setting thresholds for this model the local committee felt strongly that size alone should not be allowed to control the rating. As long as the soils were adequate, and the conflict was low, parcels of any size were deemed suitable for commercial forestry. To accomplish this objective, three criteria were written:

1. if size < 34, then total must be > 237;
2. if size ≥ 34, then if soils < 53, total must be > 180;
3. if size ≥ 34, and if soils ≥ 53, then total must be > 160.

Criterion number one says that in order for a very small parcel to qualify as primary land, it must have excellent soils and be free of land use conflicts. Criteria two and three invoke a soils standard but, unlike the agricultural LESA model, there is no absolute minimum of soil quality required. Instead, the poorer soils are allowed to be in the primary class, but only if the parcel has large enough size and is free enough of conflict to generate a high total LESA score. As both size and soil quality scores increase, more conflict can be tolerated, so the threshold for total LESA score decreases.

Summary

LESA model ratings will convey the greatest amount of information to decision makers if the objective of the model, the factors used to evaluate land resource quality, and the criteria used to determine factor ratings are all narrowly focused on a single kind of land use. SPRs are the preferred method of land evaluation because they are the most comprehensive, they can be focused on any specific type of land use, and they provide a continuous rating scale that facilitates comparisons among different soils. Disadvantages of the soil potential ratings method include the amount of time needed to develop SPRs and the need to substitute knowledgeable estimates for actual data to evaluate some factors. Other land evaluation methods, such as land capability classes, soil productivity ratings, or prime farmland ratings, may be appropriate if the LESA objective closely parallels the original objective for which those rating systems were designed.

Setting LESA rating thresholds for decision-making purposes can be done either by allowing any one factor to control the decision or by providing for some amount of factor compensation. Basing decisions simply on the total LESA score is probably the least useful method because it masks any information concerning the reasons for the final rating. An alternative is to set thresholds on each of several component factors in the LESA model and require that each and every component have values above the threshold to support a positive decision. Conversely, if the value for any one factor should fall below its threshold, that factor would control the final decision. Maximum utilization of LESA factor ratings is obtained by allowing high values for some factors to compensate for low values in other factors. This can be done by setting threshold values for certain critical factors and for the total LESA score, thereby allowing the values for other factors to vary depending on how high or low the values for the critical factors are.

References

1. Fenton, T. E., E. R. Duncan, W. D. Shrader, and L. C. Dumenil. 1971. *Productivity levels of some Iowa soils.* Iowa Agricultural and Home Economics Experiment Station and Cooperative Extension Service Special Report 66.
2. Green, G. L. 1982. *Soil Survey of Washington County, Oregon.* USDA Soil Conservation Service, Washington, D.C.
3. Huddleston, J. H. 1982. *Agricultural productivity ratings for soils of the Willamette Valley.* Oregon State University Extension Service Circular 1105.
4. Huddleston, J. H. 1984. *Development and use of soil productivity ratings in the United States.* Geoderma 32: 297-317.
5. Huddleston, J. H., J. R. Pease, W. G. Forrest, H. J. Hickerson, and R. W. Langridge. 1987. *Use of agricultural land evaluation and site assessment in Linn County, Oregon, USA.* Environmental Management 11: 389-405.
6. Klingebiel, A. A., and P. H. Montgomery. 1961. *Land-Capability Classification.* Agricultural Handbook 210. U.S. Department of Agriculture Soil Conservation Service, Washington, D.C.
7. Langridge, R. W. 1987. *Soil Survey of Linn County Area, Oregon.* U.S. Department of Agriculture Soil Conservation Service, Washington, D.C.
8. Pease, J. R. and A. Sussman. 1994. *A Five Point Approach for Evaluating LESA Models.* In: F.R. Steiner, J.R. Pease, and R.E. Coughlin (eds.) *A Decade with LESA: The Evolution of Land Evaluation and Site Assessment.* Soil and Water Conservation Society, Ankeny, Iowa.
9. Pepi, J. A. 1989. *Development of a land evaluation and site assessment (LESA) model for forestry in Lane County, Oregon.* Unpublished M.S. thesis, Department of Soil Science, Oregon State University, Corvallis.
10. Storie, R. E. 1976. *Storie Index Rating.* University of California Division of Agricultural Science Special Publication 3203.
11. U.S. Department of Agriculture-Soil Conservation Service. 1983. *National Agricultural Land Evaluation and Site Assessment Handbook.* Washington, D.C.
12. U.S. Department of Agriculture-Soil Conservation Service. 1984. *Soil Potentials for Dwellings with Basements, Stafford County, Virginia.* USDA-SCS, Richmond, Virginia.
13. U.S. Department of Agriculture-Soil Conservation Service. 1992. *National Soils Handbook, Draft.* Document 430-VI-NSH, USDA-SCS, Washington, D.C.

Soil Conservation Service photo

6 A Five-Point Approach for Evaluating LESA Models

James R. Pease
and Adam P. Sussman

Land evaluation and site assessment (LESA) rating systems are used in at least 146 jurisdictions in 31 states for land use decisions on zone changes, purchase of development rights, farmland classification, and other applications. The importance of these decisions to landowners requires that public agencies be accountable for the fairness and accuracy of the rating system. This paper proposes a set of five criteria to evaluate the validity of LESA systems. **Agriproductivity** provides a **focus** for the criteria. Factors should be related directly to agricultural productivity. **Replicability** of ratings requires objective factors that can be measured by specific definitions and procedures. Consistent ratings by different reviewers are a necessary condition for legal defensibility (*3*). **Redundancy** of factors may inadvertently over-weight certain variables and make the model more complex than necessary. **Data-based point scaling**, to the extent practical, uses empirical data to put the values, or points, associated with each factor on a firm legal footing. **Benchmarking** (comparing to a control) of LESA results provides a means to evaluate the validity of the rating. These five tests, while not exhaustive, should provide an efficient and reliable means to evaluate LESA systems. In many cases, improvements can make existing LESA systems more defensible and fairer to property owners within the jurisdiction.

The proposed evaluation procedure was tested and evaluated using the Linn County, Oregon, LESA system. Linn County is a south-central Willamette Valley county with an important agricultural sector (Figure 1). The county covers 2,297 square miles, with a population of about 90,000 (39 persons per square mile). Farmland ranges from some of the best cropland in the state on bottomlands to marginal grazing lands in the foothills and on mountain slopes. A mild climate with sufficient rain and sun produces one of Oregon's most diversified farming areas, leading the United States in ryegrass production. Vegetables, field crops, dairy products, and beef cattle are other leading cash crops.

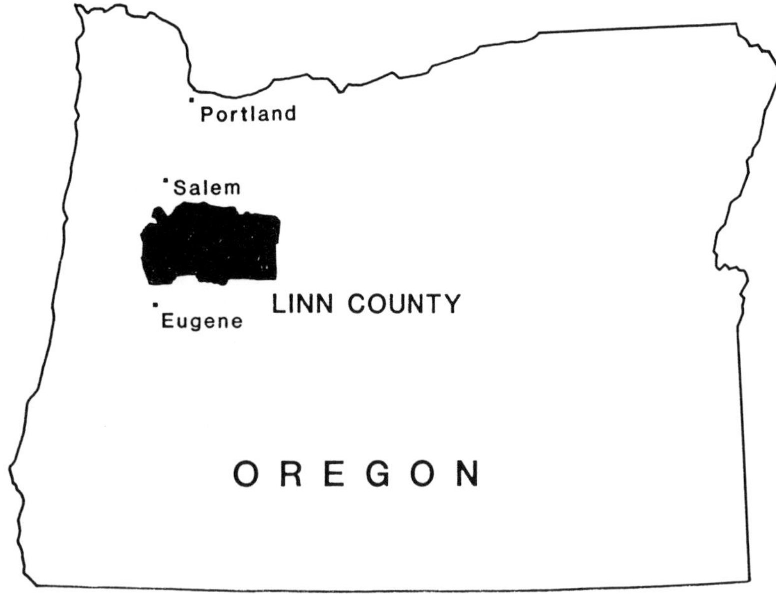

Figure 1. Location of Linn County, Oregon.

LESA criteria and procedures from a 1991 national inventory of LESA systems (*9*) also were tested under the proposed procedure. Documentation of the criteria and point allocation for 25 LESA systems in the West and Midwest were available for this purpose.

Agriproductivity Focus

An agriproductivity focus requires that all LE and SA factors relate directly to agricultural production or agricultural practices. It is recognized that not all LESA users will agree with this focus. In fact, as shown in Table 1, more than 80 percent of 25 jurisdictions in the West and Midwest use factors that do not relate directly to agricultural production or practices (*9*). For example, factors such as distance to central sewer or water, distance from urban center, compatibility with plan policies, and availability of other suitable development sites measure development potential rather than agricultural potential. It is not surprising that most jurisdictions use non-agricultural factors since they are suggested in the 1983 Soil Conservation Service (SCS) LESA handbook (*10*) for the site assessment part of the analysis. However, it is proposed that the mixing of development potential with agricultural potential in the criteria provides an amalgam of productivity value and implicit development suitability or conversion potential that confuses the rating. An alternate approach is to rate the agricultural value of a site separately from its development suitability. The two ratings could then be compared to help make policy or permit decisions.

The site assessment component of LESA can be restricted to factors that

Table 1. Site assessment (SA) criteria not focused on agricultural productivity in 25 jurisdictions in western and midwestern states.

SA Criteria (Non-Agriculture Focus)	Number (%) of Jurisdictions
Distance from central sewer	21 (84%)
Compatibility with comprehensive plan	20 (80%)
Distance from urban center	20 (80%)
Level of public service (road access)	20 (80%)
Distance to central water	15 (60%)
Availability of other suitable sites	13 (52%)
On-site waste disposal suitability	12 (48%)
Historical/cultural and recreational impacts	12 (48%)
Soil limitations for proposed use	8 (32%)
Distance from fire protection	6 (24%)
Increased governmental financial burden	5 (20%)
Consistent with municipal plan	4 (16%)
Distance/availability of elementary school space	3 (12%)
Distance from electrical extension	2 (8%)
Availability of public transit	2 (8%)

relate directly to agricultural production. Parcel size, potential conflict with surrounding uses, parcel shape, agricultural support services, on-farm investment, and irrigation water supply are examples of non-soil factors that may be important to farm productivity. These factors are easily understood by the public and provide a linkage to the land evaluation component, while retaining a focus on agriproductivity.

In the Linn County case study, SA factors measure potential perimeter conflict, non-contiguous potential conflict within a one-quarter mile area, and parcel size, all of which relate to agricultural production or potential limitations on agricultural practices. Conflicts were categorized as fully conflicting, e.g., homesites on small tracts; or somewhat conflicting, such as golf courses, schools, or commercial uses. In allocating points, somewhat conflicting was penalized one-half the points of fully conflicting. These variables capture much of the information contained in other SA criteria commonly used, such as distance to urban center, presence of sewer and water lines, and zoning and plan designations. A study to evaluate the effect of adding other variables to the system (*11*) determined that relative rankings did not change. The additional variables created more complexity without substantially changing the ratings.

Replicability

In order to be replicable, i.e., provide consistent results by different reviewers, LESA models must use measurable factors and clear definitions and procedures. A national survey of LESA systems (*9*) identified eight different non-quantifiable factors, with 76 percent of the jurisdictions in the West and Midwest using at least one subjective factor (Table 2). A simple test of the consistency of ratings can be done by a group of five to 10 persons on five to 10 sites in about a two-hour period. The results are helpful in clarifying ambiguities in definitions or procedures. In most cases, definitions and

Table 2. Subjective (non-measurable) site assessment (SA) criteria in 25 jurisdictions in western and midwestern states.

SA Criteria (Subjective)	Number (%) of Jurisdictions
Compatible with surroundinguses	19 (76)
Environmental impacts	15 (60)
Historical/cultural and recreational impacts	12 (48)
Need for additional urban land	3 (12)
Configuration/shape of the parcel	1 (4)
Potential traffic conflicts	1 (4)
Impacts on water quality	1 (4)
Impacts on mineral extraction	1 (4)

Table 3. Evaluation of the consistency of the Linn County LESA system.

Factor	Control* Score	Student Median	Student Range	Student Standard Deviation
	Terrace Landform Site #1			
Soil	99	100	99-102	1.29
Conflicting residences	27	27	0	0
Perimeter conflict	41	41	39-41	0.76
Parcel size	68	68	0	0
Total	235	236	234-236	1.49
	Foothill Landform Site #4			
Soil	100	100	98-102	1.46
Conflicting residences	15	15	0-27	8.90
Perimeter conflict	23	23	17-29	3.46
Parcel size	56	56	0	0
Total	194	196	179-208	10.54

* The control score is the score calculated by the author of the Linn County LESA system.

procedures can easily be adjusted to make the factors measurable and objective and the procedures clear to reviewers.

To evaluate the consistency of ratings for the case study, a group of eight graduate students rated five tracts in Linn County (Table 3). The ratings were generally consistent. The procedures for calculating conflicts within the one-quarter mile area could be clarified, since in one test site some reviewers miscounted the number of potentially conflicting dwelling units. One problem common to other LESA models may have been in the lack of specificity of measurement procedures. Are the distances measured in an arc from the subject parcel's corners or from the center of the parcel? Are all parcels bisected by the arc counted? These types of measurement questions need to be clearly stated in the instructions to obtain replicable results.

Redundancy of Factors

Several other research papers have reported on intercorrelation, especially with regard to SA criteria (*1, 3, 4, 5, 6*). Both LE and SA may be affected by intercorrelation. The implications of intercorrelation among LE or SA criteria may range from simply a cumbersome, unnecessarily complex system to a flawed rating because of unintended over-weighting of certain factors. Ferguson and Bowen (*4*) report that the five measures of soil quality used in the Hawaiian LESA model are highly correlated (all were above 0.85 correlation coefficient), even given the diverse soil conditions of the test parcels. This finding would indicate that one LE criterion could serve the purpose.

Since the SCS handbook (*10*) lists 36 suggestions for SA variables, and

Table 4. Simple correlation coefficients: Between LESA scores and factor ratings and among factor ratings.

	"X" County										
	LESA Score	(1)	(2)	(3)	(4)	(5)	(6)	(7)	(8)	(9)	(10)
	1										
(1) Percent agriculture within a mile	.5772*	1									
(2) Adjacent land in agriculture	.7246*	.5261*	1								
(3) Adjacent zoning	.6543*	.3016	.4441	1							
(4) Support systems	.5774*	.0455	.2007	.3731	1						
(5) L/U compatibility	.7686*	.5748*	.5387*	.5668*	.5081*	1					
(6) Distance to urban growth boundary	.4541	.4031	.1753	.3468	.3909	.3454	1				
(7) Compatibility for agricultural use	.5040*	.0879	.3036	.0974	.2017	.1598	-.0198	1			
(8) Distance to central water	.7035*	.7012*	.5186*	.3686	.5307*	.7228*	.5732*	.0080	1		
(9) Distance to central sewer	.7035*	.7012*	.5186*	.3686	.5307*	.7228*	.5732*	.0080	1*	1	
(10) Availability of public transit	-.1844	-.1024	-.3211	-.1374	-.0400	-.0924	-.1769	-.0215	-.0721	-.0721	1

* Correlation significant at the 0.01 level.
Sample size: 26

Table 5. Stepwise regression summary; dependent variable-LESA scores; independent variables-factor ratings.

"X" County

Step	Variable Entered	Variable Removed	Variable Name	R	RSQ	RSQ Increase	Number of Ind. Variables Included
1	5		Land use compatibility	0.7687	0.4348	0.5980	1
2	7		Compatible for ag use	0.8567	0.7399	0.1491	2
3	9		Distance to sewer	0.9041	0.8174	0.0775	3
4	3		Adjacent zoning	0.9469	0.8968	0.0794	4
5		5	Land use compatibility	0.9403	0.8841	-0.0066	3
6	2		Land in ag adjacent	0.9532	0.9085	0.0244	4

*Much of the variation in the county LESA scores can be explained by only two variables: (5) land use compatibility and (7) compatibility of the site for agricultural use. Together these two factors explain 74% of the variation in total scores.

local jurisdictions have been inventive in adding more, it is not surprising that a national LESA survey identified at least 40 different factors used by various jurisdictions in the SA component (*9*). Jurisdictions commonly use 10 or more SA factors.

The Ferguson and Bowen study (*4*) found that, while intercorrelation was not high among Hawaii's 10 SA factors, only four were needed to explain 95 percent of the variability in SA scores. The model would be less cumbersome and produce the same results by reducing SA from 10 to four criteria.

Table 4 displays the simple correlation coefficients for 10 SA factors in a frequently used county-level LESA model. Intercorrelation at a significant level occurs for all but two factors. Two of the factors have a correlation of 1.0. The stepwise regression summary given in Table 5 indicates that four factors explain about 90 percent (R^2) of the variation in total scores. Since two of the four factors are significantly correlated (Table 6), only two factors, surrounding land-use compatibility and compatibility for agricultural use (of the proposed use), are not intercorrelated at a significant level. These two factors explain 74 percent of variation in total scores and probably could yield the same relative rankings as the 10 factors.

Table 6. Summary table.

"X" County

	5	7	9
(7)	.1598	1	
(9)	.7228*	.0080	1
(3)	.5668*	.0974	.3686

*Correlation significant at the 0.01 level.

The correlation coefficients for SA variables in the Linn County, Oregon, case study are given in Table 7. This model uses only three SA factors, none of which are significantly correlated. It appears that the factors are measuring different things, although perimeter conflict explains much of the variation in total SA scores. A full explanation of the Linn County LESA system is given in a paper by Huddleston and Pease (*7*).

Table 7. Simple correlation coefficients: Between LESA scores and factor ratings and among factor ratings Linn County, Oregon.

	Total	1	2	3
Total	1			
(1) Surrounding non-farm dwellings	.5441*	1		
(2) % perimeter conflict	.6926*	.4633	1	
(3) Parcel size	.3375	-.1117	.2055	1

*Correlation significant at the 0.01 level.
Sample size: 25

Data-based Scaling

Data-based point scaling implies that there is some research or factual basis for how points are assigned for each factor. For example, in the Linn County case study, parcel size is an important SA factor, accounting for 50 percent of the SA points. Ranges of parcel sizes and their associated LESA points are given in Table 8. The table differentiates values for parcel sizes by landform: bottomland, terrace, and foothill. It distributes points on a scale of five acres to 100 acres on bottomlands, with 30-40 acres allocated 45 of the possible 75 points. The landforms and the point distribution were based on a survey of commercial agriculture in the county, which indicated important differences of agricultural type and scale among the landforms and also reported data on farm size and field size. The typical field size of 30-40 acres was used as a break-point in assigning 60 percent of the total point distribution. Assessor data on tax lot sizes also were used to establish upper limits on the scale.

Assigning values for potential conflicts was more problematical. Two master's degree research papers were available from Oregon State University (*2, 8*) that evaluated the potential conflict between farmers and non-farm residences. Field sizes from the survey were used to establish the threshold for farm/non-farm dwellings. Field trips with local agricultural experts were held to apply expert opinion to the potential conflict assumptions in the system, resulting in various adjustments.

The Delphi Expert Opinion benchmark test, reported in the next section, indicated that potential conflicts may be over-rated in the Linn County system. While local experts seem to agree that the presence of non-farm dwellings or other uses in the immediate vicinity of a farm does affect agricultural practices and should cause a parcel to be rated lower than a similar parcel in an area surrounded by other commercial farms, the procedures to assign points to potential conflict need more work. However, the attempt to assign points to potential conflict does make explicit the more implicit assumptions behind common SA factors such as distance to sewer or water lines or urban centers.

Table 8. Parcel size.

Bottomlands	Terraces	Hills	Points
>100	>120	>120	75
90-100	100-120	100-120	72
80-90	90-100	80-100	68
70-80	80-90	60-80	64
60-70	70-80	50-60	60
50-60	60-70	40-50	56
40-50	50-60	30-40	52
*30-40	*40-50	*20-30	45
20-30	30-40	15-20	30
10-20	20-30	10-15	20
5-10	10-20	5-10	10
<5	<10	<5	0

*Typical field size

Benchmarking

Benchmarking (comparing results to a control) of LESA ratings is an important part of a LESA validation study. The problem arises, of course, as to what to use as a benchmark. LESA incorporates the common SCS soil rating systems in its LE component. The SA component is not supported by similar tested procedures. When the LE and SA components are combined into an overall rating on a relative scale, the question still remains as to how valid the rating is. For the case studies, a Delphi Expert Opinion method was used to establish a benchmark rating for selected test sites. The procedures were applied in two case studies; the results are discussed in detail in other papers (*1, 9*). In the Linn County case study, the Delphi panel rated the LE component consistently lower than did the LESA system; two sites had limitations not addressed by the system. In one site, lack of irrigation water capacity resulted in only half of the 65-acre tract being in production in any given year. On the other site, site terrain reduced the rating by the Delphi panel, a specific limitation not considered by the LESA system.

In the SA component, small parcel size on bottomland soils was rated higher by the panel than by the LESA system. Potential conflicts with non-farm residences, while affecting ratings, were discounted by the Delphi panel, especially on sites with good soils and with certain spatial distributions of the dwellings not recognized by the LESA system.

The Delphi Expert Opinion benchmark appears to provide a reliable means to test both the LE and SA components, as well as an overall score and the relative rankings of LESA sites. While not trivial to organize and administer, it is certainly manageable by a local jurisdiction attempting to validate its LESA system. The benchmark findings should help in adjusting the LESA system, as well as providing a broader validation base for legal defensibility and public accountability.

Conclusions

The five tests outlined in this paper should contribute to developing a firmer foundation for LESA systems. Other considerations may be important as well. The LE to SA ratio recommended by the 1983 SCS handbook (1:2, LE to SA) should be re-examined. The ratio may work well in areas of homogeneous soils because then the differentiating criteria will be in the SA component. However, in areas of diverse soils, landforms, and types of agriculture, different ratios may be important. Ferguson and Bowen (*5, 6*) found that, in Hawaii, a 1:1 ratio is more appropriate, as did Huddleston et al. (*7*) in Linn County, Oregon. The Delphi panel in the Linn County case study indicated that soils should be given 2:1 weight on bottomlands, 1:1 on terraces, and 1:2 in foothills. The reasoning was that in areas of better soils, only a high degree of conflict or a serious limitation of parcel size should cause a parcel to be classified in a lower category. Conversely, in areas of poorer soils, conflict would have to be very low or parcel size very large to place the parcel in a higher category.

Since the LE:SA ratio has a significant effect on the total scores, this consideration should be examined in any LESA validation study. In areas of diversified landforms, soil types, and agricultural practices, such as Linn County, it may be desirable to weight LE:SA differently for different geographic areas of the jurisdiction. A simple map based on soil types and production activities could be prepared for calculating LESA scores.

The selection of factors for both LE and SA should consider redundancy, as previously discussed. At the least, redundant factors burden the model with unnecessary measurements and make it more difficult for the public to understand. At worst, highly correlated factors may unintentionally give too much weight to a certain concern, resulting in a "wrong" rating.

The weighting and scaling of factors also may be important in the final ratings. At the least, a rationale and some documentation should be available to explain how and why points were allocated to various factors and internally within each factor.

Ease of administration is a realistic consideration. For the busy local planning office, a rating that can be done in a few minutes using tabular and other data available in the planning office is an important concern. Consideration of the types of assessment, soils, and other maps available to the local planning office should be an important part of system development. Easily calculated LESA scores make it more likely that ratings will be done more routinely.

As with any model, LESA systems are generalizations on reality, subject to errors of both commission and omission. The overall goal should be the model-builder's one of elegance, i.e., combining simplicity with maximum information content. While perfection is not an achievable goal, we can strive to put LESA systems on as firm a foundation as our local resources permit.

References

1. Coughlin, R.E. 1994. *Sensitivity, Ambiguity, and Redundancy in LESA Systems and the Acceptability of LESA Scores.* In: F. R. Steiner, J. R. Pease, and R. E. Coughlin (eds.) *A Decade with LESA: The Evolution of Land Evaluation and Site Assessment.* Soil and Water Conservation Society, Ankeny, Iowa.
2. Daughton, K. 1985. *Presence of Farm and Non-Farm Produced Nuisances Within The Urban Fringe of Eugene and Springfield, Oregon.* Master's research paper, Oregon State University, Corvallis.
3. DeMers, M. 1989. *The Importance of Site Assessment in Land Planning: A re-examination of the SCS LESA Model.* Applied Geography (9):287-303.
4. Ferguson, C., and R. Bowen. 1991. *Statistical Evaluation of an Agricultural Land Suitability Model.* Environmental Management 15(5):689-700.
5. Ferguson, C., R. Bowen, and M. Kahn. 1991. *A statewide LESA system for Hawaii.* Journal of Soil and Water Conservation 46(4):263-267.
6. Ferguson, C., R. Bowen, M. Khan, and T. Liang. 1990. *An Appraisal of the Hawaii Land Evaluation and Site Assessment System.* Information Text Series 035, for HITAHR, College of Tropical Agriculture and Human Resources, University of Hawaii, Manoa.
7. Huddleston, J., J. Pease, W. Forrest, H. Hickerson, and R. Langridge. 1987. *Use of Agricultural Land Evaluation and Site Assessment in Linn County, Oregon.* Environmental Management 11(3):389-405.
8. McDonough, M. 1983. *A Study of Non-Farm Dwellings in an Exclusive Farm Use Zone.* Master's research paper, Oregon State University, Corvallis.
9. Steiner, F., J. Leach, C. Shaw, J. Pease, A. Sussman, R. Coughlin, and J. Pressley. 1991. *Agricultural Land Evaluation and Site Assessment: Status of State and Local Programs.* The Herberger Center, Arizona State University, Tempe.
10. U.S. Department of Agriculture-Soil Conservation Service. 1983. *National Agricultural Land Evaluation and Site Assessment Handbook.*Washington, D.C.
11. Wendolowski, W. J. 1984. *A Re-Evaluation of the Linn County LESA Model Utilizing Economic Criteria.* Research paper for Geography 559B, Oregon State University, Corvallis.

Soil Conservation Service photo

7 Benchmarking LESA Models with Delphi Expert Opinion Panels: A Case Study of Linn County, Oregon

James R. Pease
and Adam P. Sussman

iven the wide and diverse applications of the land evaluation and site assessment (LESA) system, and the fact that the U.S. Department of Agriculture requires its use by federal agencies and encourages its use by local and state governments, it is important to know how reliable, accurate, and consistent LESA systems are proving to be.

There has been some research on various aspects of LESA, such as factor selection, weighting, and intercorrelation (*2, 3, 6, 9*), consistency of ratings (*22*), and general applications (*7, 10, 19, 20, 23*). As a framework for evaluation of LESA models, an evaluation process was developed and applied to the Linn County, Oregon, LESA system (*18*). The process addressed five points: 1) the extent to which the LESA model focused on agricultural productivity potential vs. development potential, 2) intercorrelation of site assessment (SA) criteria, 3) replicability of ratings, 4) the data basis for point allocation, and 5) benchmarks for measuring the validity of the ratings. In general, the Linn County LESA model was found to focus on agricultural productivity; the criteria were all measurable, giving consistent ratings by different reviewers; there was a reasonably good data basis for point allocation; and intercorrelation of the criteria was not a problem. Results of the analyses are presented in Huddleston et al. (*10*) and Pease and Sussman (*18*).

The question remained, however, as to what could be used as a measurement benchmark when evaluating the validity and accuracy of a LESA system. In other words, in evaluating a LESA system's accuracy and reliability in distinguishing land that should be retained in agriculture and land that could be converted to other uses, what does one use for comparison?

Research Problem

The objective of this research was to develop and test a process to evaluate the consistency and validity of LESA models. The case study was the LESA model used by Linn County in Oregon's Willamette Valley. A measurement benchmark was established by a panel of local agricultural experts using the Delphi Expert Opinion method. As an additional measure of accuracy, and to examine the consistency of neighboring LESA systems, a LESA system from an adjacent county (Lane County) with similar physical and agricultural characteristics was compared to the Linn County system and to ratings of the local experts. The procedures also were applied to a second case study in Lancaster County, Pennsylvania, and are reported in chapter 8.

Linn County LESA. Linn County is a south-central Willamette Valley county with an important agricultural sector. The county covers an area of 2,297 square miles and has a population of about 90,000, an average of 39 people per square mile (see Figure 1, chapter 6). Farmland in the county ranges from some of the best bottomland in Oregon to marginal grazing land in the foothills and on mountain slopes. A mild climate with sufficient rain and sun produces one of Oregon's most diversified farming areas. Linn County leads the United States in ryegrass production. Vegetables, field crops, dairy products, and beef cattle are other leading cash crops.

In Oregon, all county governments are required to regulate uses on farmland in exclusive farm use (EFU) zones. For a complete description of

Oregon's land-use system, see papers by Pease (*15*) and Eber (*8*).

The Linn County LESA system is used in zoning permit decisions on ownership parcels zoned for exclusive farm use. The system awards a maximum of 300 points with equal weight given to land evaluation (LE) and site assessment (SA). LE is based on soil potential ratings (SPRs). The SPRs measure the net return to soil management for the production of a given crop. For the Linn County LESA, SPR tables were established by arraying the soils from 150 to 0 points based on the highest single rating of four indicator crops.

The two criteria for Linn County's SA are conflict with surrounding non-farm parcels and parcel size. When the LESA model was developed in 1983, 20 SA factors were initially considered. After extensive committee discussions, intercorrelation analysis, and field trips to view SA factors at more than 35 sites in the county, it was decided that surrounding conflict and parcel size captured most of the information of the other variables. The county also decided to limit SA factors to those affecting agricultural practices or productivity, which eliminated some SA factors used in other jurisdictions to measure development potential. Ratings from the Linn County LESA are used as background information for staff reports to the decision-making body. For a detailed description of the Linn County LESA system, see Huddleston et al. (*10*).

Lane County LESA. The Lane County, Oregon, LESA system was also examined. Lane County lies south and adjacent to Linn County and has similar physical and agricultural characteristics. The Lane County LESA system, which has not yet been implemented, was designed mainly to distinguish between primary and secondary farmland resources. Similar to Linn County, the Lane system awards a maximum of 300 points with equal weight given to LE and SA. There are, however, differences in how the two systems determine LE and SA. To determine LE, the Lane County system uses SPRs calculated from the average SPR of four indicator crops, whereas the Linn County system uses the single most profitable crop as the SPR.

The SA criteria for the Lane County system are essentially the same as Linn County, but minor refinements were added. The most notable of the refinements is the distribution of points for parcel size. Rather than awarding SA points for parcel size by landform alone, as Linn County does, the Lane system partitions the county into production areas based on soil characteristics and agricultural activities and awards points for the types and scales of commercial agriculture in each area. Small parcels in areas of row crops on well drained terrace soils would receive more points than a similar sized parcel in an area of grass seed farms on poorly drained terrace soils.

Delphi Expert Opinion Method. The Delphi method was used by the expert panel to establish benchmark ratings of the parcels. Delphi, developed in the 1950s by the Rand Corporation, is a means of systematically collecting and progressively refining information provided by a group of selected experts. Delphi is characterized by response anonymity, controlled feedback, and statistical summary of group responses. Anonymity, accomplished by the use of questionnaires, secret ballots, or on-line computers, reduces the effect of dominant individuals. Controlled feedback, i.e., conducting the exercise in a sequence of rounds between each of which a summary of the previous round is communicated to the participants, reduces the range of answers and focuses on group consensus. The less informed responses gravitate toward the more informed responses on each successive round.

Statistical summary and definition of group response is a way of reducing group pressure for conformity. More important, statistical definition of group response assures that the opinion of every member of the group is represented in the final response. For a detailed description of the Delphi method see Linstone and Turoff (*11*) and Dalkey (*4*).

Delphi has been shown to be an inexpensive and efficient method for gathering information on natural resource and land-use data (*13, 16, 17*). Delphi research conducted previously found that expert opinion was highly correlated to mail-out questionnaire data in the characterization of agricultural marketing and processing as well as in identifying characteristics such as soil types and field sizes (*13, 16*). Although these studies showed Delphi to be less well-correlated with certain financial aspects of agriculture, Delphi appeared to be a reliable method to rate agricultural productivity of ownership parcels for the purpose of establishing an evaluation benchmark.

Research Method

LESA ratings were evaluated by comparing them to ratings established by a panel of experts. It was assumed that the ratings derived by the panel of experts were the most accurate and therefore could serve as measurement benchmarks. An evaluation of this assumption was part of the research. An additional measurement benchmark was made by comparing Linn County LESA scores to the Lane County LESA system.

Accuracy and reliability of the Linn County LESA was determined based on the difference between ratings by the Delphi panel and ratings by the LESA system. To carry out the validation, a four-step approach was taken:

1) Five ownership parcels in Linn County were selected that represented diverse physical and spatial characteristics. Table 1 gives a description of the sites. Factors considered in the site selection included, but were not limited to, soil type, landform, current agricultural activities, surrounding development, and location within the county.

Table 1. Description of study sites.

Linn County LESA Study Sites			
Site #	Size (in acres)	Landform	Current Use
1	95.2	Terrace	grass seed
2	13.2	Terrace	residence/grazing
3	13.4	Bottomland	fallow
4	49.2	Foothill	grazing/timber
5	65.4	Bottomland	row crops

2) A panel of agricultural experts was shown the five sites during a two-hour field trip; later they were asked to rate the parcels in terms of "Soil Quality" (LE), "Other Factors" which may affect the ability to conduct agricultural operations (SA), and "Overall" (LESA). "Other Factors" were not specifically defined, but panelists were asked to list separately the other factors they felt affected agricultural practices or productivity. The Delphi method was employed by the panel to establish median ratings.
3) The investigators then completed LESA ratings for the same five ownership parcels using the Linn County LESA system and the Lane County LESA system.
4) Once all the ratings were completed (Delphi, Linn County LESA, and Lane County LESA) the results were compared. Using the panel ratings as the benchmark and the Lane County LESA as an additional comparison, the reliability of the Linn County LESA ratings was analyzed.

Panel Selection. Delphi panelists for the study were selected in consultation with Linn County agricultural extension agents and other USDA personnel. The panel, when completed, consisted of a diverse group of farmers, a Linn County planning commissioner, a representative from the Farmers Home Administration, a credit officer from Farm Credit Services, a farmland tax assessor, an agricultural instructor, an extension agent, and an Agricultural Stabilization and Conservation Service official, for a total of 14. This group represented a wide range of knowledge on agricultural practices and agricultural land uses. Research on the relationship of group size to range of responses has found that groups of 10 to 17 are adequate for providing accurate results (*4*).

Additional Worksheets. To gain additional information on site assessment and LE to SA ratios, panelists were also asked to complete two worksheets. Following the third iteration of site characteristics ratings for each site, the panelists were asked to note the three most important factors that caused them to rate the parcel as they did, and whether they saw those factors as an advantage or disadvantage to the site. At the conclusion of the entire rating session, the panelists used another worksheet to describe how they would weight soil quality relative to "Other Factors" in the overall rating. This weighting was done by landform.

Results

Delphi Process. The median and interquartile range of the panel's scores are displayed in Table 2. Convergence of the interquartile range, signifying group consensus, after two or three rounds was observed in all cases except for "Overall" rating for ite 5, where it remained unchanged from its Round I narrow spread. Changes in the median values from Round I to Round II occurred six of 15 times and, where three iterations were conducted, changes from Round II to Round III occurred four of 10 times. In general, the Delphi method proved to be an effective tool for gaining group consensus.

Comparison of Linn County LESA and Delphi Ratings. The Linn County LESA ratings were compared to the panel's ratings by looking at numeric differences between the two ratings, testing statistically to see whether there was a significant correlation between the relative ranking of the five sites by the two methods, and by examining the relative weights given to LE and SA. The Delphi panel used a 100-point scale for all ratings, which were later converted to the LESA's 300-point scale.

Numeric Differences. Differences between the Delphi panel and Linn County LESA ratings are described by difference (Delphi minus Linn) and percent error [(Delphi (A) minus Linn (A1) divided by Delphi (A) x 100)]. Results from a comparison of the scores are displayed in Tables 3-5. Comparing the soils ratings (Table 3), it can be seen that the Linn County LESA consistently rated all sites higher than the panel with the exception of site 1 where there was an absolute difference of only 0.75 points. Excluding site 1, the soil ratings by the panel and the LESA system differed by an average of -21.75 points. The standard error of the average difference was 1.14, indicating that the Delphi panel was quite consistent in its lower rating of the sites as compared to the LESA rating.

It is interesting to note that site 1, where the absolute difference is only 0.75 points, is the predominant type of landform and agricultural operation (grass seed) found in Linn County. On the other hand, foothill sites such as site 4, which had the largest absolute difference (25 points), are generally perceived as less valuable farmland and may be used for several different types of lower-value agricultural activities.

Sites 3 and 5 received 149 of a possible 150 points for LE from the LESA model, indicating they represented sites with the best soils in the county. The Delphi panel, however, awarded 127.5 points to each, which indicates they

Table 2. Linn County Delphi panel scores, by round.

	Soil Quality			Other Factors			Overall		
	Round 1	Round 2	Round 3	Round 1	Round 2	Round 3	Round 1	Round 2	Round 3
Site 1									
Upper quartile	72	70	68	83	80	78	80	75	74
Median	65	65.5	66.5	76	76	75	71	71	71.5
Lower quartile	62	65	65	65	69	69	66	69	70
Site 2									
Upper quartile	75	70	68	60	52	50	60	55	55
Median	65	65	65	47.5	47.5	45	52.5	50	50
Lower quartile	50	55	68	40	45	44	44	40	40
Site 3									
Upper quartile	86	86	85	80	75	72	73	70	70
Median	85	85	85	65	60	60	66	65	62.5
Lower quartile	80	80	80	40	50	50	55	60	60
Site 4									
Upper quartile	60	55	--	60	52	52	55	55	--
Median	50	50	--	51	50	50	50	50	--
Lower quartile	50	50	--	45	46	46	48	50	--
Site 5									
Upper quartile	90	90	--	85	80	--	85	85	--
Median	84.5	85	--	80	80	--	80	80	--
Lower quartile	75	80	--	70	75	--	79	79	--

Table 3. Analysis of "Soil Quality Ratings." Delphi panel ratings vs. Linn county LESA system ratings.

Site Number	Size (in acres)	Landform (A)	Delphi Rating* (A1)	LESA Rating**	Difference Delphi-LESA	% Error A-A1/A x 100
1	95.2	Terrace	99.75	99	+0.75	0.75%
2	13.2	Terrace	97.50	117	-19.50	20%
3	13.4	Bottomland	127.50	149	-21.50	16%
4	49.2	Foothill	75.00	100	-25.00	33%
5	65.4	Bottomland	127.50	149	-21.50	16%

* The Delphi rating is the median "Soil Quality Rating" given by the 14 panelists. Delphi Ratings were multiplied by 1.5 to fit the Linn County LESA system (150 points possible).
**The LESA rating is the Soil Potential Rating using the Linn County LESA system.
Note: Sites 1-3 had three Delphi iterations; Sites 4-5 had two iterations.

did not consider the sites the best in the county. Site 3 was a small site (13.3 acres) located in an area of mixed parcel sizes. It was a long, narrow tract between two homesites and was fallow at the time of the field trip. Site 5, a large field imbedded in a prime farm area, had a problem familiar to one of the panelists. The tract had an inadequate supply of irrigation water, which resulted in only half the tract being irrigated in a given year. Although these could be considered SA factors, the panel may have penalized the LE portion for some of them. These site-specific adjustments illustrate the advantage a group of local experts has over a general LESA model, which cannot reflect a wide variety of site-specific factors.

A comparison of "Other Factor" ratings (Table 4) shows that, for sites 1 and 4, LESA SA ratings are higher than Delphi ratings, while they are lower for sites 2, 3, and 5. The largest difference between the two ratings is for bottomland site 3, where the Delphi panel score was 52.0 points higher (percent

Table 4. Analysis of "Other Factor" ratings. Delphi panel ratings vs. Linn County LESA system ratings.

Site Number	Size (in acres)	Landform (A)	Delphi Rating* (A1)	LESA Rating**	Difference Delphi-LESA	% Error A-A1/A x 100
1	95.2	Terrace	112.5	136.0	-23.5	20%
2	13.2	Terrace	67.5	42.0	+25.5	37%
3	13.4	Bottomland	90.0	38.0	+52.0	57%
4	49.2	Foothill	75.0	94.0	-19.0	25%
5	65.4	Bottomland	120.0	95.0	+25.0	20%

*The Delphi rating is the median "Other Factor Rating" given by the 14 panelists. Panelists were asked to rate the parcels for OTHER FACTORS that affect the ability to conduct agricultural operations. Delphi scores were multiplied by 1.5 to fit the scale of the Linn County LESA system (150 points possible).
**The LESA rating is the score given for Site Assessment using the Linn County LESA system (SA).
Note: Sites 1-4 had three Delphi iterations; Site 5 had two iterations.

error of 57) than the SA. This discrepancy points out the differences in the panel's perception of the impact of surrounding non-farm dwellings and the assumptions of conflict in the LESA model.

The Linn County LESA system assumes that low density populations are less likely to object to agricultural practices or cause conflicts. It also assumes that conflicts are likely to occur when non-farm residences are located adjacent to or nearby the subject parcel. To quantify the degree of conflict between residential development and agricultural practices, the SA subsystem counts the number of non-perimeter conflicting residences (conflicting residences are those located on parcels smaller than typical farm field size within a quarter of a mile) and also measures perimeter conflict. For site 3, 18 conflicting residences were located within 0.25 miles and 44 percent of the parcel perimeter was in conflict. This resulted in a low overall compatibility score of 18 points out of 75 possible and a low score for parcel size, giving an overall SA of 38 points out of a possible 150 points. In comparison, the equivalent "Other Factors" score by the panel (90 out of 150) may indicate that the experts discounted the potential conflict and small parcel size. This is an interesting point in that the potential for conflict is an important assumption underlying most farmland protection policies. However, as noted previously, the panelists may have incorporated the small parcel size and elongated shape in their lower LE rating.

Overall ratings for the sites by the two methods (with the exception of foothill site 4) are much closer (Table 5). Looking at differences in score by landform, the two terrace sites 1 and 2 were both rated higher by LESA. For bottomland sites 3 and 5, the difference between ratings (Delphi-Linn) ranges from as little as 0.5 points for site 3 to -4.0 points for site 5. Foothill site 4, however, differs from the Delphi panel by 44.0 points, reflecting the discrepancy in ratings for soils and other factors.

Table 5. Analysis of "Overall Ratings." Delphi panel ratings vs. Linn County LESA system ratings.

Site Number	Size (in acres)	Landform	Delphi Rating* (A)	LESA Rating** (A1)	Difference	% Error Delphi-LESA A-A1/A x 100
1	95.22	Terrace	214.5	235.0	-20.5	9%
2	13.18	Terrace	150.0	159.0	-9.0	6%
3	13.36	Bottomland	187.5	187.0	+0.5	0.2%
4	49.20	Foothill	150.0	194.0	-44.0	29%
5	65.43	Bottomland	240.0	244.0	-4.0	1%

*The Delphi rating is the median "Overall Rating" given by the 14 panelists. The Delphi ratings have been multiplied by 3 to fit the scale of the Linn County LESA system (300 points possible).

**The LESA rating is the Overall Score a parcel received using the Linn County LESA system.

Note: Sites 1-3 had three Delphi iterations; Sites 4-5 had two iterations.

Relative Ranking. The Linn County LESA system was analyzed to see whether its relative ranking of the five sites was significantly correlated to that of the Delphi panel. Correlation of ranks was calculated using the Spearman Coefficient of Rank Correlation Equation (*14*). However, because of the small number of observations, combined with ties in ranking, the sample coefficient of correlation may deviate from the "true" coefficient of correlation. Therefore, the calculated coefficients and their associated P values can be seen as only approximate. Additionally, because LESA scores are linearly dependent, a test of the statistical significance of rank correlations of all three factors (Soil, Other, and Overall) would be a redundant test. It was therefore decided to calculate the statistical significance of rank correlation only for Overall ratings (Table 6). A correlation of -1 signifies perfect disagreement and +1 signifies perfect agreement.

Table 6. Relative rank of sites by Delphi panel and Linn County LESA.

Overall Ratings			
Site # Rank	Delphi Relative Rank	LESA Relative In Rank	Difference
1	2	2	0
2	4*	5	1
3	3	4	-1
4	4*	3	1
5	1	1	0

Coefficient of rank correlation = 0.82 (p = .1007)
* Signifies a tie in ranking.

Considering the relative rankings of Soil Quality scores, Delphi panelists, and Linn County LESA ratings ranked bottomland soils (sites 3 and 5) the highest. The Delphi panel ranked foothill site 4 soils the worst, whereas the LESA system ranked terrace site 1 the worst. It should be noted, however, that the LESA relative rank for the foothill site differs from the panel by only a 1 point score difference. Terrace site 1, ranked lowest by LESA, has a poorly drained soil type limited to grass seed production, while site 4 is limited to pasture and other lower per acre value uses. Using Spearman's equation, the rank correlation of the soil ratings was calculated to be 0.68, showing some evidence of agreement in relative soil rankings. In the relative ranking of sites by other factor scores, while no two sites were ranked exactly the same by the two scoring methods, the coefficient of rank correlation was calculated to be 0.60, again showing some evidence of agreement.

Rank correlation appears strongest for the Overall ratings. Both scoring methods rank bottomland site 5 the highest and terrace site 1 the second highest. Using Spearman's equation, a coefficient of rank correlation of 0.82

(P = 0.1007) for Overall ratings was calculated. Although not considered statistically significant, considering how small the sample is, it seems likely that larger samples would yield small P values. Overall, it appears that the LESA system and the panel of experts ranked the parcels for soil quality, site characteristics, and overall ratings in a similar way.

A further comparison of the panel and LESA ratings was made using threshold values incorporated into the Linn County LESA system. In 1984, while testing the system on 23 sites in the county, threshold values for good, marginal, and non-agricultural land were determined for each LESA factor, as well as for the overall score (Table 7). Because the panelists did not break their Other Factor scores out by conflict and size, a comparison of Other Factor threshold levels cannot be made. However, evaluation of soil ratings found that differences in threshold levels occurred only for site 4, where the panel rated the site as non-agricultural (75 points) compared to marginal (100 points) by the LESA system. There were no differences in threshold levels in the Overall ratings.

Table 7. Linn County LESA threshold levels.

	Thresholds			
Threshold	Soils	Conflict	Size	Total
Levels				
Good	>80	>52	>45	>200
Marginal	50-79	18-51	10-44	100-200
Non-Ag.	<50	<18	<10	<100

LE to SA Weights. Worksheets at the end of the rating session were used to investigate the Linn County LESA LE to SA ratio. The Linn County LESA system gives equal weight to LE and SA in all situations. This differs from the 33 percent (LE) to 67 percent (SA) ratio recommended in the 1983 LESA handbook (*21*) and used by most jurisdictions. The panel of experts was asked to indicate, by landform, how they would weight LE and SA points. In general, the panelists gave more weight to LE in bottomlands, slightly more or equal weight to LE in terrace landforms, and equal or less weight to LE in foothills.

The LE to SA ratios indicated by the panel were applied to the Linn County LE and SA LESA scores and to the Delphi panel scores to determine whether it would decrease the gap between the two ratings. Table 8 compares the panel and the adjusted LESA scores. For bottomland sites 3 and 5, where soil quality is generally high, it was found that increased LE weights increased overall scores and increased the gap between Delphi and LESA. Although the panelists were not asked to weight their scores given to Soil

Table 8. Comparison of Delphi and LESA Overall scores (when normalized to the LE to SA ratio indicated by the panel*).

	Results Weighted by Landform		
Site #	Delphi	LESA	Difference Delphi-LESA
1	210	228	-18
2	171	174	-3
3	236	243	-7
4	150	190	-40
5	251	271	-20

*The Delphi panel was asked to indicate preferred LE to SA weighting for each landform. These weights were applied to both Delphi and LESA scores to obtain a normalized value. For Terrace Sites #1 and #2 the preferred LE to SA ratio was 60% to 40%, Bottomland Sites #3 and #5 the preferred LE to SA ratio was 75% to 25%, Foothill Site #4 the preferred LE to SA ratio was 40% to 60%.

Quality and Other Factors to arrive at the Overall Rating, it is theoretically possible to determine the weights they implicitly used by calculating the ratio between their scores on the three factors. For example, for bottomland site 3, the imputed weights calculated were Soil Quality, 10 percent and Other Factors, 90 percent. Although panelists stated they would give more weight to LE it appears that, in rating bottomlands, more weight was given to Other Factors. For bottomland sites, LESA at the 50 percent-50 percent ratio was closest to the panel, which is in agreement with actual LESA weighting and the overall Delphi panel score (Table 5).

Giving slightly more weight to LE in terrace sites brought the LESA score and panel score into closer agreement for both sites 1 and 2 (Table 8). By comparison, the imputed weight given by the panel for site 1 was 37 percent for Soil Quality and 63 percent for Other Factors. For site 2 the imputed weights were Soil Quality, 32 percent and Other Factors, 68 percent.

Comparison of Lane County LESA and Delphi Ratings. Another method of testing the accuracy of the Linn County LESA was to apply a LESA system from an adjacent county to the five sites. If the LESA from an adjacent county (Lane County) was better correlated in terms of score and relative ranking, it could provide insight into weaknesses in the Linn County LESA.

Numeric Differences. A comparison of soil ratings by Delphi and the Lane County LESA show absolute differences ranging from -8.25 to -28.5. Similar to the Linn County LESA, the Lane County LESA consistently rated the soils higher than did the Delphi panel, in spite of the fact that the Lane LESA uses average SPRs rather than the highest of four indicator crops as the Linn County LESA does. The ratings for Other Factors by Delphi, and

Lane County LESA did not vary in a consistent fashion as did the soil ratings. However, the difference in Other Factors ratings for bottomland site 5 was 0.

Large differences in Overall scores were found between Delphi and the Lane County LESA. Similar to the soil ratings, Lane County LESA Overall ratings for all sites were higher than the panel's ratings. The Overall scores differed by an average of -39.5 with the smallest absolute differences found between terrace site 1 and bottomland site 5 (-19.5 and -24.0 points respectively).

Relative Ranking. A comparison of the relative ranking of the sites by Delphi and the Lane County LESA was carried out. Using Spearman's equation of rank correlation, a coefficient of 0.87 was calculated for relative soil rankings, providing some evidence for agreement. The ranking of sites by Other Factors was found to have a coefficient of rank correlation of 0.60. The rank correlation for Overall scores is almost 1. Spearman's equation yielded a correlation of 0.97 ($P = 0.054$) providing strong evidence for correlation of the relative rankings of the five sites.

Comparison of Linn LESA, Lane LESA, and Delphi

A comparison of all three ratings for Soil Quality is displayed in Figure 1. From this figure, it can be seen that, with the exception of site 1 (where the Linn LESA and the panel are almost exactly the same), both LESA systems consistently rated soils higher than the panel. Focusing on the differences between the LESA systems, it was found that, although the two systems calculate the SPRs used in LE differently, one using the average and the other using the highest of four indicator crops, the end results varied only by a maximum of 9 points. It should be noted that, when applying the Lane County system to the Linn County sites, some of the site average SPRs were unavailable. For sites 1 and 2 some average SPRs were estimated by a USDA Soil Conservation Service soil scientist.

Considering that both LESA systems use quantitative, data-based SPRs to determine LE, and that both were consistently higher than the ratings of the panel as well as consistent with each other, it appears that there may be limitations to comparing absolute soil ratings with expert opinion. The SPRs for both systems include specific data on crop yields, crop prices, and management practices. Lacking such specific data, absolute differences in Delphi panel soil scores would be expected.

Also, the panel of experts was able to adjust its scoring for site-specific problems that are not considered by the LESA model. For example, site 5 had a problem with inadequate volume of irrigation water, known to the pan-

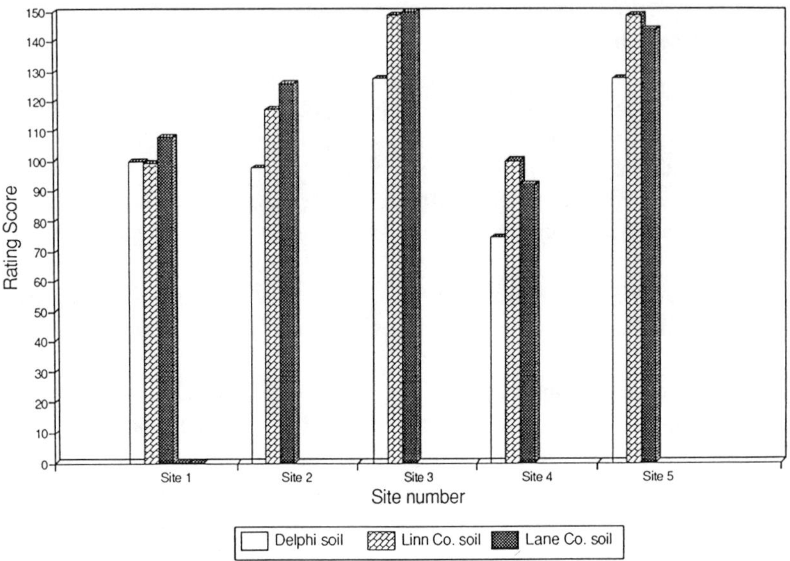

Figure 1. Comparison of Soil Quality ratings by Delphi, Linn, Lane.

elists but not accounted for by the LESA model. This most likely caused the LE rating to be lower for the panel than the LESA model. Another possible explanation of the difference in ratings may be that the LESA rating is based on a table of per-acre soil potential numbers, which will be the same wherever the soil occurs. The panel may have incorporated factors other than soil quality.

However, examining the relative ranking of sites by the panel and the LESA systems, it can be seen in Figure 1 and in earlier calculations of coefficients of rank correlation that there was general agreement in relative rankings. Overall, there is consistency between the two LESA systems, absolute but consistent differences between the panel and the LESA systems, and agreement in relative ranking for all three.

Figure 2 displays a comparison of Other Factors ratings by the Delphi panel and the two LESA systems. From this figure it can be seen that the correlation between panel scores and SA scores is highly variable. However, with the exception of site 4, the Lane County SA scores are more closely aligned with the panel's and, except for site 1, Lane County SA scores are higher than those of the Linn County system. Because SA ratings by panelists were not broken out and weighted by categories, i.e., conflict and size, it is impossible to tell exactly why the panelists gave a parcel a particular score. However, it appears that refinements in the Lane County LESA are

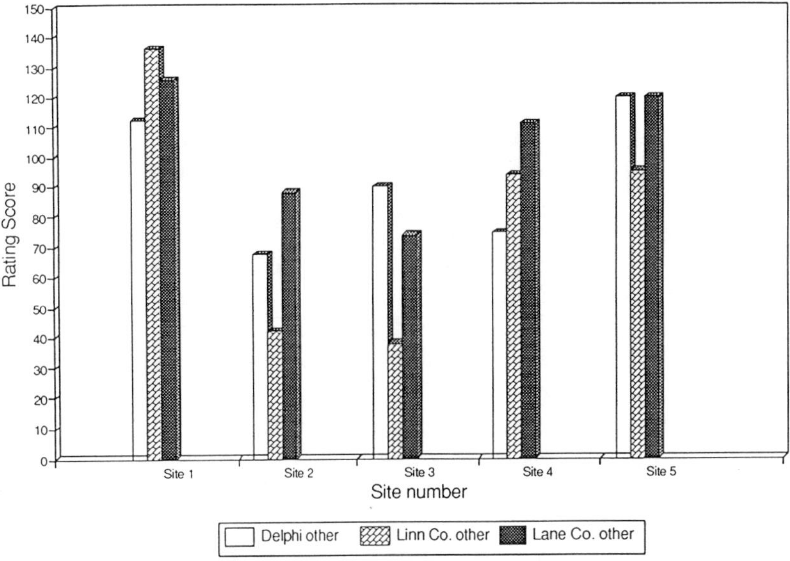

Figure 2. Comparison of Other Factor ratings by Delphi, Linn, and Lane.

responsible for the closer alignment with the panel ratings.

The Lane County LESA system, developed almost four years after the Linn LESA, puts less emphasis on the conflicts associated with non-resource dwellings in farm areas and refines the evaluation of parcel size to include consideration of not only landform but also the production area within the county. For site 1, a 95.2 acre grass seed field with little surrounding conflict, the two LESA systems rate the "conflict" almost identically. But, in the evaluation of size, because the site was found in a production area of poorly drained soils, the Lane system rated the parcel lower than the Linn system and closer to the panel's rating. Site 2, 13.2 acres of terrace land, was awarded 10 of 75 possible points for size by the Linn County system. In comparison, the Lane LESA system, which yielded absolute ratings closer to the panel, rated the site based on its location in a production area of well-drained terrace soils and awarded 45 of 75 possible points for size. Panelists characterized disadvantages of the site in terms of its small size and irregular shape; shape is not considered by either model.

Differing emphasis on conflict and the method for evaluating size appear to have caused large differences between the panel and the Linn County LESA for site 3. Site 3, a 13.4 acre parcel located on bottomland soils, is surrounded by several non-farm parcels. When evaluated for conflict by the Linn County system, a score of 18 out of a possible 75 points was awarded.

Additionally, the small size of the parcel was responsible for a size evaluation of 20 out of 75 possible points. Although worksheets by the panelists indicated that the size of the parcel and the number of surrounding neighbors were disadvantages of the site, the site was penalized to a much lesser degree by the panelists than by the LESA model. A comparison between the two LESA systems shows that Lane County's slightly less emphasis on conflict combined with the refinements in size evaluation bring the panel into much closer agreement with the Lane model than with the Linn County model.

As with the other sites, site 5 had closer agreement between the panel and Lane County. The Linn County system emphasis on conflict and its method of rating size resulted in a lower score as compared to Lane County. Lane County LESA and the panel were in perfect agreement for site 5 (Figure 2).

The only exception to the Lane LESA system being closer to the panel was site 4. In this case, less emphasis on conflict by the Lane model over-rated the parcel compared to the panel. Evaluating panelists' worksheets, the disadvantages of the site were indicated as steep slopes and lack of irrigation, neither of which is addressed directly by the LESA models. As mentioned earlier, it appears that the low scores awarded site 4 by the panel compared to either LESA model are probably due to the panel's discounting the relative value of foothill sites, useful mostly for pasture, compared to bottomland and terrace cropland found in most of the county.

For Overall ratings (Figure 3) it can be seen that, with the exception of site 4, while the LE and SA parts of LESA may reflect differences between the panel and the Linn County system, the Overall ratings between the two are very closely aligned. In comparison, the Lane LESA consistently over-rated the parcels when compared to a local expert panel.

Summary of Findings

The Delphi method provides a reasonable benchmark for evaluating LESA ratings. The Delphi procedure focused on the agricultural productivity of the site in both the LE and SA evaluations. Non-farm development was considered only to the extent that it impacted agricultural practices. If a LESA system does include urbanization suitability factors, a separate Delphi procedure would probably be warranted.

In this study, because panelists were asked to rate LE, SA, and Overall LESA on a 100-point scale, it was not clear to them that the Overall rating was an additive combination of LE and SA. For this reason, there appears to be little linkage between the parts of the ratings when compared to the whole. This lack of linkage was evident in the differences found in the preferred LE to SA weights indicated by the panelists vs. the imputed weights.

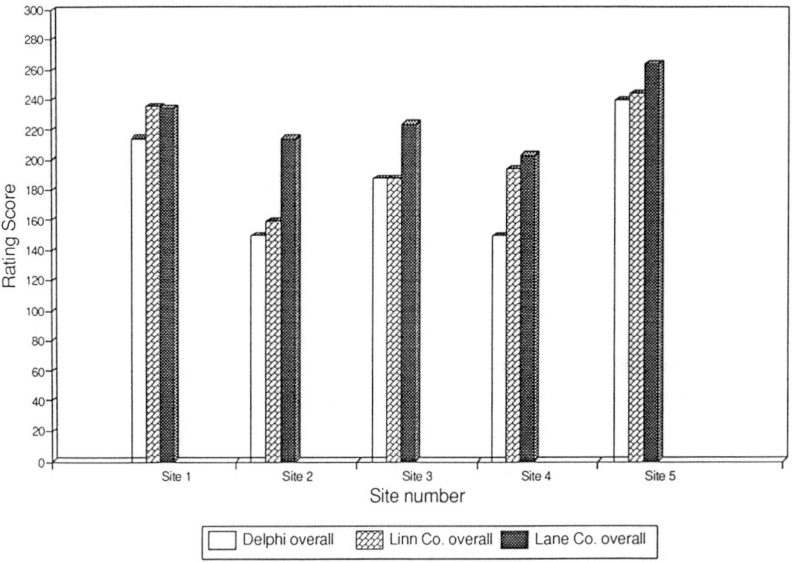

Figure 3. Comparison of Overall ratings by Delphi, Linn, Lane.

To improve the methods used, we suggest that the panel should rate soil quality and site assessment factors separately on a 100-point scale. Factor weights for different landforms or other geographic subareas should be determined by the Delphi procedure. Overall scores can then be calculated from the factor ratings and weights and by a comparison to LESA ratings. This provides an evaluation of LE and SA factor ratings, the weighting given to each factor, and a comparison of Overall ratings.

In addition to these comparisons, the relative ranking of several sites should be compared. Given time and budget limitations, this study compared only five sites. A comparison of 30 or more sites would provide a better basis for relative ranking comparisons, although it may be necessary to compensate the panelists for the time required by the procedure.

It was found that the ratings given by the Delphi panel were logical and specific to site conditions. Certain problems or limitations that affected the panel's rating of a specific site were not recognized by the general LESA model. This result, of course, is expected of any generalized rating system intended to be relatively simple to administer and easy to understand. It does, however, lend credence to the assumption that the panel's ratings were more accurate.

In counties with diverse farming activities, the use of agricultural subareas helps to fine-tune the parcel size ratings. The use of landforms (e.g., bottomlands, terraces, foothills) is one approach. The subareas should reflect differences in type and scale of agriculture.

In spite of widespread assumptions about the negative effects of non-farm homesites on farming operations, the expert panel discounted the conflict potential even beyond the conservative ratings of the LESA models. In Lane County, potential conflict was linked with parcel size, causing fewer points to be deducted for conflicting residences around larger parcels. Nevertheless, the Delphi finding would indicate that penalties for conflict should be investigated further for both Linn and Lane County LESA systems. This finding is supported by two independent studies of farm/homesite conflict, one for Linn County (*12*) and one for Lane County (*5*). These studies included interviews with farmers and surrounding non-farm residents and concluded that, while non-farm residences in farm zones does give rise to some problems, the impact on agricultural practices is minimal. A similar conclusion can be reached by examining data in a 1990 study of conflicts in EFU zones commissioned by the Oregon Land Conservation and Development Commission (*1*). In this study, about 10 percent of a statewide random sample of commercial farms reported a problem with a dollar cost and about five percent reported neighbor complaints about farm practices.

Parcel size, while a significant variable in relative ranking, also needs to be re-examined. In areas of prime soils, even small parcels (10-20 acres) appear to have more value than assigned in the LESA models. While the Lane County LESA model did include refinements to place more value on small parcels in areas of productive soils, the point distribution needs to be re-examined.

One option to simplify the benchmark procedure would be to evaluate only the SA portion, since LE is derived from consistent data sources and procedures. In this case, the Delphi panel could be given the LE ratings for test parcels in each subarea, and asked to provide an SA rating on a 0-100 scale. A second Delphi procedure could be used to derive the LE to SA weights for each subarea. This option would shorten the Delphi procedure and focus more attention on validating the SA factors.

A benchmark evaluation using a local expert panel in a systematic procedure is an important part of a LESA validation procedure. When used in conjunction with other evaluation criteria, it can lend great insight into an effort to improve the basis for LESA ratings of resource lands.

References

1. Berg, H., D. Cleaves, and E. Schmisseur. 1991. *Farm and Forest Land Research Project: Relationship, Nature, Frequency, and Cost of Conflicts Between Farm/Forestry Operators and Residentials.* Oregon Department of Land Conservation and Development, Salem.

2. Bowen, R., C. Ferguson, M. Khan, and T. Liang. 1990. *An Appraisal of the Hawaii Land Evaluation and Site Assessment System.* Information Text Series 035, for HITAHR, University of Hawaii, Manoa.
3. Coughlin, R. E. 1994. *Sensitivity, Ambiguity, and Redundancy in LESA Systems and the Acceptability of LESA Scores.* In: F. Steiner, J. Pease, and R. Coughlin (eds.) *A Decade with LESA: The Evolution of Land Evaluation and Site Assessment.* Soil and Water Conservation Society, Ankeny, Iowa.
4. Dalkey, N. 1969. *The Delphi Method: An Experimental Study of Group Opinion.* Rand Corporation, Santa Monica, California.
5. Daughton, K. 1985. *Presence of Farm and Non-Farm Produced Nuisances Within The Urban Fringe of Eugene and Springfield, Oregon.* Master's research paper, Oregon State University, Corvallis.
6. DeMers, M. 1989. *The Importance of Site Assessment in Land Planning: A re-examination of the SCS LESA Model.* Applied Geography (9):287-303.
7. Dunford, R., R. Roe, F. Steiner, W. Wagner, and L. Wright. 1983. *Implementation of LESA in Whitman County, Washington.* Journal of Soil and Water Conservation 38(2):87-89.
8. Eber, R. 1984. Oregon's Agricultural Land Protection Program. In: F. Steiner and J. Theilacker (eds.) *Protecting Farmlands.* AVI Publishing Co., Westport, Connecticut.
9. Ferguson, C., and R. Bowen. 1991. *Statistical Evaluation of an Agricultural Land Suitability Model.* Environmental Management 15(5):689-700.
10. Huddleston, J., J. Pease, W. Forrest, H. Hickerson, and R. Langridge. 1987. *Use of Agricultural Land Evaluation and Site Assessment in Linn County, Oregon.* Environmental Management 11(3):389-405.
11. Linstone, H., and M. Turoff. 1975. *The Delphi Method: Techniques and Applications.* Addison Wesley Publishing Co., Reading, Massachusetts.
12. McDonough, M. 1983. *A Study of Non-Farm Dwellings in an Exclusive Farm Use Zone.* Master's research paper, Oregon State University, Corvallis.
13. Nelson, D. 1984. *The Characterization of Commercial Agriculture: A Test of the Delphi Expert Opinion Method.* Master of Science thesis, Oregon State University, Corvallis.
14. Ostle, B., and L. Malone. 1988. *Statistics in Research: Basic Concepts and Techniques for Research Workers.* Iowa State University Press, Ames.
15. Pease, J. 1982. *Commercial Farmland Preservation in Oregon.* GeoJournal 6(6):547-563.
16. Pease, J. 1984. *Collecting Land Use Data.* Journal of Soil and Water Conservation 39(6):361-364.
17. Pease, J., and R. Beck. 1984. *Characteristics of Commercial Agriculture in Washington County Obtained by a Delphi Group Estimation Method.* Extension Special Report No. 734, Oregon State University Extension Service, Corvallis.
18. Pease, J., and A. Sussman. 1994. *A Five Point Approach for Evaluating LESA Models.* In: F. Steiner, R. Coughlin, J. Pease (eds.) *A Decade with LESA: The Evolution of Land Evaluation and Site Assessment.* Soil and Water Conservation Society, Ankeny, Iowa.
19. Stamm, T., R. Gill, and K. Page. 1987. *Agricultural Land Evaluation and Site Assessment in Latah County, Idaho, U.S.A.* Environmental Management 11(3):379-388.
20. Tyler, M., F. Steiner, D. Roe, and L. Hunter. 1987. *Use of the Agricultural Land Evaluation and Site Assessment System in Whitman County, Washington.* Environmental Management 11(3):407-412.
21. U.S. Department of Agriculture-Soil Conservation Service. 1983. *National Agricultural Land Evaluation and Site Assessment Handbook.* Washington, D.C.
22. VanHorn, T., G. Steinhardt, and J. Yahner. 1989. *Evaluating the Consistency of Results for the Agricultural Land Evaluation and Site Assessment (LESA) System.* Journal of Soil and Water Conservation 44(6):615-620.
23. Wright, L. W. Zitzmann, K. Young, and R. Googins. 1983. *LESA Agricultural Land Evaluation and Site Assessment.* Journal of Soil and Water Conservation 38(2):82-86.

Soil Conservation Service photo

8 Sensitivity, Ambiguity, and Redundancy in LESA Systems and the Acceptability of LESA Scores

Robert E. Coughlin

In evaluating a particular land evaluation and site assessment (LESA) system, four issues should be investigated.

First, how sensitive are LESA scores to the many weights that are built into the system? Committees typically assign such weights both to factors and to land evaluation (LE) and site assessment (SA) scores.

Second, to what extent do ambiguities in interpreting LESA scores actually result from the fact that final scores are made up of a variety of mixes of LE and SA characteristics?

Third, to what extent do LESA models contain redundant factors, which add to the complexity of rating but bring little additional independent information into the evaluation?

Fourth, to what extent do people knowledgeable about farmland and farmland protection find that the LESA scores yielded by the local system are reasonable, that is, consistent with the judgments they would make as experts?

This chapter investigates each of these questions in turn by examining the specifications of particular LESA systems and studying the results of applying these systems to samples of sites. It is the interaction between the system itself and the characteristics of the sites to which it is applied that determine the scores that a LESA system yields.

The LESA systems chosen for this investigation are not claimed to be typical of all systems in use. Similar analyses should be applied to other systems before general conclusions are drawn. At this stage, it may be more useful to think of the ensuing analysis as an example of the kind of investigation a jurisdiction should make to ensure that their LESA system is yielding its intended results.

The Analytical Structure of the LESA System

The purpose of the LESA system is to consider a number of disparate factors, combine them in a consistent way, and obtain a score that is helpful to people making decisions about particular sites in agricultural use. The LESA system has the form of a point system consisting of a linear combination of weighted factors. The factors are classified as land evaluation (LE) factors and site assessment (SA) factors. LE factors are concerned with soil quality for agricultural production. SA factors are concerned with other considerations that contribute to the suitability of an area for retention in agricultural use, such as, economic viability of the farm in question, existence of urban infrastructure and pressure for development, and the nature of zoning and other public policy measures in effect (*9*). Typically, there are one to four LE factors and 11 to 16 SA factors in a LESA system (*7*).

For a given site, each factor is usually rated on a scale of one to 10 points by a committee or staff. The uniform 1-10 scale is chosen to make rating easy. The initial ratings are then multiplied by weights designed to reflect the relative importance of each factor. This is the first step of the weighting process.

The second step of the weighting process is to assign weights to LE factors as a group and weights to SA factors as a group.

Two methods are common for assigning weights to the SA factors. The classical method, set out in the LESA handbook (*8*) and the Wright and

Zitzmann article (*9*), combines the two steps of the weighting process. It suggests that the factor weights in the SA portion be adjusted so that when summed they yield a total maximum of 200 points (*8*). The SA score for a given site may, therefore, range anywhere from 0 to 200. It is added to the LE score, for which a maximum score of 100 is suggested, to yield a total LESA score of between 0 and 300.

The second method treats the two weighting steps separately, and is referred to as the two-step method. Following this method, the SA weights do not have to be constrained to yield a particular total when multiplied by the assigned points on the 0-10 scale. For a given site, the first step is to divide the total weighted points by the maximum number of weighted points possible. In step number two, the resulting fraction is multiplied by the SA weight (e.g. 70) to yield the SA score (ranging between 0 and 70 in this example). The SA score is added to the LE score (which would have a maximum of 30 in this example) to yield a LESA score within the range of 0 to 100. There is some intuitive merit to a 100 point scale, because it is the most common scale used in our culture.

Figure 1, reflecting the two-step method, lays out the analytic structure of the LESA system. The higher the LESA score, the more desirable it is to retain the land in agriculture.

Note that LESA is a neutral system, a way of combining a variety of considerations or factors. Whether the scores it produces will favor sprawl development, strict protection of agricultural regions, or something in between depends on the factors that are included and the weights given to them and to LE and SA as entities.

Using LESA Scores in Making Decisions. LESA is used to help make a variety of decisions. The LESA handbook (*8*) points out that it may be necessary to design a separate LESA system for each use. Most of the jurisdictions surveyed use their LESA system for only one purpose (*7*). Few jurisdictions have developed more than one system, each addressed to a different problem.

The type of decision being addressed suggests slightly different formulations of the LESA system. A typical application involves deciding what land should be eligible for inclusion in an agricultural district or put into or taken out of agricultural zoning. This type of decision suggests that LESA would be applied to:

Identify all sites, with a LESA score > k.

A second common application for which LESA is used is to determine what locations for a proposed public facility will have acceptably small impacts on the local farm economy. Here, LESA would be used to:

Identify all sites, with a LESA score < k.

Both of these applications require that a threshold or cut-off level of

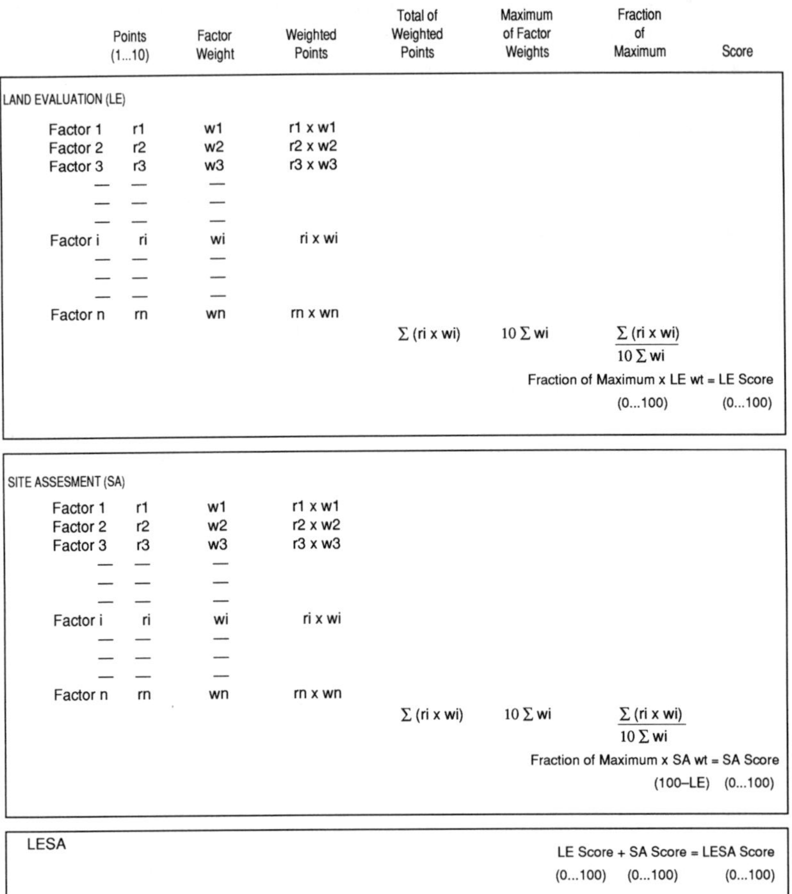

Points (1...10)
Factor Weight
Weighted Points
Total of Weighted Points
Maximum of Factor Weights
Fraction of Maximum
Score
LAND EVALUATION (LE)
Factor 1 r1 w1 r1 x w1
Factor 2 r2 w2 r2 x w2
Factor 3 r3 w3 r3 x w3
Factor i ri wi ri x wi
Factor n rn wn rn x wn
Σ (ri x wi)
10 Σ wi
Σ (ri x wi) / 10 Σ wi
Fraction of Maximum x LE wt = LE Score
(0...100) (0...100)
SITE ASSESMENT (SA)
Factor 1 r1 w1 r1 x w1
Factor 2 r2 w2 r2 x w2
Factor 3 r3 w3 r3 x w3
Factor i ri wi ri x wi
Factor n rn wn rn x wn
Σ (ri x wi)
10 Σ wi
Σ (ri x wi) / 10 Σ wi
Fraction of Maximum x SA wt = SA Score
(100–LE) (0...100)
LESA
LE Score + SA Score = LESA Score
(0...100) (0...100) (0...100)

Figure 1. Analytical structure of LESA system with suggested nomenclature.

LESA be defined. For example, 75 might be so defined based on the judgment of local experts. Sites with a higher LESA score would be recommended for retention in agricultural use and sites with a lower score would be recommended for conversion to other uses. Setting one precise cut-off level, however, may assume more accuracy of LESA than in fact is warranted. It may be more appropriate to specify a "fuzzy" threshold instead of a sharp one. For example, instead of specifying one cut-off of 75, divide LESA scores into three domains, setting the following ranges:

If LESA is

greater than 77	keep in agriculture based on LESA score, give minor weight to other factors;
between 73 and 77	LESA score indicates keep in agriculture, but give major weight to other factors in making decision;
less than 73	allow to go out of agriculture, give minor weight to factors other than LESA score.

The Clarke County, Virginia, Planning Commission uses criteria of this sort in determining whether a farm is eligible for inclusion in an agricultural district. Farms with LESA scores of 70 or more are eligible to join the district. Farms rated between 60 and 70 are eligible if they are located near existing towns. Farms scoring below 60 are generally not eligible.

Another type of decision is—what farms should be given highest priority for the purchase of conservation easements (sometimes called the purchase of development rights)? Typical conservation easement programs are voluntary, that is, eligible farmland owners may offer to sell easements on their farms. The administering agency often uses LESA to rank the offers according to how well each measures against the program's goals. Usually, a cut-off LESA score is not relevant, because the number of good farms offered for easement sale is much greater than the budget can afford. Instead, the LESA application is formulated to:

Rank all sites in order of LESA score.

In this application, the cut-off that is relevant is determined by the budget available and the easement costs of the highest ranked sites. Once again, it may be desirable to define a fuzzy threshold as a gray area, such as, sites ranking above the gray area generally would be accepted based on their LESA score, sites below it would be rejected, but sites within the gray area would be studied more carefully, giving major consideration to factors other than LESA and changing their priorities as appropriate.

Because LESA scores embody a mix of ratings on a number of factors, sites may be chosen for retention in agriculture that are rated very low on certain critical factors. This problem of ambiguity of interpretation is discussed in the "Ambiguity in LESA Scores" section below. One way to address this inherent problem is to choose only sites whose ratings on the critical factors is above some stated minimum. For example, to qualify for consideration in a purchase-of-development-rights program, the system could specify that all sites must have a stated minimum LE score. Then, the qualifying sites would be ranked by their SA scores. This formulation is in the nature of:

Choose sites such that aggregate LESA scores are maximized, subject to

LE $\geq$ k, or more generally, subject to weighted factor i $\geq$ k.

In chapter 5, Huddleston discusses the use of such constraints or "thresholds."

Sensitivity of the LESA System

The weights assigned by the committees that formulate LESA systems obviously have an important effect on the outcomes of LESA analyses. This section explores how sensitive LESA scores are to changes in factor weights and to changes in LE and SA weights.

Effects of Variation in Factor Weights. To explore the effects that a change in factor weights would have, we have analyzed factor ratings for a sample of sites from two jurisdictions, doubling the weight of each factor in turn. Figure 2 shows the results for the LESA system of the Clarke County (Virginia) Planning Commission. Figure 3 shows results for the system of the Chester County (Pennsylvania) Agricultural Land Protection Board.

The Clarke County analysis (Figure 2) shows the SA total for each of 30 sites (Sites A...Z, a...d) as factors are presently weighted (axis P in the figure) and as the weight of each individual factor is multiplied by 2 and the weights of all other factors remain unchanged (axis 2x in the figure). For example, the SA score with all factors weighted as at present is connected by a straight line with the SA score when the weight of the Area-of-Farm factor is doubled from 7 to 14 (see the first column of Figure 2). For site A, SA is changed from 89 to 86.1

The effects on an SA score of changing the weighting of a factor are not as simple to predict as might have been expected. This is because the SA score depends on several factors include the following:

- The initial size of the weighted rating on the factor whose weight is changed.
- The weighted ratings on all other factors relative to the given factor.
- The increase in weight of the given factor.

Table 1 provides examples of the computation. Site C received the largest possible number of points on the Area-of-Farm factor—7; the effect of doubling the weight of that factor was to increase SA by 1.7 points.

Site E received a very low number of points on the Area-of-Farm factor—2.31; doubling the weight of that factor decreased SA by 6.9 points.

Sites c, R, and A all received the same number of points on the Area-of-Farm factor (4.69), but the relative size of that factor differs for the three sites. For site c, the rating on the Area-of-Farm factor was large in relation to the sum of the ratings on other factors; for site R, it was moderate; for site A, it was relatively small. Accordingly, doubling the weighting of the Area-of-Farm resulted in an increase in SA for site c, little change for site R,

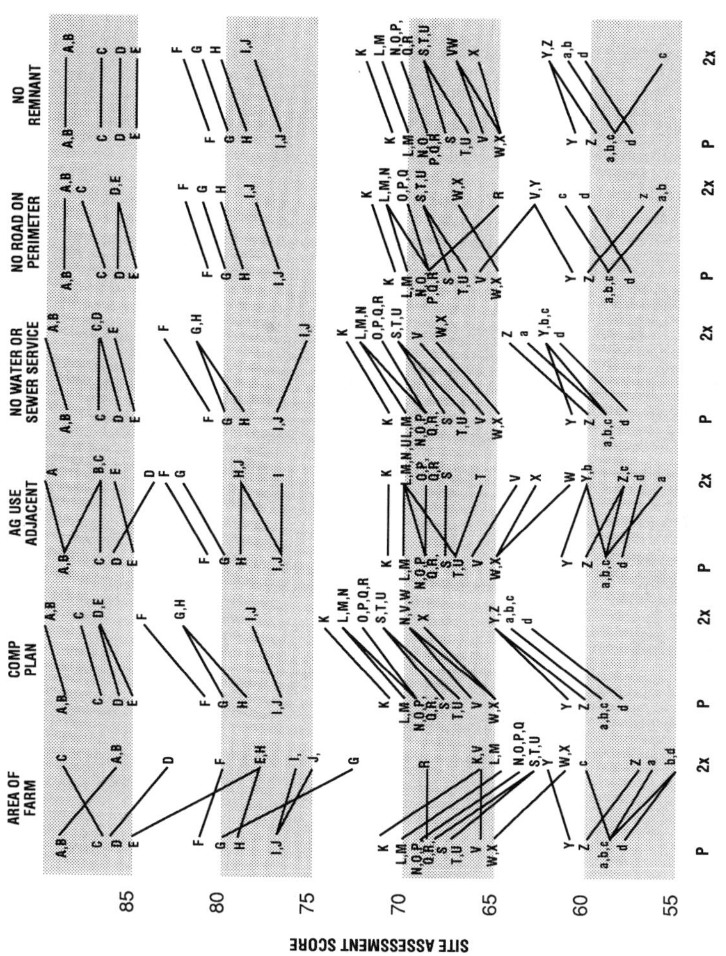

Figure 2. Effect on site assessment score of multiplying each factor by two, Clarke County, Virginia, planning commission system.

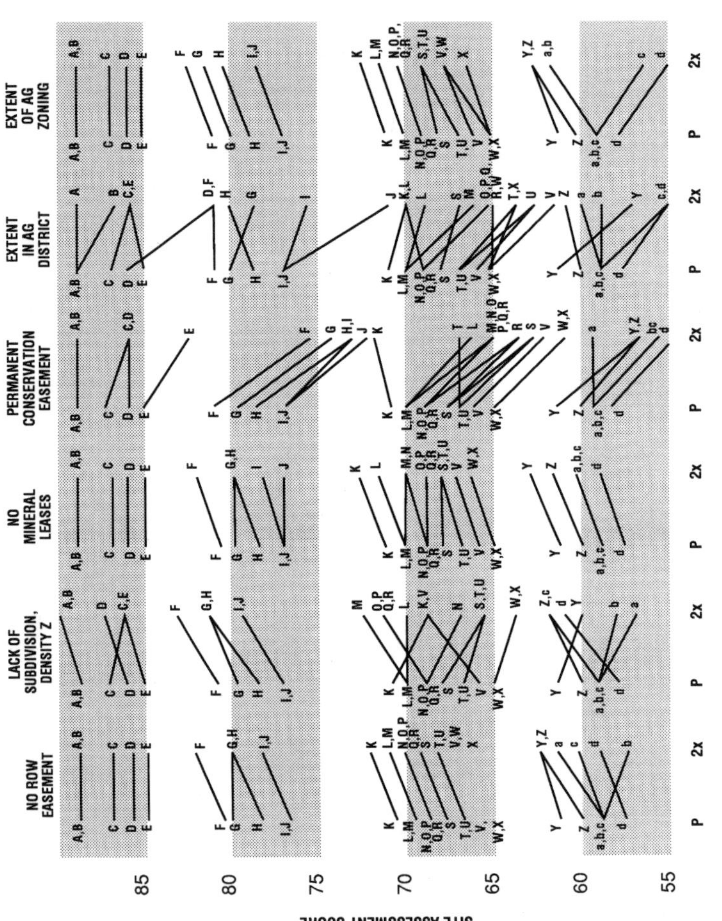

Figure 2 (continued). Effect of site assessment score of multiplying each factor by two, Clarke County, Virginia, planning commission system.

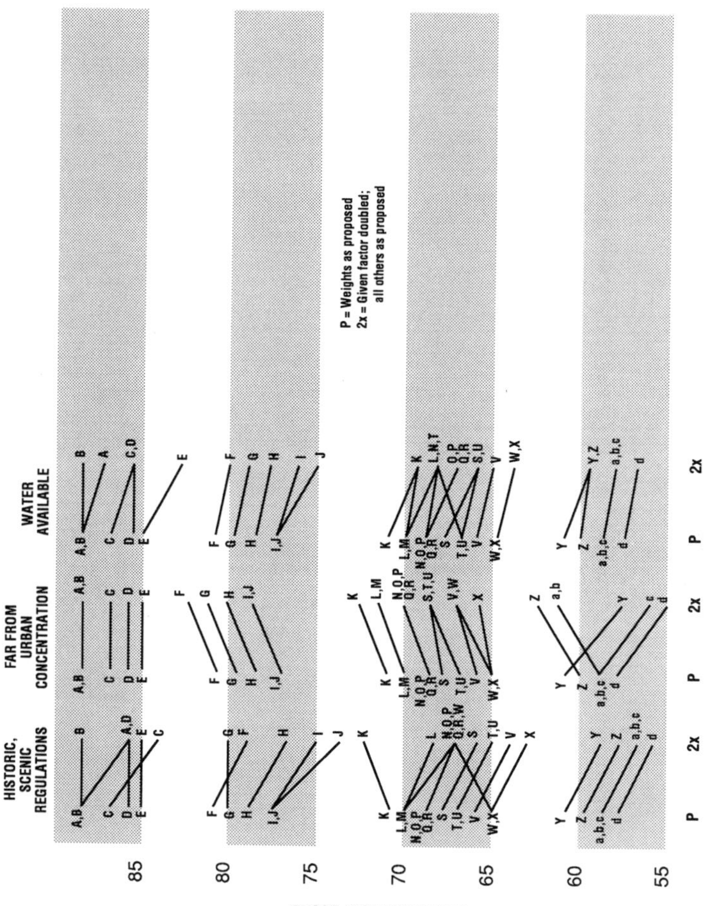

Figure 2 (concluded). Effect on site assessment score of multiplying each factor by two, Clarke County, Virginia, planning commission system.

Table 1. Effect on SA score of doubling the weight on one factor: Examples using the area-of-farm factor, Clarke County, Virginia, system.

	Weighted Points*		SA Score Initial Weighting	SA Score Area-of-Farm Factor Weighted 2x	Difference 2x Minus Initial
Site	Area-of-Farm Factor	All Other Factors			
C	7.00	32.35	(7.00+32.35)/(45.3) x 100 = 86.9	14.00 + 32.35)/(45.3 + 7) x 100 = 88.6	1.7
c	4.69	21.90	(4.69 + 21.90)/(45.3) x 100 = 58.6	(9.38 + 21.90)/(45.3 + 7) x 100 = 59.8	1.2
R	4.69	26.45	(4.69 + 26.45)/(45.3) x 100 = 68.7	(9.38 + 26.45)/(45.3 + 7) x 100 = 68.5	-0.2
A	4.69	35.60	(4.69 + 35.60)/(45.3) x 100 = 88.9	(9.38 + 35.60)/(45.3 + 7) x 100 = 86	-2.9
E	2.31	36.10	(2.31 + 36.10)/(45.3) x 100 = 84.8	(4.69 + 36.10)/(45.3 + 7) x 100 = 77.9	-6.9

*under initial weighting, the maximum number of points for the Area-of-Farm factor was 7.00.

and a decrease for site A.

Doubling a factor weight is probably as large a change as a local government is likely to make to its LESA system. Figure 2 indicates that for the Clarke County system, such a change for any one factor changes the SA scores of some sites substantially, but changes many sites only moderately, if at all. Under the original weighting, the sites in the Clarke County sample fell into four groups:

Sites A through E, which have SA ratings of 85 or above;
Sites F through J, which have SA ratings of 77 to 81;
Sites K through X, which have SA ratings of 65 to 71;
Sites Y through d, which have SA ratings of 56 to 61.

Although there were some changes in ranking (easily seen by the lines that cross in Figure 2) caused by the doubling of the weighting on each factor, the four major groupings remained distinct. This suggests that for some applications, with a single cut-off criterion that falls between such major groupings, changes of this scale in the weighting of a single factor may have little effect on the classification of areas. But in other applications, such as a purchase-of-development rights program that sets priorities by ranking sites, changes in factor weightings could have greater effects on what sites are chosen.

Figure 3 presents a similar set of results for the Chester County LESA system. This figure plots effects on the total LESA score instead of effects on just the SA portion, as was done in Figure 2 for Clarke County. Again, for this level of change in weights, there are relatively few changes in ranking of the various sites.

Effects of Variation in LE:SA Weights. Many of the LESA systems in use follow the handbook's suggestion (*8*) that LE be assigned a maximum score of 100 and SA a maximum of 200. (Of the LESA systems in the eastern United States that were analyzed, 43 percent followed this pattern). On the basis of 100, this assignment amounts to LE:33 and SA:67. The basis for this ratio is not presented, even though the LE:SA ratio is a basic assumption of the system.

Ratings on a sample of 37 sites from Lancaster County, Pennsylvania, provide an opportunity to trace what happens as the weights on LE and on SA are varied. The Lancaster County system actually has three major segments, Quality of Farmland (which is comparable to LE), Likelihood of Conversion, and Other Factors (which together constitute SA) instead of the classical two components, LE and SA. In this exploration, we vary the weights on the first two segments, Quality of Farmland and Likelihood of Conversion, while keeping constant the third segment, which is by far the smallest with a maximum score of only five percent.

When the Lancaster system was first formulated, a weight of only 25 percent was given to Quality of Farmland. After using this formulation for a

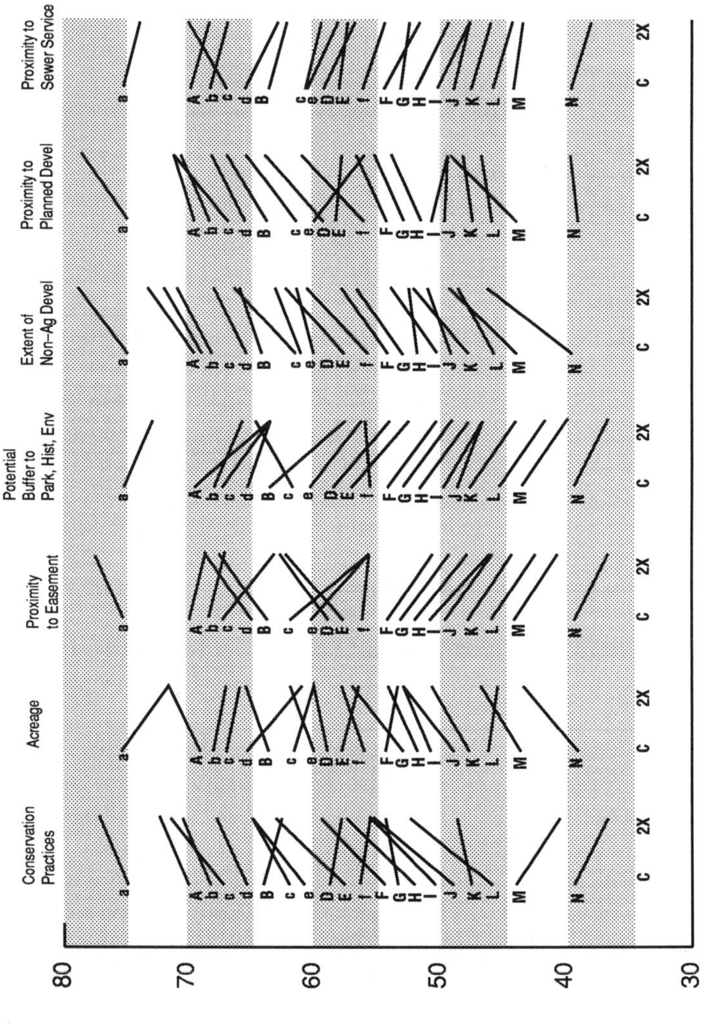

Figure 3. Effect on LESA score of multiplying each factor weight by two, Chester County, Pennsylvania, agricultural land preservation board system.

period of time, the Agricultural Preservation Board decided that Quality of Farmland had been given too little weight. Therefore, in 1991, the board revised the system to increase the weight of Quality of Farmland to 35 percent. The executive director of the board has suggested a further increase to 50 percent (*2*). Figure 4 presents the effects on a sample of sites of these alternative weights. In addition, it shows the effects of giving Quality of Farmland a weight of 60 percent. As one progresses through these examples, the weight on Quality of Farmland is increased and, correspondingly, the weights on Likelihood of Conversion is decreased:

	Quality of Farmland (LE)	Likelihood of Conversion (SA)	Other Factors
Original Weights	25	70	5
Current Weights	30	60	5
Alternative 1	50	45	5
Alternative 2	60	35	5

It is evident in Figure 4 that changing the relative weights results in significant changes in total LESA scores. In the figure, it may be helpful to look at three situations, including sites with LESA scores that remain approximately constant as the LE weights are increased, those sites with LESA scores that decrease substantially, and sites with LESA scores that increase substantially. Weighted ratings for LE, SA, and "Other" for sites exemplifying these three situations follow:

	Original Weighted Ratings		
	LE	SA	"Other"
LESA generally unchanged by increase in LE weight			
Site B	94.4	91.1	46.4
Site M	75.9	72.2	67.9
LESA decreased by increase in LE weight			
Site N	63.0	75.7	46.4
Site S	61.1	68.6	46.4
LESA increased by increase in LE weight.			
Site I	100.0	59.8	46.4
Site g	100.0	33.7	46.4

The LESA scores of sites B and M are changed very little by the change in LE and SA weights because their LE and SA weighted ratings are almost equal. Therefore, there is about an equal trade off when the weight of one is increased and that of the other is correspondingly decreased.

The LESA scores of sites N and S decreased as the LE weight was increased because their LE weighted ratings were smaller than their SA weighted ratings. As a result, the incremental increase in LE weight multiplied by the total of LE weighted ratings was not enough to offset the corre-

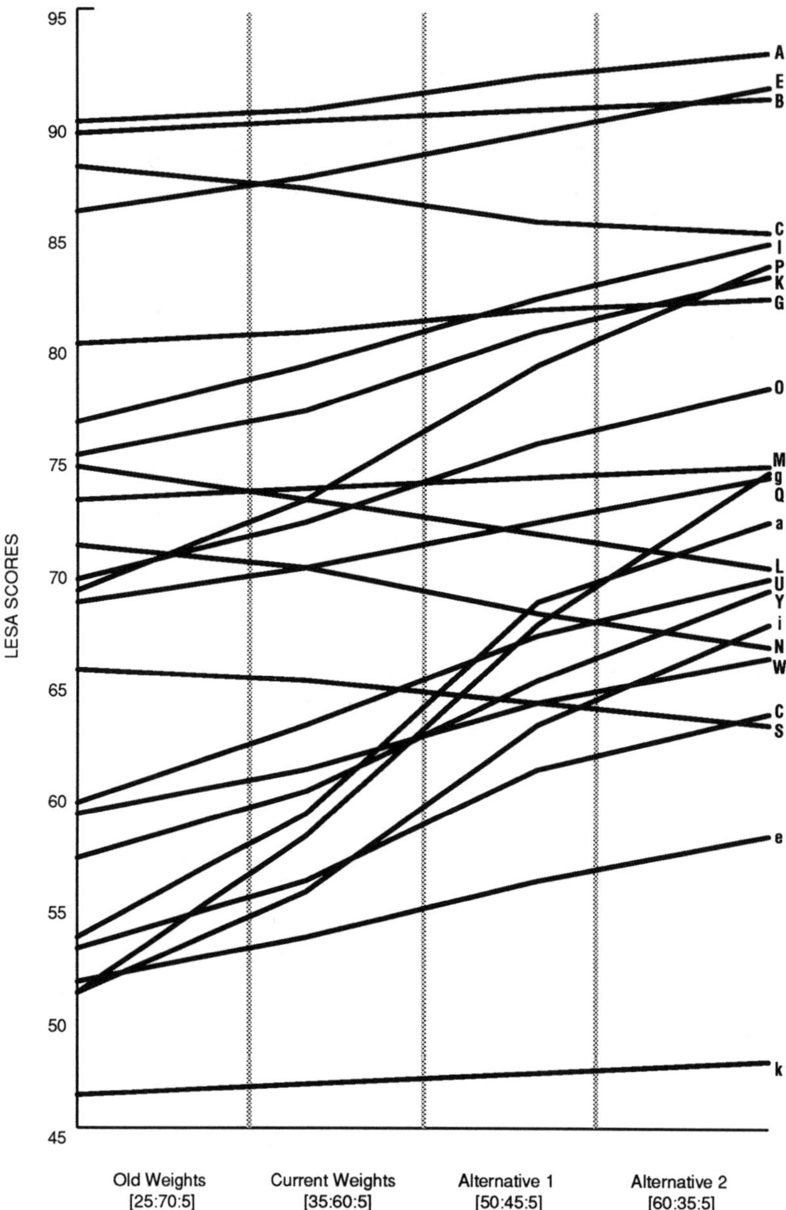

Figure 4. LESA scores for various LE:SA weights, Lancaster County, Pennsylvania, agricultural preserve board system.

sponding incremental decrease in SA weight multiplied by the larger total of SA weighted ratings.

Finally, the LESA scores of sites I and g increased as the LE weight was increased. For these sites the LE weighted rating was greater than the SA weighted rating, and when multiplied by the increase in weight, more than offset the corresponding decrease in weight applied to the SA weighted rating.

The major changes in LESA scores that result from changes in the LE and SA weights emphasize that formulators of LESA systems should not adopt the 100:200 formulation of the handbook uncritically, but instead should choose the LE:SA weights only after careful analysis.

Ambiguity in LESA Scores

A basic property of any point system involving more than one factor is that any particular final score could be made up of a variety of mixes of scores on the factors. Consider a system made up of two factors, where each is given equal weight:

	Factor 1	Factor 2	Final Score
Site 1	20	80	50
Site 2	80	20	50
Site 3	50	50	50

In this example, all three sites receive the same final score, but each has greatly differing characteristics. It is not clear in what sense the three sites are equivalent.

This inherent ambiguity of scores operates at both the factor level and at the LE:SA level. Figure 5, based on thirty sites in Clarke County, is an example of the low correlation between total LE weighted ratings and total SA weighted ratings (the correlation coefficient is a low -0.199). The interpretation of sites along the diagonal is relatively easy: on both LE and SA they are rated very high, moderately high, very low, or whatever. The sites that are far from the diagonal are harder to interpret, and there are many of them. Some rate high on LE and low on SA; others are low on LE and high on SA, with many variations in between. As examples, consider three Clarke County sites that yield almost equal LESA scores when LE is weighted 33 and SA is weighted 67:

Site No.	LE Total Wtd. Points	SA Total Wtd. Points	LESA Score
J	45.0	79.0	67.8
Y	81.8	60.7	67.6
I	67.0	67.7	67.5

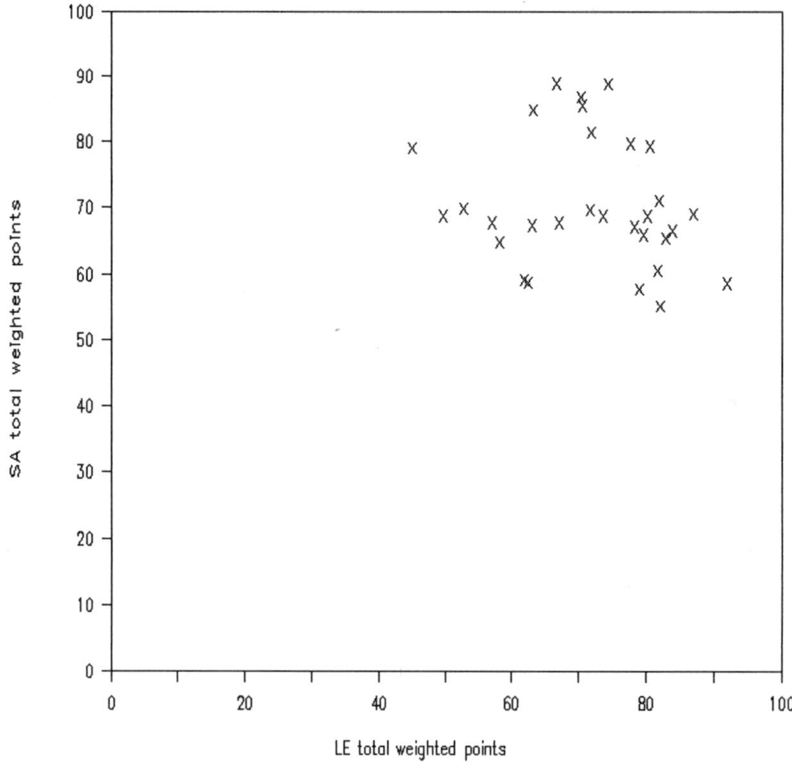

Figure 5. LE vs. SA at 30 sites in Clarke County, Virginia.

Unquestioning use of LESA scores may lead to ill considered action if the unstated weights underlying a policy differ from the weights incorporated in the LESA score. For example, the choice between protecting site J or site Y appears to be equal based on the LESA score, but site J evidently has very poor soils, while site Y evidently has very productive soils.

LE and SA are intended to measure different aspects of a site, so low correlations between LE and SA ratings are to be expected. In fact, if the two were highly correlated, there would be no need to treat LE and SA separately. The ambiguity created by combining LE and SA may best be dealt with by setting threshold values of one (or both) that must be met for a site to qualify for a given policy action. The question of setting thresholds in LESA systems is explored thoroughly by Huddleston in chapter 5 of this book.

If a LESA system is well designed in relation to the types of decisions that are to be based on its scores, knowledgeable people will agree that the final scores are appropriate even though they arise from very different mixes of characteristics. If the system is not well designed, its results will not be well accepted. One of the advantages of involving local experts and public officials in the process of formulating and testing the LESA system is to assure that LESA scores will be widely accepted.

Possible Redundancy of Factors

The purpose of SA is to attempt to measure very complex relationships, therefore a large number of factors may be necessary to measure them satisfactorily. The number of SA factors ranged from 5 to 31 in 47 LESA systems analyzed in the eastern U.S. Half of them had between 11 and 16 factors and the median number was 13.

If two or more factors are measuring the same thing, however, the LESA system is unnecessarily complex and, probably, unnecessarily expensive to implement. It also may inadvertently give more weight to a particular consideration than the designers of the system intended. To identify such redundant factors we analyzed weighted points for samples of sites in Chester and Lancaster Counties in Pennsylvania, and Clarke County, Virginia, using the LESA systems of each county respectively.

Correlations Between Factors. The analysis consists, first, of computing simple correlation coefficients between all pairs of variables. If two variables are highly correlated, the value of one can be estimated accurately given the value of the other. The results are given in Tables 2 through 4. Correlation coefficients that are significant at the 0.01 level are underlined. This level means that there is only one chance in 100 that such relationships could have occurred by chance.

In the tables, factors are grouped by the general categories: Quality-of-Farm factors, Conservation and Other Policy factors, and Risk-of-Development factors. Correlation coefficients between factors in any one of these groups are found in the "triangles" that lie just beneath the diagonal in the tables. Because factors within any one of these groups have some logical relationship, one might expect them also to be statistically related. Correlations between factors in different groups are found in the "rectangles" that make up the remainder of the tables. Correlations in these rectangles are expected to be lower than in the triangles, because there generally are no logical connections between such factors.

This expectation is borne out in the tables for Chester County and Lancaster County. In the Chester County table, no significant correlations are found in the rectangles, while four significant correlations are found in the triangles. In the Lancaster County table, only one significant correlation is

Table 2. Simple correlation coefficients: Between LESA scores and factor ratings and among factor ratings, Chester County, Pennsylvania, agricultural land preservation board system.

		Dependent Variable	Independent Variables							
			Quality-of-Farm Variables			Conservation Policy Variables		Risk-of-Development Variables		
		LESA Score	Soil Capabil	Conserv Practices E	Acreage F	Prox to Easement C	Potentl Buffer D	Non-Ag Devel A	Prox to Plan Dev B	Prox to Sewr Svc G
	Soil capability	-0.234	1							
E	Conservation practices	0.377	0.351	1						
F	Acreage	-0.042	-0.087	-0.189	1					
C	Proximity to easement	0.536	-0.264	0.122	-0.238	1				
D	Potential buffer	0.527	-0.210	0.140	0.069	0.063	1			
A	Extent of non-ag devel	0.428	-0.227	-0.172	-0.200	0.072	0.107	1		
B	Prox to planned devel	0.564	-0.176	-0.157	-0.125	0.159	-0.012	0.372	1	
G	Proximity to sewer svc	0.318	-0.212	-0.060	-0.237	-0.087	0.110	0.320	0.422	1

Underlined correlation coefficients are significant at the 0.01 level, that is, coefficients >0.30.
n = 70
Capital letters (A...G) refer to factors as designated by Chester County.

Table 3. Simple correlation coefficients: Between LESA scores and factor ratings and among factor ratings, Lancaster County, Pennsylvania, agricultural preserve board system.

	Dependent Variable	Independent Variables												
		Quality-of-Farm Variables				Conservation & Other Variables				Risk-of-Development Variables				
	LESA Score	Acreage B2	Soil Capabil B3	Farm Prod. Sales B4	Adeq Bldgs B5	Prox. to Easemnt. B1	Stwrdshp. of Land C1	Hist. Scenic C2	Prior Applic C3	Non-Ag Devel A1	Non-Ag Zoning A2	Prox. Sewr. Svc. A3	Road Front. A4	Urgency A5
B2 Acreage of farm	0.272	1												
B3 Soil capability	0.390	-0.086	1											
B4 Farm product sales	0.269	0.445	0.125	1										
B5 Adequacy of bldgs.	0.239	0.393	0.224	0.259	1									
B1 Proximity to easement	0.213	0.047	0.087	-0.136	0.193	1								
C1 Stewardship of land	0.200	0.099	0.100	0.307	0.252	-0.295	1							
C2 Hist., scenic, env.	0.172	0.106	-0.116	-0.045	-0.166	-0.165	0.176	1						
C3 Prior applic.	-0.110	0.158	-0.276	0.154	0.040	-0.280	0.196	0.319	1					
A1 Non-ag devel in area	0.606	-0.031	0.216	0.206	-0.039	-0.340	0.418	0.159	0.074	1				
A2 Non-ag zoning	0.728	0.074	0.003	0.222	0.004	-0.095	0.118	0.343	0.154	0.662	1			
A3 Proximity to sewer sv	0.781	0.353	0.237	-0.034	-0.004	0.227	0.129	0.169	-0.155	0.414	0.548	1		
A4 Extent of road front.	0.295	0.282	0.024	0.148	0.353	0.052	-0.141	-0.210	-0.161	-0.111	-0.009	-0.067	1	
A5 Urgency	0.287	-0.041	-0.037	-0.181	0.040	0.134	0.010	0.319	-0.028	0.074	0.154	0.251	0.093	1

Underlined correlation coefficients are significant at the 0.01 level, that is, coefficients > 0.40.
n = 37.
Capital letters (A1..C3) refer to factors as designated by Lancaster County.

Table 4. Simple Correlation Coefficients: Between LESA scores and factor ratings and among factor ratings Clarke County, Virginia, planning commission system.

		Dependent Variable	Independent Variables												
			Quality-of-Farm Variables		Conservation and Other Variables				Little-Risk-of-Development Variables						
		LESA Score	Area 1	Water 13	Easement 5a	Ag Dist. 5b	Ag Zoning 5c	Scenic, Historic 5d	Lack W/S 4q-i	Lack Road 4a-ii	No Remnant 4a-iii	No ROW 4a-iv	Lack Subdiv 4b	Adj Ag 3	Urban Far 6
1	Large area	0.481	1												
7	Water available	0.391	0.268	1											
5a	Permanent easement	0.517	0.364	0.693	1										
5b	Extent in ag district	0.348	0.026	-0.166	0.246	1									
5c	Extent of ag zoning	0.382	-0.033	-0.202	0.144	0.291	1								
5d	Scenic, historic regs	0.484	-0.089	0.378	0.341	0.234	0.134	1							
4a-i	Lack of water/sewer	0.039	-0.405	0.034	-0.070	0.092	-0.068	0.126	1						
4a-ii	Lack of road on bdry	0.416	0.026	0.259	0.077	-0.014	-0.120	0.224	-0.113	1					
4a-iii	No isolated remnant	0.257	-0.190	-0.140	0.100	0.202	0.695	0.093	-0.047	-0.083	1				
4a-iv	No ROW easement	0.253	0.144	0.107	0.100	-0.087	-0.050	0.093	-0.047	0.415	-0.355	1			
4b	Lack of subdiv, zoning	0.464	0.392	0.245	0.046	-0.180	-0.218	0.068	0.224	0.183	0.152	0.227	1		
3	Adj land in ag use	0.622	0.178	0.031	0.089	0.119	0.245	0.115	0.135	0.410	0.170	-0.043	0.437	1	
6	Far from urban conc.	0.446	-0.141	-0.104	0.180	0.363	0.802	0.167	0.477	-0.149	0.557	-0.062	-0.045	0.306	1

Underlined correlation coefficients are significant at the 0.01 level, that is, coefficients >0.45.
n = 28
Number codes (1...7) refer to factors as designated by Clarke County.

found in the rectangles, while four are found in the triangles. In the Clarke County table, the pattern is less clear. Two significant correlations appear in the triangles, while three appear in the rectangles.

In the Chester County table, all three Risk-of-Development factors are significantly intercorrelated. They also appear to be logically related. Therefore, just one of these factors would probably be sufficient; the inclusion of more than one of these factors adds little information to the system.

In the Lancaster County table, as in the Chester County table, three factors in the Risk-of-Development group are significantly correlated with each other. The Lancaster factors are similar to the Chester factors:

Chester County	**Lancaster County**
Extent of Non-Agricultural Development in the Area.	Same
Proximity to Sewer Service	Same
Proximity to areas Designated for Development on Co. Plan	Proximity to Areas Zoned for Developed Uses

In the Risk-of-Development section of the Clarke County table, Lack of Water or Sewer and No Highway Remnant are significantly correlated with Far from Urban Concentration, but are not correlated with each other.

Some other significant correlations occur in the triangles depicting the interrelationships among Quality-of-Farm variables. The Chester County table has one significant correlation: between Soil Capability and Conservation Practices. Perhaps there is a causal connection here, such as, farmers with good soil invest in practices that will protect their asset.

In the Lancaster table, Acreage of Farm is significantly correlated with Farm Product Sales. The logical relationship is evident. Perhaps Farm Product Sales per Acre should be substituted to gain a variable that is less strongly correlated with Acreage and that measures productivity rather than total output. But, of course, it might turn out to be significantly correlated with Soil Capability.

No significant correlations were found among Conservation Policy variables in any of the three county systems.

Turning now to the "rectangular" sections of the tables, Chester County has no significant correlations. Lancaster County has only one: between Extent of Non-Agricultural Development within a Mile and Stewardship of Land. The causal relationship between the two is not compelling. In the Clarke County table, the Existence of Agricultural Zoning is significantly correlated with Far from Urban Concentration (where some logical connection might be expected) and with No Isolated Highway Remnant (where there appears to be less basis for a logical relationship).

Overall, there are relatively few significant correlations to be found in Tables 2, 3, and 4. The numbers of significant correlations (at the 0.01 level) can be summarized as follows:

Chester Co.: 5 correlations significant out of 28 possible, or 14.3 percent

Lancaster Co.: 5 out of 78 possible, or 6.4 percent

Clarke Co.: 5 out of 78 possible, or 6.4 percent

These results are similar to those of Ferguson and Bowen (*3, 4*) for the State of Hawaii system, but differ from those of Pease and Sussman who found that a much larger percentage of factors were significantly intercorrelated. (See chapter 6 in this volume).

Regressions between Factors and the LESA Score. Tables 2 through 4 also report the correlations between factors and the LESA score (column 1). Significant correlations are much more common here than among factors.

Table 5 presents summary regression statistics for the three systems. All three require only a few variables to reach high levels of statistical explanation of the LESA score. The Lancaster County system requires only three variables to reach an R of more than 0.9; the Chester and Clarke County systems require six. One could argue that the additional factors (variables) add little to the final rankings of the LESA scores. Therefore, they could be eliminated from the systems with little loss in discrimination among sites and with some reduction in the cost of application of the system. This contention, however, should be tested.

Acceptability of Results

Insights gained through analysis of the structure of the LESA system, such as those presented in the previous sections, are valuable for designing new or revised LESA systems whose results will more closely approximate the intentions of the designers.

The ultimate test of a LESA system, however, is whether its results—the levels and rankings of LESA scores—will be accepted as reasonable by people knowledgeable about farmland and planning. If LESA results are consistent with the judgments of such experts, then it is reasonable to assume that they will be well received by such experts and by a wider range of government officials, civic leaders, lawyers, and others involved in using LESA in the decision-making process. To the extent that LESA scores are not in accord with the judgments of local experts, the use of the LESA system will be limited at best.

To compare the scores from a LESA system with the evaluations of a group of experts, we asked 14 experts with extensive knowledge of

Table 5. Stepwise regression summary table: Dependent variable-LESA scores, independent variable-factor scores.

Step No.	Variable Entered	Variable Name	Multiple R	Multiple RSQ	Increase in RSQ	No. of Independent Variables Included
A. Chester County (PA) agricultural land preservation board system						
1	B	Prox to plan devel	0.564	0.318	0.318	1
2	D	Potential buffer	0.777	0.604	0.285	2
3	C	Prox to easement	0.883	0.779	0.175	3
4	E	Conserv. practices	0.945	0.894	0.115	4
5	A	Prox to non ag devel	0.971	0.943	0.049	5
6	F	Acreage	0.994	0.989	0.046	6
7	G	Prox to sewer svc.	1.000	1.000	0.011	7
B. Lancaster County (PA) agricultural preserve board system						
1	A3	Prox to sewer svc	0.781	0.610	0.610	1
2	A1	Non-ag zoning	0.859	0.739	0.129	2
3	A12	Road frontage	0.923	0.852	0.113	3
4	B3	Soil capability	0.958	0.917	0.065	4
5	B2	Acreage	0.971	0.942	0.026	5
6	A1	Non-ag development	0.977	0.955	0.013	6
7	C1	Prox to easement	0.993	0.987	0.031	7
8	A5	Urgency	0.997	0.993	0.006	8
9	C1	Stewardship of land	0.999	0.997	0.004	9
10	B4	Farm product sales	0.999	0.999	0.001	10
11	C2	Hist., scenic, env	1.000	0.999	0.001	11
12	B5	Adequacy of bldgs	1.000	1.000	0.000	12
C. Clarke County (VA) planning commission system						
1	3	Adj ag	0.622	0.387	0.387	1
2	5a	Permanent easement	0.776	0.602	0.215	2
3	5d	Historic, scenic regs	0.823	0.678	0.076	3
4	1	Large area	0.880	0.774	0.096	4
5	-3	Adj ag (removed)	0.860	0.740	-0.034	3
6	6	Far from urban conc	0.912	0.831	0.091	4
7	4a-ii	Lack road on bdry	0.942	0.888	0.056	5

Note: Letter and number codes under Variable Entered refer to factors as designated by each system.

Lancaster County to make general evaluations of five sites, and compared their evaluations with the LESA scores computed for each site. (See chapter 7 for a similar evaluation of the Linn County, Oregon, LESA system). These experts included board members and staff from the Lancaster County Agricultural Preserve Board and the Lancaster Farmland Trust, soil conservationists and other professionals from the soil conservation district, professionals from the state Cooperative Extension Service, and professional planners on the staff of the county planning commission.

We instructed these experts about the objectives of the exercise, took them on a field trip to view the five sites, and returned them to a meeting room where they made their evaluations.

Working in the Lancaster County context required that the experts be reminded that the Lancaster LESA system is designed to identify tracts that should be given the highest priority for easement purchase. The Lancaster system differs markedly from many other LESA systems. While most LESA systems give the highest ratings to tracts that are least likely to be developed, the Lancaster system gives the highest ratings to tracts that are under the greatest threat of development. Both types of systems are rational given the policy contexts in which they are applied. In most counties, there is little regulatory power to prevent development of farmland. There, it is sensible to work with the real estate market and give low agricultural ratings to land under heavy pressure of development and give the highest ratings to land that is unlikely to be developed. In Lancaster County, however, 35 townships have enacted zoning ordinances that have placed more than 272,000 acres in agricultural zones and very little of this land has since been rezoned to other uses (*1*). The Lancaster County Agricultural Preserve Board, therefore, relies on zoning to protect most agricultural land in the short term and seeks to concentrate its budget for acquisition on farms that are under strong pressure for development. By purchasing easements on such farms it hopes to create a band of permanently preserved land that will discourage the extension of water and sewer lines into the land beyond that is protected by zoning only. Therefore, the board gives the highest ratings to land most likely to be converted to non-farm uses. Daniels reports on the Lancaster program in chapter 11 of this volume.

We used an iterative method for reaching group consensus that restricted discussion but allowed the evaluators to learn the range of evaluations by the group as a whole before making their second, third, or fourth round evaluations. Using this Delphi method (*5, 6*), after the group scores a site for the first time, staff administering the study computes the median and interquartile range of the scores given by the experts and presents them to the group. Each expert can take this information into account to the extent desired in assigning second-round scores. The Delphi method restricts discussion among participants during the scoring session so that dominant personalities will not influence others. The developers of the Delphi method argue that participants who are uncertain about their scores will adjust them toward the group norm, while participants who are more certain of their scores will not be swayed by information on the group's scores.

The same procedure is followed for subsequent rounds. Two or three rounds of scoring were completed for each site, depending on the degree to which the interquartile range of scores narrowed in the course of previous rounds and on the amount of time remaining for the session. Regardless of whether two or three rounds of scoring were completed, each member of the panel gave round 4, and final, scores to all sites. In this fourth, and final, round, the staff encouraged each panel member to consider all sites relative to each other, rather than in isolation as they had in the previous rounds.

The medians and interquartile ranges of the final scores are given in Table 6, where they are set alongside the scores derived through application of the county's LESA system. In order to be comparable with the panel's Land-Quality and Other-Factors scores, which are on the basis of 100, the LE and SA scores are also put on a 100 basis, instead of as a given number of points out of a maximum of 35 possible for LE and out of 65 for SA.

The LESA system includes explicit weights for combining LE and SA scores to form the LESA score. The panel members, in contrast, were asked simply to assign an Overall score in addition to scores on Land and Other Factors. It is, however, theoretically possible to determine the weights they implicitly used by determining the ratios between their median scores on Land, Other Factors, and Overall. Because of the pattern of results, however, it was possible to do this satisfactorily only for site 1. Its imputed weights were Land:0.33 and Other:0.67, very similar to the LESA weights of Land:0.35 and Other:0.65. Sites 3 and 5 received the same scores for Other and Overall, thus suggesting imputed weights of Land:0.0 and Other:100.0. Sites 2 and 4 received the same scores for Land, Other, and Overall, so the imputed weighting cannot be determined.

There are several ways to compare the median scores of the panel and the scores from the LESA computation. In Table 7, absolute and relative (percentage) differences are presented. Generally, the Land scores were lower than the LE scores, the Other-Factor scores were higher than the SA scores, and the Overall scores were higher than the LESA scores. The relative differences were much greater for the component parts than for the summary scores. For four of the sites, the Overall and LESA scores were within six percent of each other. For the other site (site 1), however, the panel's score was 27 percent higher.

Another way to compare the two sets of scores is to determine how closely they are correlated as a first step in deriving a regression equation that

Table 6. Scores by panel and scores from LESA computation.

		Scores by Panel			LESA Scores		
		Land	Other	Overall	LE	SA	LESA
Site 1	Upper quartile	85	95	90			
	Median	75	90	85	59.0	71.1	66.8
	Lower-quartile	70	65	70			
	Imputed wt.	0.333	0.667	—			
	Q-Q	15	30	20			
	(Q-Q)/median	0.200	0.333	0.235			
Site 2	Upper quartile	80	75	72			
	Median	70	70	70	100.0	59.6	73.7
	Lower-quartile	65	65	65			
	Imputed wt.	indeterminate		—			
	Q-Q	15	10	7			
	(Q-Q)/median	0.214	0.143	0.100			
Site 3	Upper quartile	85	85	85			
	Median	83	80	80	100.0	66.3	78.1
	Lower-quartile	75	75	78			
	Imputed wt.	0	100	—			
	Q-Q	10	10	7			
	(Q-Q)/median	0.120	0.125	0.088			
Site 4	Upper quartile	90	85	85			
	Median	80	80	80	84.8	70.7	75.6
	Lower-quartile	70	75	75			
	Imputed wt	indeterminate		—			
	Q-Q	20	10	10			
	(Q-Q)/median	0.250	0.125	0.125			
Site 5	Upper quartile	90	95	90			
	Median	85	90	90	100.0	77.6	85.4
	Lower-quartile	80	80	84			
	Imputed wt.	0	100	—			
	Q-Q	10	15	6			
	(Q-Q)/median	0.118	0.167	0.067			

Under Lancaster County's "New System" of LE:SA weights LE given a maximum score of 35 and SA is allowed a maximum of 65. In order to put these scores on a comparable basis with the panel's scores, the LE scores were divided by 35 and multiplied by 100, and the SA scores were divided by 65 and multiplied by 100.

Table 7. Absolute and relative differences between median panel scores and LESA scores.

	Scores by Panel			LESA Scores			Panel minus LESA			Panel divided by LESA		
Site	Land	Other	Overall	LE	SA	LESA	LE	SA	LESA	LE	SA	LESA
1	75	90	85	58.97	71.05	66.82	16.03	18.95	18.18	1.27	1.27	1.27
2	70	70	70	100.00	59.60	73.74	-30.00	10.40	-3.74	0.70	1.17	0.95
3	83	80	80	100.00	66.26	78.07	-17.00	13.74	1.93	0.83	1.21	1.02
4	80	80	80	84.77	70.65	75.59	-4.77	9.35	4.41	0.94	1.13	1.06
5	85	90	90	100.00	77.57	85.42	-15.00	12.43	4.58	0.85	1.16	1.05

would predict the value of the LESA score given the value of the panel's score, or vice versa. With only five observations, however, it is not possible to ascribe significance to statistical measures, so instead of performing a correlation or regression analysis, we have simply plotted the final scores of the panel against the scores from LESA computation. The results are given in figures 6, 7, and 8. The plots suggest that the correlation between Other Factors and SA appears to be quite strong (Figure 7), but the correlation between Land and LE is weakened by site 2 (Figure 6) and that between Overall and LESA is weakened by site 1 (Figure 8).

It is difficult to draw conclusions from such a small sample, but it seems fair to say that there is a reasonable correspondence between the evaluations of the panel and the scores of the LESA system. Some sites, however, may be over- or under-valued by the Lancaster County LESA. Site 1 is an example of a site that should have received a higher LESA score if one assumes that the panel's Overall evaluation of it was valid. This conclusion from our Lancaster exercise is consistent with the survey responses (*7*) to the question—how often does your LESA system reliably distinguish between land that should remain in agriculture and land that should be converted to other uses? In answer,

10.9 percent said	"Always"
68.0 percent said	"Most of the time"
18.8 percent said	"Not very often"
2.3 percent said	"Never."

Conclusions

The research reported here suggests the following:

1. Careful attention should be paid not only to LESA scores but also to the criteria with which they are applied in decision making.

2. When a variety of considerations are combined into one index, the result is likely to contain some ambiguities. If a minimum level of some factors or of LE or SA is considered important, LESA should be reformulated to require that a site meet those minima as an eligibility test. Choice based on LESA scores would be made from among the sites that meet the stated minima.

3. LESA scores are necessarily inexact. Therefore, cut-off criteria for choice of parcels should be of the "fuzzy" variety, not the sharp, knife-edge variety. The level of accuracy of LESA scores suggests that they should be stated to only one decimal place at the most.

4. LESA models are used to aid decision making concerning particular

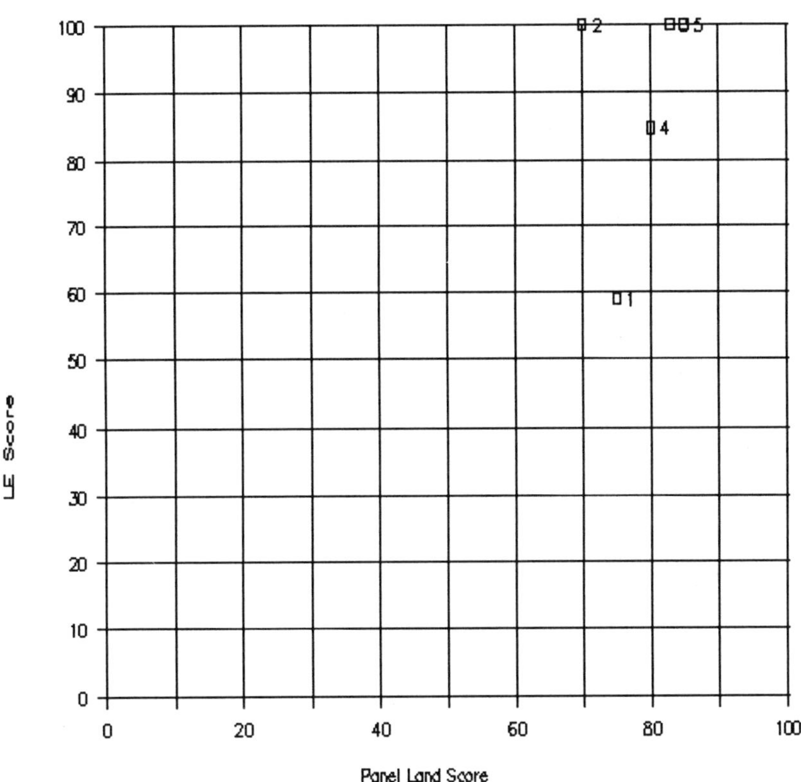

Figure 6. Panel land scores vs. LE scores.

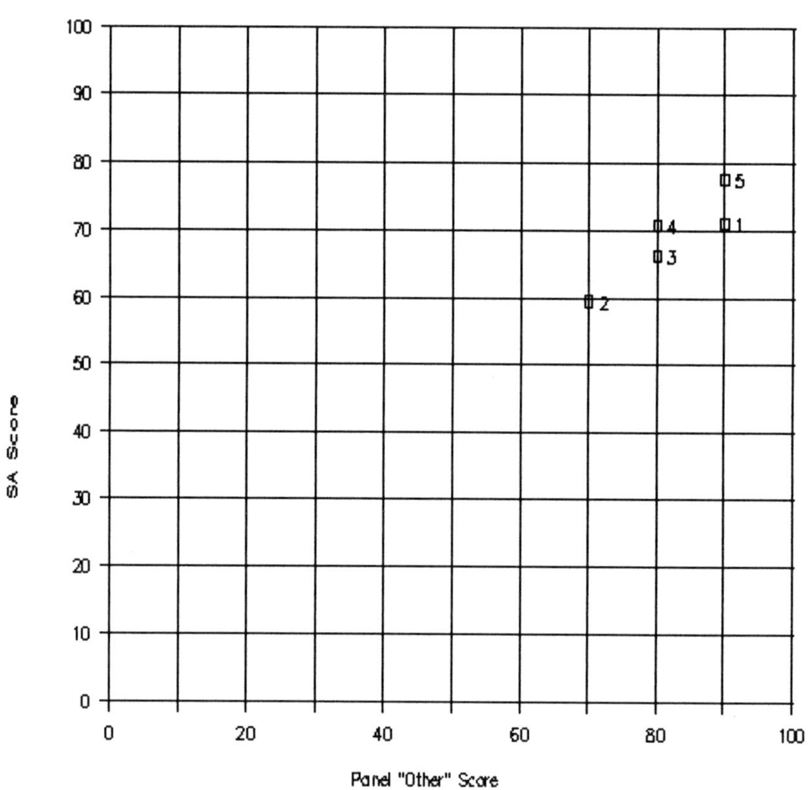

Figure 7. Panel Other-Factors scores vs. SA scores.

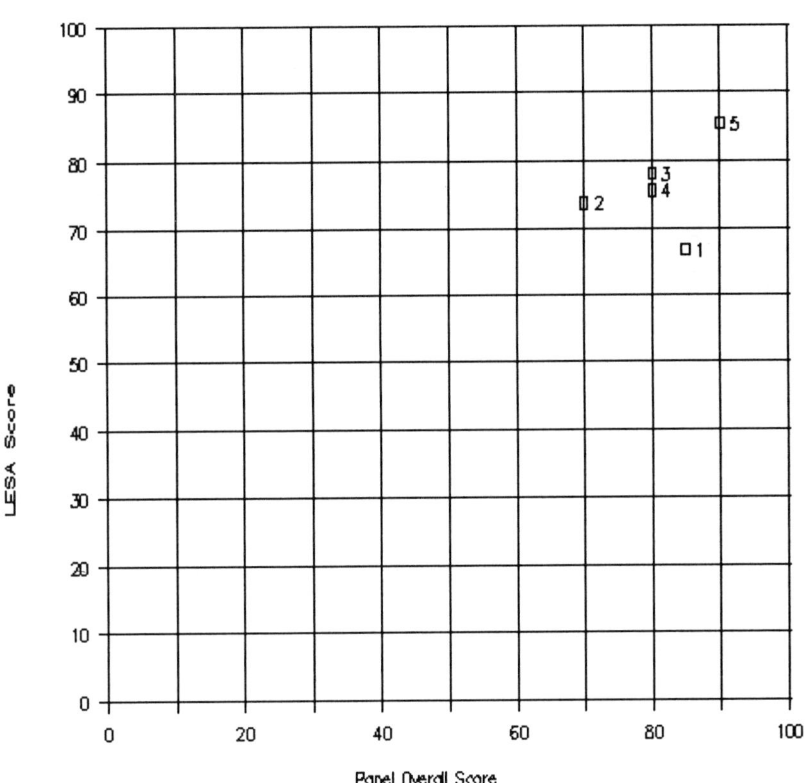

Figure 8. Panel Overall Scores vs. LESA scores.

questions. Therefore, systems should be designed with a particular type of question in mind. A jurisdiction should develop special purpose models as necessary (e.g. for PDR, agricultural zoning, etc.) instead of a single all-purpose model.

5. It is harder to predict the effect on a particular site of changing factor weights or LE:SA weights than one might have suspected.

6. Changes to LE:SA weights can have substantial effects on the ranking of sites; changes in factor weights are less likely to have substantial effects. LE:SA weights, particularly, should be chosen carefully.

7. There appears to be relatively little intercorrelation among LE factors, but often, two or more SA factors are intercorrelated. Generally, possible reduction in the number of SA factors should be explored. Certainly, systems with more than a dozen factors should be examined.

8. Panels of local experts can be used to determine whether LESA scores are likely to be accepted as valid in a community.

9. Jurisdictions should conduct extensive tests of their LESA systems and adjust them accordingly to ensure that resulting LESA scores are reasonable and that the systems are not excessively complex and costly.

References

1. Coughlin, R. E. 1992. *The Adoption and Stability of Agricultural Zoning in Lancaster County, Pennsylvania.* Research Report Series: No. 15. Department of City and Regional Planning, University of Pennsylvania, Philadelphia.
2. Daniels, T. 1990. *Using LESA in a Purchase of Development Rights Program.* Journal of Soil and Water Conservation 45(6):617-621.
3. Ferguson, C. A., and R. L. Bowen. 1991. *Statistical Evaluation of an Agricultural Land Suitability Model.* Environmental Management 15(5):689-700.
4. Ferguson, C. A., R. L. Brown, and M. A. Kahn. 1991. *A Statewide LESA System for Hawaii.* Journal of Soil and Water Conservation 46(4):263-267.
5. Linstone, H. A., and M. Turoff (eds). 1975. *The Delphi Method.* Addison-Wesley Publishing Co., Reading, Massachusetts.
6. Pease, J. R. 1984. *Collecting Land Use Data.* Journal of Soil and Water Conservation 39(6):361-364.
7. Steiner, F., J. R. Pease, R. E. Coughlin, J. C. Leach, J. A. Pressley, L. S. Papazian, A. P. Sussman, and C. Shaw. 1991. *Agricultural Land Evaluation and Site Assessment: Status of State and Local Programs.* The Herberger Center, Arizona State University, Tempe.
8. U.S. Department of Agriculture-Soil Conservation Service. 1983. *National Agricultural Land Evaluation and Site Assessment Handbook.* Washington, D.C.
9. Wright, L. E., W. Zitzmann, and R. Googins. 1983. *LESA - Agricultural Land Evaluation and Site Assessment.* Journal of Soil and Water Conservation 38(2):82-86.

9 Hawaii's LESA Experience in a Changing Policy Environment

**Richard L. Bowen
and Carol A. Ferguson**

awaii was one of the first state governments to embrace land evaluation and site assessment (LESA) and remains the only state to develop an area-wide LESA system for all agricultural land within its jurisdiction. LESA offered a means to improve state zoning decisions by identifying agricultural lands warranting a high level of protection from urbanization pressures. Hawaii's experience with LESA provides a number of lessons for improving the method and current practices, including use of geographic information systems (GIS) for comprehensive assessment as well as extended applications to address new policy concerns. A changing policy environment over time requires continuous adaptation of a LESA system to support land use decision making.

Creating a Statewide LESA

The movement to establish a statewide LESA system began in 1983 with the appointment by the state legislature of a special commission. The Hawaii LESA commission was comprised of the heads of relevant state and county government agencies, along with representatives from major farm organizations, other sectoral interests, and the general public. Its overall mandate was to develop standards, criteria, and procedures to identify "important agricultural lands" (IAL) using the LESA method, and to map IAL areas on the major islands. In addition, the commission was to recommend actions and legislation to integrate LESA into the existing land use regulatory framework. After two and a half years of study, deliberation, and public hearings, a final report (*10*) was issued in time to be considered by the 1986 legislative session. Further details on the commission's work and the Hawaii LESA system may be found in our earlier publications (*6, 7, 8*).

Land Evaluation (LE). During its tenure, the Hawaii LESA commission was able to specify and map the LE component of the system. Five LE factors were selected from existing national and state soil interpretive systems (see Table 1). To derive an LE score, all five soil rating systems (LE factors) are first converted to percentage ratings using a common 100-point scale, then

Table 1. Hawaii LESA factors and weights.

Factor	Weight
LAND EVALUATION	
1. land capability classification	1.0
2. agricultural lands of importance to the state of Hawaii	1.0
3. soil potential index	1.5
4. modified Storie index	1.0
5. overall productivity rating	1.5
SITE ASSESSMENT	
1. conformity with county plan, policy	15
2. availability of irrigation facilities/services	10
3. proximity to urban infrastructure, services	7
4. presence of on-site agricultural improvements	7
5. conformity with state agricultural programs, projects	7
6. access to agricultural facilities, services	4
7. economical parcel size, location, configuration	4
8. compatible agricultural land uses with region	4
9. adequacy of off-site drainage	1
10. impact of nearby non-agricultural land use	1

aggregated with a weighted average to produce a score ranging from 0 to 100. LE factors 3 and 5 are given 50 percent greater weight then the other three factors because they are considered more direct measures of productivity.

In the Hawaii system, LE scores correspond directly to soil types (series and phases) and soil mapping units. Therefore, the LESA commission was able to create a statewide inventory of LE-rated lands based on existing soils information. Using manually drawn overlays, preliminary LE maps of Hawaii's agricultural lands were prepared by the commission staff.

Site Assessment (SA). The commission chose to restrict the SA component of the LESA system to site attributes that directly or indirectly impact site suitability for agricultural uses. After reviewing the national handbook as well as other LESA systems on the mainland, it adopted 10 SA factors deemed most appropriate to Hawaii's situation. Four of the 10 relate to conditions affecting farm productivity and profitability: irrigation, on-site farm improvements, access to agricultural services, and layout of the parcel. Another four factors address potential conflicts with adjacent lands: proximity to urban facilities, compatibility with other agricultural uses, drainage, and impacts from a non-agricultural use. The final two factors assess conformance of a site's use with government policies, specifically county development plans and state agricultural programs.

The commission went on to develop short, descriptive characterizations with factor ratings (1-10 points) and weights (1-15) for each factor. A weighted average was used to compute a total SA score ranging 0 to 100. Due to lack of time and readily available data, the commission could not produce statewide maps of SA-rated lands. Instead, factor characterizations were arranged in expected combinations to form 24 "prototype" representative farming situations. The prototypes were used to make a qualitative evaluation of alternative SA factor point and weighting schemes, and to select the ratio with which to combine SA and LE scores. The commission ultimately gave equal weight to each component in computing a final LESA score.

After the commission disbanded in 1986, the state legislature appropriated funds to continue with LESA development. The University of Hawaii was contracted to implement a mapped version of the system using an existing GIS in the College of Tropical Agriculture and Human Resources. Statewide computerized mapping of LESA factors took three years. Further analysis and evaluation of the system were reported in 1989 and 1990 (*13, 15*).

LESA for State Zoning of Agricultural Land

Zoning is the main policy tool used in Hawaii to protect agricultural land from urbanization pressures. Hawaii is unique among states in its two-tiered, state-county system of zoning. Under Hawaii's state system of zoning, all land in the state is classified into one of four land-use districts. The state is responsible for management of lands in the conservation district, while county governments manage the urban district. Management of the agricultural and rural districts is shared by the two levels of government. The Hawaii Land Use Commission (LUC) administers state district designation and must approve a petition to reclassify a parcel from one district to another. County zoning operates similar to other local zoning systems in the U.S. A landowner must obtain both state and county zoning approvals to change a parcel's use from agriculture to another use.

Pre-LESA Zoning Policy. State zoning began in 1961 with the passage of Hawaii's pioneering land-use law (*14*). At that time, sugarcane and pineapple plantations dominated Hawaii agriculture, and both the plantations and unionized agricultural labor had strong political clout. The major concern behind the law was that land speculation, fueled by a rapidly emerging tourism economy, would lead to the demise of plantation agriculture (*3, 14*).

During the early years of the land-use law, LUC zoning decisions generally favored growth. Approval rates for reclassifying parcels from agriculture to the urban district were high, reflecting this pro-growth attitude. Tourism development was encouraged as long as it did not disturb the beauty of Hawaii's natural landscape. Urban growth was encouraged in compact developments efficiently served by public infrastructure and services (*2*).

By the 1970s rapid population growth and its perceived threat to the environment and quality of life in Hawaii was a major public concern. Although agriculture had declined sharply in relative economic importance, residents recognized its environmental contribution in maintaining green, open space. State zoning was administered more strictly, as reflected in lower approval rates in agricultural district reclassifications (*12*). In 1978 the electorate amended the state constitution calling for greater statutory protection of farmland (*10*). The Hawaii legislature responded five years later by establishing a state LESA commission in 1983 to identify important agricultural lands and recommend measures to protect them.

Identifying Important Agricultural Lands. When the LESA commission was created, much of the land zoned in the state agricultural district was of poor quality and of little significance to the agricultural economy. To manage important agricultural lands, the commission proposed that the district be drastically reduced to encompass only areas with acceptable LESA scores. The unimportant land of the district would be transferred to the urban district, to be managed exclusively by the county governments. State control over land use would be less extensive but more focused. Following the initial downsizing of the agricultural district, it would presumably be more difficult for developers to gain LUC approval to reclassify parcels to non-agricultural uses, thereby increasing protection.

The commission recommended that only one-third of agricultural district lands be retained as IAL. The quantity of farmland to be protected was determined by projecting the size, in terms of acreage, of various agricultural industries on each island. Actual and 1990 commission-targeted IAL acreages are shown in Figure 1 and targeted acreages by island given in Table 2. A total of 650,000 acres was targeted for the IAL in 1990. Sugarcane was projected to experience a moderate decline while pineapple was expected to remain steady. Moderate growth was forecast for all other export crops. The production of all locally consumed commodities was expected to increase based on state population growth and economic feasibility. The beef cattle industry was an exception, where it was assumed that only half of existing grazing and pasture lands would be needed to meet production goals under more intensive management. These lands also can be considered a reserve for further expansion of cultivated crops.

LESA threshold scores were established so that the amount of agricultural land with LESA scores above the threshold would match the production goals for each island (see Table 2). These lands would be retained in the new IAL district. The threshold score varied considerably depending on the production goal and quality of land. The island of Hawaii is the newest island in the Hawaiian chain and its soils are of poorer quality than other islands, thus its LESA threshold score was considerably lower.

Table 2. Hawaii LESA production goals and threshold scores by island.

	Production Goals (acres)	LESA Threshold Score*
Hawaii	356,519	55
Kauai	65,743	63
Lanai	12,700	75
Maui	132,495	61
Molokai	26,689	67
Oahu	55,890	71
State total	650,000	—

*Using simplified LESA model with 4 SA factors.

From Figure 1 it can be seen that 1990 target production acreages were not reached for most agricultural industries. The only industry exceeding the target acreage was grazing, which can be explained by an insufficient shift to intensive grazing practices. The greater than expected decline in sugarcane and pineapple acreage and less than expected increase in tree and food crops reinforces the recommendation of the LESA commission that future goals and threshold scores be periodically reviewed and adjusted to reflect changing economic conditions.

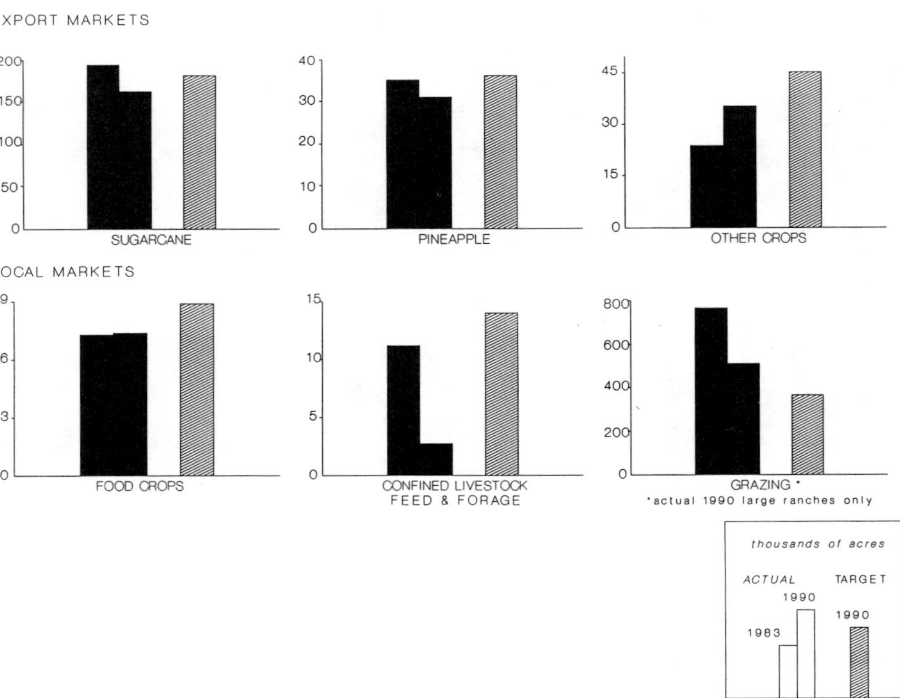

Figure 1. Actual cropped and LESA target acreage for the agricultural district, by market outlet and commodity group.

A demonstration of the Hawaii LESA system for the island of Oahu is shown in Figure 2a, generated by the University of Hawaii LESA-GIS. The LESA commission targeted 56,000 acres for 1990 Oahu agriculture which, with the full LESA model (10 SA factors), produced an IAL threshold score of 68. Areas with LESA scores of 85 or greater (darkest shade) are "prime" farmlands most suitable for agricultural use. Lower rated but still IAL areas are shown with medium shading. Under the commission's proposal, poor quality agricultural lands (lightly shaded) would be merged with the present urban district (see Figure 2b).

Impediments to System Adoption

Legislation to implement LESA commission recommendations has been before the Hawaii legislature since 1987 but none of the various bills submitted have passed. This failure has little to do with the technical specification of the LESA model and much to do with how land-use law changes would affect the state, the county governments, landowners, and other interest groups.

The first impediment to LESA adoption was the lack of maps accurately delineating the agricultural lands to be placed in the new IAL district. Legislators, government officials, and landowners could not fully comprehend how LESA would affect them or their constituents without maps. The LESA commission was able to produce only "illustrative generalized IAL maps" based largely on LE scores. The legislature provided additional funds for the development of a LESA-GIS and LESA maps were available by the 1989 session. That LESA legislation did not pass in 1989 or subsequent years means that more formidable impediments persisted. The remainder of this section discusses some of these other impediments.

A lack of a solid political base of support can partially explain the lack of legislative action since 1987. The Hawaii Farm Bureau is the major interest group supporting LESA but conflicting views within its membership have not permitted it to take a strong stance. Positions of farmers tend to reflect their status as landowners or tenants and the location of their land. For lands slated to remain in the IAL district, pressures to convert agricultural land to non-agricultural uses and land values can be expected to decline, favoring lessees and penalizing landowners. On the other hand, land values and conversion pressures could be expected to rise on lands to be excluded from the IAL, favoring landowners but reducing the prospects of the lessees for continued access.

Conflicts among government interests are also responsible for legislative inaction. The commission's proposal would have transferred 1.3 million

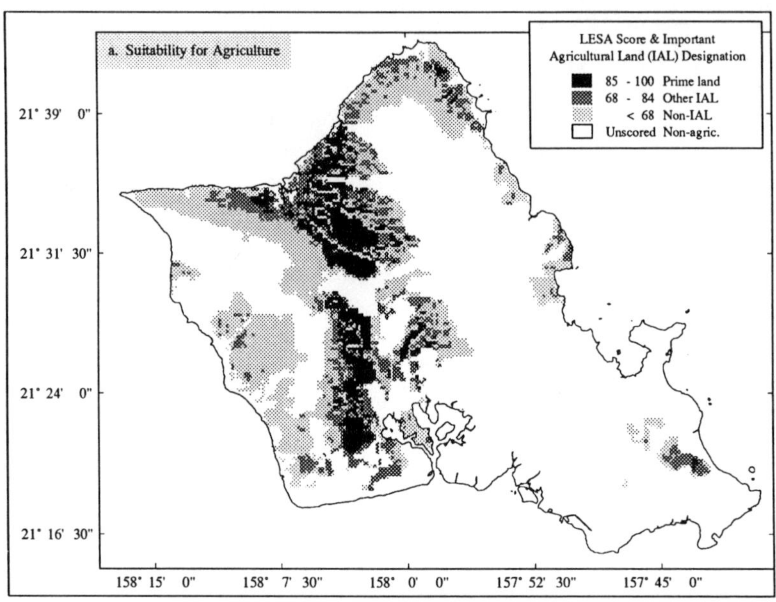

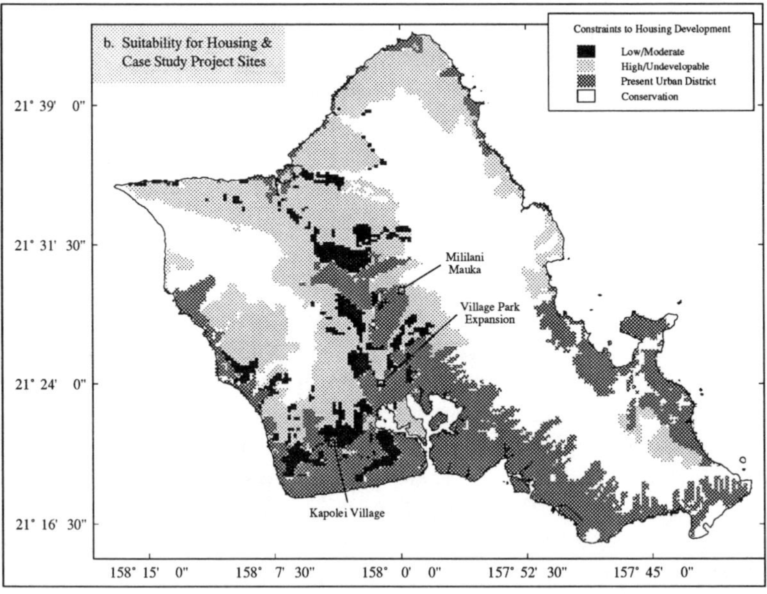

Figures 2a and 2b. Maps of land suitability ratings for Oahu's present agricultural district.

acres from joint state-county control to exclusive control by the counties. A new Office of State Planning countered in 1989 with a proposal to place these non-IAL lands in a new "open" district, which would continue joint state-county management and require landowners to obtain state LUC approval for conversion to urban uses. This struggle for land-use control between the counties and the state governments, part of the long-standing issue of county "home rule," remains an impediment to the adoption of a LESA-designated district.

Another impediment has been the expanding role of the state government in promoting "affordable housing." Shortly after the LESA commission was established, the provision of "affordable housing" became an important policy issue. By the time the LESA commission finished its work, a new state administration came into power committed to expanding the supply of housing for moderate- and low-income families. The state became an aggressive housing promoter by purchasing land and entering into agreements with developers to build affordable housing tracts. Many of the planned housing projects were sited on important agricultural lands. The Office of State Planning (OSP) was responsible for both affordable housing and agricultural land protection policies, and the conflict between the two policies may have prevented the agency from strongly pushing its own LESA legislation.

LESA and Affordable Housing

Emergence of the Affordable Housing Issue. For state zoning policy, the period from 1975 to 1982 can be characterized as one of "limited growth." Housing development in Hawaii slowed because of a lagging economy, as well as more restrictive zoning for urban expansion. During the 1980s however, demand for housing rose sharply. Increasing real incomes and family formation by the "baby-boom" generation resulted in a population "boomlet" and strong pressures for more detached, single-family units. Housing prices in Hawaii had been well above those of the U.S. mainland for a long time. But given the lack of inventory, by the end of the decade, rising demand was pushing housing prices beyond the reach of even middle-income families (*1, 9*).

During the period of LESA-GIS development, the OSP contracted with a private firm to determine which lands in Oahu's agricultural district would be best suited for affordable tract housing (*4*). Maps from this study were digitized into the GIS containing LESA. This allowed for additional analyses comparing land suitability for agriculture with land suitability for housing.

Land Suitability for Housing vs. Farming. In the OSP-sponsored study, land suitability for housing was assessed based on possible limitations from four main factors: slope, erosion hazard, commuting times, and soil shrinkswell. Lands in Oahu's agricultural district at that time were classified by the degree of constraints to housing development—low, moderate, or high. Parcels with some limitation from any of the first three factors were assigned the moderate constraint rating. High constraint lands had moderate-severe limitations from one of the four main factors, or from another secondary factor (flood hazard, airport noise, or dedicated agricultural use). Some areas in the agricultural district were separately judged undevelopable, either better suited for the conservation district or already committed to another use (e.g., military reserves). These were excluded from the housing suitability analysis.

Figure 2b shows the distribution of housing ratings across Oahu's agricultural district, along with parcels previously zoned for urban uses (excluding any subsequent reclassifications between districts). The best housing areas are those presenting only low or moderate constraints to development (darkest map shade) and are limited to about 25,000 acres (less than 20 percent) of the agricultural district. Most sizable concentrations of these higher-rated housing lands are found adjacent to the urban district (medium shade). Other locational factors favor housing construction in these areas. Public utilities and other infrastructure could be provided at less expense by extending and expanding current lines. Also, these lands are owned and/or operated as plantations for sugarcane or pineapple production and are available in large contiguous tracts preferred by developers of suburban-type housing.

Close comparison of the two maps in Figure 2 and information presented in Figure 3 reveals noticeable overlap in agricultural district lands well-suited for both farming as well as housing. Figure 3 presents the distribution of housing suitability ratings within LESA-score land classes. One-third, or 18,000 acres, of important agricultural lands, received one of the two highest housing ratings. However, only 6,800 acres, about 10 percent of non-IAL lands, offer favorable opportunities for affordable housing development. In addition, developable non-IAL lands are generally located further from the urban core in more dispersed sites and therefore are less suitable for tract housing. This confirms the growing conflict between protecting agricultural land in districts by LESA and meeting affordable housing goals for the island of Oahu.

Case Study of Planned Housing Developments. Besides one-time downsizing of the agricultural district, the LESA commission proposed the system be used in Land Use Commission consideration of subsequent petitions to reclassify IAL parcels. To evaluate LESA's utility for this purpose, three Oahu sites were selected from among the petitions submitted during that time period. Large-scale suburban housing developments were planned for these former plantation lands. As shown in Figure 2b, all case study sites were adjacent to already urbanized areas, a factor that would favor rezoning

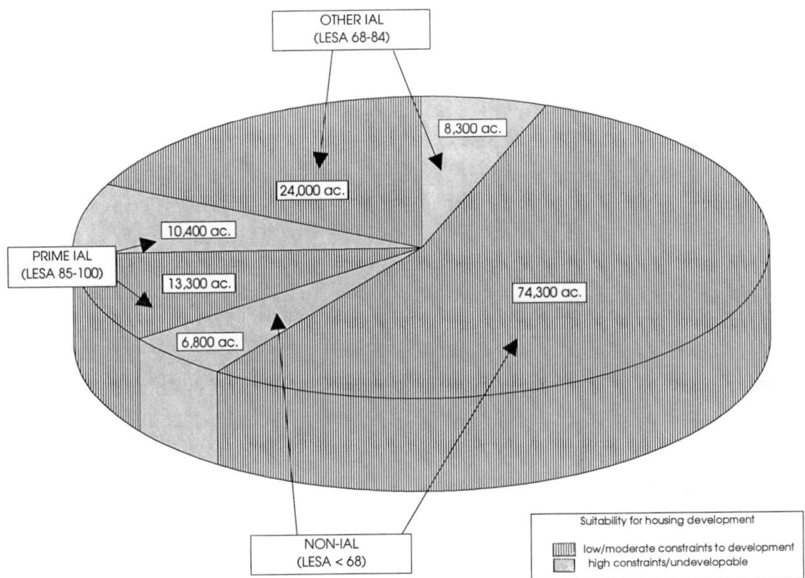

Figure 3. Land suitable for housing developed in Oahu's present agricultural district, by LESA important agricultural land (IAL) designations.

approval. In addition, two of the projects were extensions of previously approved developments, while the third was part of an envisioned "Second City" promoted by both state and county governments.

Case study sites were evaluated with respect to relative suitability for housing development or continued use in agriculture. Statistics of land suitability ratings are given in Table 3. LESA scores were generally quite high, indicating the three areas were well-suited for farming. However, the scores depend on SA factor ratings for county zoning of the project, which can be obtained before petitioning the state LUC. Prior county approval would have lowered the LESA values on any rezoned parcels resulting in none of the project areas being rated prime farmland, though more than half the acreage at each site would still be classified as IAL. At the same time much of the petitioned acreage was suitable for housing development, presenting a trade-off between government support for agriculture and for housing.

More detailed analysis of GIS raster data revealed considerable variability in land quality within each site. The LESA handbook (*15*) suggests using the mean score in these situations. But for the three study sites, the mean LESA values are nearly equal and mask important differences. Alternative summary statistics include the median score and the percentage of area designated IAL. However, each of these three measures results in a different ranking of projects as to the best farmland to be preserved.

Table 3. Evaluation of three petitions to rezone agricultural district land for housing development.

Evaluation Criteria (units)	Kapolei Village		Mililani Mauka		Village Park Exp.	
Petition site						
Agricultural use	sugarcane		pineapple		sugarcane	
Rezoned area			acres			
requested	830		1,200		627	
approved	830		723		548	
Agricultural suitability						
Important agricultural			percent of approved area*			
land (IAL) designation	(a)	(b)	(a)	(b)	(a)	(b)
prime	49%	0%	55%	0%	7%	0%
other IAL	46	79	25	72	79	86
non-IAL	5	21	20	28	14	14
			0-100 scale*			
LESA score	(a)	(b)	(a)	(b)	(a)	(b)
mean	80	73	79	70	78	70
median	82	76	89	80	81	72
Housing suitability			percent of approved area			
Low/moderate constraints	70%		60%		7%	
High constraints/undevelopable	30		40		+	

*For SA factor on conformance with county development plan, agricultural suitability computed with: (a) actual ratings at the time of petition, (b) revised ratings if entire area zoned for non-agricultural uses.
+Remaining area not rated.

Case study results and later analysis (*5*) indicate rezoning of the agricultural district based on LESA is unlikely to relieve the pressures to urbanize more farmland. None of the projects evaluated would have been viable using only non-IAL parcels. The fact that the LUC approved most of the petitioned acreage reflects government priority given to housing.

Lessons for System Development and Use

Experience in Hawaii suggests several areas for modifying current national LESA guidelines. Also, improvements in common practices would facilitate development of empirical models and increase their effectiveness.

The largest obstacle is vagueness and/or subjectivity in the handbook (*15*) definitions of the SA factors. Use of GIS technology places even higher definitional requirements on LESA. Factor criteria must be specified in terms of quantifiable land attributes (preferably only one per factor) for which spatial information is readily available. Clearer factor definitions in the LESA handbook would reduce, but not entirely eliminate, the ambiguity for future developers of LESA systems. Some adaptability for local conditions is necessary and desirable. Guidelines with specific examples of such adjustments would be helpful.

Evaluation of the Hawaii system indicates that a simpler model specification can provide satisfactory area-wide assessments. Only four of the original 10 SA factors, those with more variable and thus discriminating ratings, accounted for virtually all differences in relative scores. These key factors were tacitly recognized earlier by the LESA commission through the assignment of higher weight values. To an even greater extent, all five LE factors, though based on different national and local soil evaluation systems, proved highly intercorrelated. In this case, Hawaii's weighted-average scoring system is easier and as effective as the recommended soil grouping procedures.

Model simplicity also may be served by less elaborate weighting of the separate LE and SA components. The ratio used to combine LE with SA assumes greater importance in area-wide applications than in individual parcel applications because conditions are likely to vary more. An appropriate value will depend on variability of land versus site attributes embodied in the two components. In the Midwest, soil quality may be relatively homogeneous over large areas, and so SA factors may need greater weight to provide differentiation. In places like Hawaii, with high variability in soil types, LE should be given more weight.

The housing case studies reveal that developers can manipulate how LESA is applied in zoning decisions by extending project boundaries to include extraneous low-score areas and obtaining county rezoning first.

These actions would lower the LESA score for the entire parcel and possibly affect the decision on whether to reclassify the parcel out of agriculture. The first possibility can best be exposed by maps showing the distribution of scores across a site, which might also suggest to planning authorities ways to modify the zoning request. As for the second possibility, state governments should clarify by law whether county zoning changes should occur before or after state zoning decisions.

Hawaii was fortunate to be able to tap an existing computerized GIS and database in developing statewide LESA maps. Given high GIS start-up costs, it would be difficult to justify establishing such a system for LESA alone. But as demonstrated in the previous section, extended applications can help spread out the costs, making GIS an efficient long-run choice in some situations. In Hawaii, GIS mapping capabilities would be essential in using LESA to rezone the agricultural district. Carefully designed LESA maps can improve public understanding for other agricultural land policies as well. To maximize GIS power and flexibility, however, we have found it useful to link with other statistical and graphics software to provide additional analyses and display formats, including composite figures with maps and high-resolution output.

A final consideration is the institutional framework underlying a LESA system. Hawaii has encountered continuing problems and delays resulting from transitory arrangements and fragmentation of responsibilities for LESA design, implementation, and use. Better coordination and continuity across the different phases would have improved the final product. Moreover, institutionalizing LESA would establish a base of political support for acceptance and maintenance of the system.

Looking Toward the Future

The history of political and economic development and agricultural land preservation are intimately entwined in Hawaii. In the early years after statehood in 1959, when attitudes were both pro-growth and protective of agricultural land, LESA would have been a useful tool for guiding development. LESA was introduced in Hawaii during a period of high concern for the environment and related quality of life. LESA was seen not only as a tool for protecting important agricultural land but useful for protecting open and green space and limiting urban and resort development. In today's policy environment, LESA alarms policy makers for its potential to stymie government-sponsored housing projects and the attainment of affordable housing goals.

Public support for government protection of agricultural land tends to increase when the agricultural sector is booming and to wane when the sector is in recession or permanent decline. Nationally, concern over losses of prime agricultural land increased during the late 1970s when agricultural income and land prices rose sharply. The concern nearly disappeared at the national level in the 1980s as the farm crisis produced falling income and a precipitous drop in agricultural land values. Ward (*16*) has accused the Reagan administration of "benign neglect" of LESA, probably since agricultural land protection was seen as counter to the priority goals of economic growth and deregulation. With large declines in the past decade in land devoted to sugarcane and pineapple and only a small fraction being replaced by diversified crops, the concern for agricultural land protection has declined in Hawaii too. Because of weak political support, conflicts among state and county governments, and strong opposition by large landowners, proposals for incorporating LESA into state land-use law have not passed the state legislature. If legislation does pass in the next few years, it will likely be in a form that will have little impact on land use decision making.

One can expect conversion of good farmland to continue in the 1990s, with or without LESA legislation. The state housing program relies on the initiative of private developers, who will naturally propose projects on the most easily developable land. Despite the home rule arguments against LESA, county governments could exert considerable influence over site selection through the heavily weighted SA factor on county zoning. But preservation of agricultural land has never been a major concern at the county level, particularly in Honolulu where urbanization pressures are greatest. Thus, the balance between competing land uses and the rate of farmland conversion will remain largely a matter of state policy.

Technically the Hawaii LESA model is not controversial. However, the inclusion of housing and other urban considerations, or the joint development of other land suitability rating systems, would make LESA more palatable to policy makers. We believe that separate land rating systems are superior to a single integrated system, because the latter can be difficult to interpret. Separate rating systems more clearly show the trade-offs in rating the same land for different uses, allowing policy makers to assign their own relative weights.

GIS technology is rapidly improving and costs are declining. Its use for LESA and related applications is bound to increase. Although it would generally be difficult to justify developing a GIS solely to implement LESA, incorporation of LESA into an existing GIS and computerized database may be cost-effective. With more and more data becoming available in GIS format, the development of SA factors and land rating systems for nonagricultural uses will become easier. SA factors will need to be developed with GIS in mind. And databases developed for LESA will be useful for many other purposes.

Looking toward the future, rising concerns over water quality as related to agriculture and impending government regulation of non-point source pollution have added other dimensions not critical when LESA was first created. The discovery of widespread agricultural contamination of the nation's aquifers and increasing public concern over surface water quality make this an important factor for system development. The positive contribution of agriculture to environmental goals, such as provision of open and green spaces, might also be recognized in the model. Some LESA factors indirectly reflect off-site environmental concerns but there is further need for factors that provide explicit measurement.

Environmental concerns in some locations could be sufficiently strong to justify adding a third component to LE and SA. It would likely consist of land factors (e.g., soil erodibility) and site factors (e.g., vulnerability of underlying aquifer). Specifically, it is less important to protect agricultural lands overlaying shallow aquifers or on highly erodible soils where chemical leaching and soil erosion threaten to pollute our waters. Such areas have been identified in Hawaii on the same GIS used for LESA (*11*), and could easily be incorporated into a revised LESA model.

At the same time, the argument for protection of agricultural land should be stronger in areas where agriculture provides cultural or aesthetic benefits. Whether it is affordable housing, water quality, or some other emerging policy issue, a LESA system must adapt to new issues.

References

1. Bank of Hawaii. 1991. *Construction in Hawaii 1991.* Honolulu.
2. Bosselman, F.P., and D. Callies. 1971. *The quiet revolution in land-use control.* Council on Environmental Quality, Washington, D.C.
3. DeGrove, J.M. 1984. *Land growth and politics.* Planners Press, Washington, D.C.
4. DHM, Inc. 1987. *Evaluation of Oahu state agricultural district.* Hawaii Office of State Planning, Honolulu.
5. Ferguson, C.A., and M.A. Khan. 1992. *Protecting farmland near cities: Trade-Offs with affordable housing in Hawaii.* Land Use Policy 9(4):259-271.
6. Ferguson, C.A., and R.L. Bowen. 1991. *Statistical evaluation of an agricultural land suitability model.* Environmental Management 15(5):689-700.
7. Ferguson, C.A., R.L. Bowen, and M.A. Khan. 1991. *A statewide LESA system for Hawaii.* Journal of Soil and Water Conservation 46(4):263-267.
8. Ferguson, C.A., R.L. Bowen, M.A. Khan, and T. Liang. 1990. *An appraisal of the Hawaii land evaluation and site assessment (LESA) system.* Information Text No.35. Hawaii Institute of Tropical Agriculture and Human Resources, University of Hawaii, Honolulu.
9. Hawaii Department of Business, Economic Development and Tourism. 1991. *The State of Hawaii Data Book.* 1991. Honolulu.
10. Hawaii Land Evaluation and Site Assessment Commission. 1986. *A report on the state of Hawaii land evaluation and site assessment system.* Legislative Reference Bureau, Honolulu.
11. Khan, M.A., and T. Liang. 1989. *Mapping pesticide contamination potential.* Environmental Management 13(2):233-242.
12. Lowry, K., M. Awaya, K. Higham, T. Luke, A. Mitsuda, P. Olsen, H. Sonomura, and G. Uchida. 1977. *Analysis of alternative land-use management techniques for Hawaii.* In Growth Management Issues in Hawaii. Hawaii Department of Budget and Finance, Honolulu.
13. Martin, J.C., C.A. Ferguson, and R.L. Bowen. 1989. *Evaluation and application of the land evaluation and site assessment (LESA) system in Hawaii.* Hawaii Office of State Planning, Honolulu.
14. Myers, P. 1976. *Zoning Hawaii: An analysis of the passage and implementation of Hawaii's land classification law.* Conservation Foundation, Washington, D.C.
15. U.S. Department of Agriculture-Soil Conservation Service. 1983. *National agricultural land evaluation and site assessment handbook.* Washington, D.C.
16. Ward, Robert M. 1991. *The U.S. Farmland Protection Policy Act; another case of benign neglect.* Land Use Policy 8(1)63-68.

The authors acknowledge the assistance of M. Akram Khan of the Department of Agricultural Engineering , University of Hawaii, in producing the GIS maps.

35 ACRES AVAILABLE

SECTION III

Applications of LESA

Soil Conservation Service photo

Soil Conservation Service photo

10 LESA and the Illinois Farmland Preservation Act

James D. Riggle

In 1980 the National Agricultural Lands Study (NALS) released its finding that more than 90 capital development or spending programs of the federal government converted farmland or directly led to the conversion of farmland, usually by a state or unit of local government (*4*). These programs included direct spending for the federal-aid highway system and housing programs operated by the Department of Housing and Urban Development (HUD) and the Farmers Home Administration (FmHA) in the U.S. Department of Agriculture (USDA). Less visible but more numerous were grant-making programs to promote "economic development" or "rural development," many of which also were administered by HUD and USDA. These development grants typically are made to states and local governments, but also are available to nonprofit and other non-governmental organizations.

Through its programs that distribute or redistribute wealth and income, the federal government plays a major role in determining, or at least influencing, land use and development patterns across the country. Many of the public facilities and services that make farmland conversion economically feasible for the private sector simply could not be afforded and would not be undertaken by states and local communities on their own.

In July of 1980 Illinois Governor James Thompson issued an executive order for the "Preservation of Illinois Farmland." Governor Thompson's order recognized economic and environmental reasons for establishing a policy to protect farmland. Agriculture is the top industry in Illinois, currently producing more than $9 billion per year in crops and livestock, and providing more than a million full-time jobs (*3*). Moreover, the policy foresaw the current dilemma of attempting to sustain high yields on poorer quality soils, saying, "With less prime farmland available there will tend to be greater reliance on marginally productive land, resulting in greater soil erosion, increased fertilizer requirements, and increased environmental damage" (*5*).

The NALS report contained another finding that provided the foundation for farmland protection programs of the type Illinois adopted and ultimately spelled the need for a decision-making tool such as the land evaluation and site assessment (LESA) system. NALS found that for every acre of farmland actually converted, that is, paved over or built-up, another acre was rendered "unfarmable" because of an unregulated or inefficient pattern of development (*4*).

The lack of a clear public policy requiring state agencies to regard productive land as a finite natural resource resulted in programs that treated all open land merely as a commodity waiting for "development" to happen. At the same time, all land was viewed as equal, with regard to both quality and location, resulting in a tendency to convert prime land, which was by definition easier and cheaper to build on. Ironically by 1980, eleven years after the passage of the National Environmental Policy Act (NEPA), it had become easier to convert prime farmland from a public policy standpoint because prime land inherently had fewer of the environmental sensitivities NEPA was designed to regulate.

The focus of Illinois' farmland protection policy was to regulate the spending decisions of its own agencies. Governor Thompson's executive order said, "Agencies of the Executive Branch perform numerous functions which effect (*sic*)... the conversion of prime agricultural land. Decisions on state grants and capital improvements may have significant impact on the conversion process, yet often they may not adequately recognize that agricultural land is a finite resource that can be irretrievably diminished as a result of State actions" (*5*).

The goal of the Illinois policy was "to ensure that State actions do not unnecessarily encourage the conversion of prime farmland to non-farm uses, particularly when there are alternatives available that are less destructive..." (*5*). Thus it became "the policy of the State of Illinois to protect, through the administration of its current programs and regulations, the State's prime agricultural land from irreversible conversion to uses that result in its loss as an environmental or essential food production resource" (*5*).

Illinois' program was initiated by executive action for several reasons. The legislative process can be argumentative and slow, and the lack of a farmland protection program was viewed by the governor and then Illinois Director of Agriculture John Block as a problem requiring immediate action. The agencies affected by the executive order were correctly expected to range from skeptical to hostile in their view of the need for such constraints on them. An executive order was intended as a prelude to legislative action, to provide time for state agencies to develop a program and demonstrate it. In July of 1982 the Illinois General Assembly adopted the Illinois Farmland Preservation Act, incorporating all the provisions adopted under the executive order.

All Illinois state agencies responsible for programs that directly converted farmland or that issued licenses or permits allowing others to do so were required to prepare formal policies including two principal elements. Departments had to analyze the impacts of their "programs, regulations, procedures, and operations" on agricultural lands. And, the policies were required to "detail measures that can be implemented by the agency which will mitigate conversions to the maximum extent practicable" (*5*).

Several important assumptions about the farmland conversion process and land development in general were made before adopting a land protection policy that rests principally on the state regulating itself. First, such a policy was required to "level the playing field" in the face of existing governmental policies and regulations, notably NEPA requirements and the provisions of Section 4-f of the U.S. Transportation Act of 1966. These restrictions on wetlands, habitats, parks, and publicly owned lands had the effect of directing capital developments onto agricultural lands. The level of concern for agricultural lands had to be raised to equal or nearly so that of other "protected" lands.

Second, in large agricultural states like Illinois, the vast majority of privately owned open land is in agricultural use. It is nearly impossible to conduct the business of the public sector without converting some farmland. Hence, the buzzword "unnecessary" was included in Illinois' policy to signal affected agencies that the intent of the regulations was not to prohibit their legitimate activities, but to cause their land acquisition and taking actions to be done as conservatively as possible.

Finally, there was a growing recognition that government programs converted farmland directly and indirectly. That is, the capital spending decisions of governments at all levels provided incentives and opportunities for the private sector to convert farmland that otherwise would not exist. For example, the acquisition of a public park or recreation area might create the opportunity to develop a hotel or residential subdivision by capitalizing on the public facility, thereby converting more farmland. Highway interchanges might shorten commuting times enough to make a residential development feasible. The Illinois policy was designed to account for such indirect conversions and to stipulate measures to avoid them.

The Givings Issue

This concern with government-caused, indirect farmland conversion is particularly relevant to the current debate raging over private property rights and the takings issue. In fact, Illinois' regulatory approach to farmland protection and similar efforts deal with the exact opposite of public takings, that is, what might be called "givings." Government capital spending and development create opportunities for land use change and can alter the pattern of economic development in any particular area.

Resulting increases in the market value of land lead to speculative acquisitions and development proposals made possible only because of the provision of government facilities and services. This in turn leads to expectations by landowners that higher land values are linked to private "rights" to profit from public investments. The Illinois policy attempts to temper both the extent of indirect conversion (the "givings issue") and landowners' rising expectations by requiring its agencies to condition or modify their decisions to minimize these effects.

Curiously, the federal government seems to have taken the opposite approach, even suggesting that landowners might have a right to develop their land with public funds. In the final rule implementing the federal Farmland Protection Policy Act (Subtitle I of Title XV of the Agriculture and Food Act of 1981, Public Law 97-98) USDA claims that federal agencies cannot "modify any project solely to avoid or minimize the effects of conversion of farmland to nonagricultural uses" (*2*). This is because, USDA and the Office of Management and Budget (OMB) claim, "the Act does not authorize the Federal Government in any way to regulate the use of private or nonfederal land, or in any way affect the property rights of owners of such land"

(*2*). The logical extension of this assertion is that somehow landowners have a right to have public projects built on their land, precisely what the Illinois program is trying to limit.

Authority to oversee the development of individual agency policies, and responsibility for their implementation under the executive order for the Preservation of Illinois Farmland were delegated to a small bureau in the Illinois Department of Agriculture (IDOA). Under an executive order no formal rules or regulations were required to establish state agency policies. Without such limitations, virtually every project or program decision of every affected agency was potentially subject to review and mitigation. Yet the order itself had come from the governor with an explicit promise that it would not obstruct the operation of state government.

By any measure Illinois is a big state, including its physical area of more than 55,000 square miles and its population of 11.4 million. The government of a state that size generates a huge number of projects in any given year that would consume farmland or cause problems for agriculture. In the early 1980s the state as a whole proposed roughly 10,000 projects each year that would have required a farmland impact analysis. The Illinois Department of Transportation (IDOT) alone proposed as many as 3,000 projects per year.

In practice it turned out that the vast majority of all projects were minor, verging on insignificant. Highway projects are dominated by rehabilitation, maintenance, and repair efforts, which even if they require small amounts of land confer far more benefit than harm on the farming industry. Most conservation and recreation land acquisitions are minor additions to existing facilities, or the willing sale of an inholding.

Thresholds of significance and performance standards were necessary for each type of capital project to identify and dismiss from review those with no serious direct or indirect conversion potential. For example, if the right of way for the smallest possible new public road required five acres per mile, anything less was exempt from review, understanding that it could not result in opening a new road and all the attendant indirect effects. A rural electric transmission right of way employing single-pole structures instead of the troublesome four-legged steel towers likewise passed without review.

After exempting insignificant projects from formal review, IDOA staff face an average of 1,000 projects per year that are analyzed individually. Timeliness is an extremely important consideration in reviewing proposed farmland acquisitions. Many projects never get off the drawing board or do not make it to budgetary review, making an analysis a waste of time. However, once a project is given a budget, subsequent changes in planning and design increase its costs in time and money.

The Illinois Bureau of the Budget (BOB) defines an early planning stage at which all projects are numbered and tracked for budgetary purposes (this stage coincides with the procedures of the old federal Circular A-95 review process). IDOA staff are notified when projects with a significant potential farmland impact enter the early planning stage.

Because most, if not all, major farmland conversion projects are claimed to be economic developments that will provide jobs, increase the tax base, or both, undue delays quickly create political problems by way of the state agency, a legislative sponsor, or a constituent beneficiary. State agency projects, procedures, and operations are to be mitigated or modified to protect farmland to the maximum extent practicable. In practice, this means that several major conversion projects will be approved every year because no feasible alternative exists or safety standards dictate specific capacities or designs. In those instances where viable alternative sites or corridors do exist, a preference must be stated accurately and quickly. This is where the LESA system becomes most valuable.

For two reasons, Illinois was able to adopt the LESA system quickly after it was field tested. The director of IDOA's farmland protection bureau was a member of the national LESA implementation team, lending a familiarity with the system that did not exist elsewhere. The state farmland protection program itself was designed to select among alternative project proposals each of which was expected to make trade-offs among land quality and the potential for direct and indirect farmland conversion.

Illinois has approximately 25 million acres of cropland, about 80 percent of which is prime farmland, and the largest number of acres of Class I prime land of any state. Thus it is highly likely that any major project will convert prime land. A decision-making tool was needed that would provide objectivity and reliability in judgements about the long-term effects of developments.

Illinois Land Evaluation

In preparing the land evaluation component of the statewide LESA system Illinois was fortunate to have high quality soils information available and the cooperation of technical staff in the state office of USDA's Soil Conservation Service (SCS). SCS staff arranged Illinois' soil types into ten groups with the most similar crop production capabilities.

The soil groups were prepared by comparing individual soil types against three criteria: land capability, important farmland status, and soil productivity. Land capability classifications group soils according to their limitations caused by erodibility, wetness, internal soil problems, and climate. Designation as prime, important, or other farmland indicates the soils' inherent suitability for food and fiber production. Soil productivity under the highest level of management is available from a grain crop index explained in a

University of Illinois publication titled "Circular 1156" (*6*).

Each of the ten LESA soils groups is assigned a relative value indexed to a possible score of 100. The best soils (assigned to Group 1) are given a relative value of 100. The poorest soils (Group 10) receive a relative value of zero. When alternative sites for a proposed state project are reviewed using the LESA system the number of acres of each soil type is multiplied by the relative value of its group. The relative values for all soil types are added together and divided by the total number of acres in the site under review, resulting in a score that represents the land evaluation portion of a LESA project analysis and is added to site assessment factor values.

Soils information that is incorporated into the land evaluation component of a LESA system will come from similar sources in any state or local government that chooses to develop a system to assist in making land-use decisions. Some states and localities will have better and more highly developed soils information. For example, counties that do not have modern soil surveys may have to rely on older soil association maps. Iowa, like Illinois, has a productivity index called the corn suitability rating (CSR), but such indices are not available everywhere. State and local decision makers should obtain the most up-to-date soils information available and seek assistance from soil scientists and agronomists at their respective land-grant universities.

Illinois Site Assessment

The second component of a LESA system is a set of site assessment factors. Unlike land evaluation data, site assessment factors are by nature more subjective and may vary significantly among different jurisdictions and levels of government. Before discussing the site assessment criteria of Illinois' LESA system, it is necessary to distinguish between two basic types of public capital projects: corridor projects and site specific projects. Each of these broad project types requires that a different weight be placed on the LESA system components.

Examples of site specific projects include airports, housing developments, and industrial and recreational parks. These projects have great potential to cause indirect conversion or spin-off developments. They also may create serious negative fiscal impacts through subsequent demands for public services if site assessment factors are neglected when a location decision is made. This type of project should coincide with local land-use plans and zoning ordinances where they exist to encourage a compact and efficient pattern of development. When projects such as airports and parks are purposely sited in outlying areas the opportunity for mitigation and buffering through the use of agricultural conservation easements is great, both to limit indirect land conversion and maintain compatible adjacent land uses.

Corridor projects include highways, pipelines, sewers, electric transmission rights-of-way, and rail lines. By their nature corridor projects are relatively narrow, long, and essentially linear in design. Whereas site specific projects may take one or a few farms entirely, corridor projects can sever and take parts of hundreds of farms. Alternative corridors may be separated by many miles, offering an opportunity to emphasize land evaluation factors and minimize the conversion of prime and important farmlands.

Highways may seem an exception to this corridor project rule of thumb. However, rather than the highway corridor itself, interchanges and access points are what allow the highway to cause additional conversion and development. Thus, the road corridor itself should be evaluated to minimize its impacts on productive soils and ongoing farm operations. Access to roads, whether new proposals or existing facilities, should be evaluated separately with site assessment factors weighted more heavily.

The Illinois LESA system uses 16 site assessment criteria for site specific projects and eight slightly modified criteria for corridor projects. Proposed project alternatives are scored higher in the absence of site assessment factors, or conversely receive lower scores if urban development is planned, logical, or imminent. The following site assessment factors are illustrative, neither all inclusive for Illinois' system nor prescriptive for states or localities that may be considering adopting LESA. Illinois law also grants incorporated municipalities a planning area or sphere of influence one and one-half miles beyond their corporate limits, thus dictating the "distance" factor in Illinois' site assessment factors.

The distance of a proposed project to city limits or the urban fringe is regarded as a measure of agricultural viability. Sites more than a mile and a half from the city limit receive maximum value while adjacent sites receive zero. This factor is intended to promote a more compact and contiguous development pattern, holding the amount of land between the existing urban fringe and a new project to a minimum.

Public sewer and water systems on a proposed project site receive zero points whereas a site a mile and a half or more from such existing facilities gets maximum protection value. Existing public facilities are most efficient and cost-effective when used to capacity. And the availability of such services reduces the land area needed to accommodate any given amount of additional development by avoiding wells and septic systems.

The type of road providing access to a site is considered. An earthen road scores highest. A limited or controlled access road (highway or freeway) gets no points. A rural road, especially a dirt road, would need to be improved for any urban development or capital project, thereby creating the possibility of additional land conversion and development. Thus, projects on already improved roads are preferred.

Important concerns in Illinois are the existing land use or the planning and zoning designation of areas adjacent to a proposed project site. Highest values are given to sites planned and zoned for agriculture or in farm use on all sides. Illinois statutes and case law require that adjacent land uses be taken into account in decisions on requests for rezonings or land-use changes. Once a non-farm use is introduced, farmland conversion is made easier and more likely.

Illinois allows landowners to create voluntary agricultural areas (known elsewhere as agricultural districts or agricultural security areas). Parts or all of a proposed projects site may be protected by an agricultural area designation. Fully protected sites receive full points while the absence of a security area nets zero. This is consistent with the law, which provides land in agricultural areas with greater protection from government takings.

Larger sites get a higher protection value than small sites. Proposed takings of 100 acres or more are at the top of the scale and sites less than 20 acres are at the bottom. This factor is intended to protect commercially viable parcels, based on the experience that larger fields are more likely to be purchased or rented for farming as opposed to potential housing sites.

The presence of an agricultural infrastructure is regarded as an important indicator of the viability of agriculture. The existence of facilities and services such as grain elevators, implement dealers and mechanics, and feed and seed stores is highly rated. The absence of such an infrastructure was thought to be a good indicator that the long-term economic sustainability of farming is uncertain.

The compatibility of the proposed project with an ongoing agriculture industry is considered. A state park is viewed as more compatible and scores higher than a housing development. This factor recognizes that industrial side effects of farming, such as noise, dust, and odors, are likely to generate complaints and nuisance suits from non-farm neighbors. These are considered common influences on farmers' decisions to sell or retain their land.

The government agency making a project proposal can influence the LESA evaluation of all proposed alternatives by cooperating in good faith with the state farmland protection policy. If a proposed project includes alternatives on less productive land, the entire project is scored higher; if not, no points are awarded. For example, a coal-fired electric generating plant might be proposed on three separate 1,000-acre sites, containing 20, 50, and 100 percent prime farmland respectively. Not only does this proposal make selecting a preferred site easier, it demonstrates that the notion of protecting farmland is being incorporated in the operating procedures of the taking agency.

Whether prior governmental actions have committed a site for development is regarded as so important that the score for this factor is weighted by a factor of two. This factor addresses plans for utilities or roads that have not been implemented and considers permits and licenses that are granted or denied by a regulatory or non-taking agency (such as the state Environmental Protection Agency). Thus, a site proposed as a landfill or quarry will be assigned a much higher protection value before certain permits are issued than it would after the fact.

The Illinois LESA system allows a maximum 300 points to be awarded any project proposal. In considering corridor projects, equal weight is given to land evaluation and site assessment factors, otherwise site assessment factors are weighted twice as heavily (200 possible points) in the final analysis. This bottom line evaluation criterion reflects the fact that such a high percentage of Illinois is prime farmland, recognizing that little development of any type can be done without converting highly productive land but that indirect or secondary conversion can be greatly limited.

One of the most important characteristics of LESA as a model is its flexibility. States or localities with little prime land resources may choose to weight land evaluation criteria as a controlling factor in land-use decisions.

Illinois' County LESA Systems

In Illinois, as in most states, day-to-day land-use decisions are made at the local level. Officials charged with administering the state's farmland protection program recognized at the outset that community support for their efforts would be crucial to the ultimate success of the program. The state agreed to provide counties with technical assistance in making routine land-use decisions, and in developing their own local LESA systems.

The advantage of having local LESA systems is twofold. A greater degree of rationality is introduced in the land use decision making process. The factors determining land-use decisions and changes are agreed upon in advance, reducing the possibility of political influence, and increasing reliance on the capabilities of the natural resource base.

Second, Illinois allows a local LESA system, adopted by the county government and approved by the state office of the Soil Conservation Service, to be used in place of the state LESA system in evaluating proposed state projects. This allows much more detail to be incorporated into LESA, refining the state factors to address local conditions specifically. It also reinforces the local commitment to communities' comprehensive plans and land-use ordinances, by lending a measure of local control over state capital development decisions.

Currently, 29 Illinois counties operate state-approved LESA systems. (In the 1991 nationwide survey, only 26 LESA systems were reported in Illinois. Three LESA systems have been adopted since then. See Table 1 in chapter 4 for the 26 systems reported in 1991.) Since the beginning in May 1984, steady progress has been made on this ongoing initiative, with the most recent county system approved in July 1992. Local LESA systems in Illinois are concentrated in the northern and central parts of the state, including most of the top-producing agricultural counties.

Conclusions

As a public policy issue, the need to protect prime and important farmland from premature or unnecessary conversion to urban and built-up uses has been somewhat controversial over the last 10-12 years. The substance of the objection to land protection efforts usually focuses on the number of acres of land converted in a given year, and whether those losses have an effect on the output of the agricultural economy. These arguments miss the nature of the issue entirely.

The "national" issue is the sum of thousands of specific land-use decisions made in states and localities across the country—particular places where people spend their lives. In this sense, the number of acres of farmland converted in the United States every year is an abstract concern. State governments and local communities have a strong and legitimate interest in their "share" of farmland conversion, the effects of which have permanent implications for their economies and quality of life.

It is extremely important to distinguish among different types and capabilities of land. Prime and important farmlands are more inherently productive, requiring fewer purchased inputs to maintain the same yields than does marginal land. As Illinois' policy statement noted, a greater reliance on marginal land not only results in higher production costs, but also requires more numerous and expensive soil conservation measures for adequate environmental protection. Thus, efforts to retain as much prime and important farmland in agricultural uses for as long a time as possible make economic and environmental sense.

The recognition of land as a limited natural resource, as opposed to a commodity, is perhaps the most compelling argument for strong programs to manage its use. Land is limited by the simple fact that it cannot be manufactured, or replaced once it is committed to a permanent use. Our remaining agricultural lands serve numerous purposes in addition to farming, including future urban uses, groundwater recharge, forestry, wildlife habitat, and recreation. The key to a successful long-term land protection program is to avoid wasting good land, assuring land is developed at the highest practical density, and that adjacent land uses are compatible with agriculture. This notion is conveyed in Illinois' conditioning its farmland preservation goals on the prevention of unnecessary and irreversible land conversion. These are implicit signals acknowledging that decisions committing land permanently to one use reduce the amount of a basic resource available for all uses.

The Illinois Farmland Preservation Act should be viewed as one among several methods to incorporate in a comprehensive farmland protection program. The Illinois program is a management decision-making system. It does not require local governmental actions, nor does it necessarily result in long-term land preservation. Illinois selected a course of action designed to minimize the amount and quality of agricultural land converted directly or indirectly by government agencies, and to do so for the lowest administrative costs. As an indication of this approach's potential for success, the program was recognized in the *Congressional Record* after its first two years of operation for having saved 2,000 acres of prime land from public acquisition and $10 million tax dollars on two projects alone—a highway and a flood control reservoir—savings in land and money that can hardly be ignored by any state (*1*).

References

1. *Congressional Record*-U.S. Senate, June 21, 1984, p.S 7912.
2. *Federal Register* 49 (130): 27716.
3. Illinois Department of Agriculture, Bureau of Agricultural Statistics. November 1991.
4. National Agricultural Lands Study. 1981. *Final Report.* U.S. Government Printing Office, Washington, D.C. p.11.
5. Thompson, J. R. 1980. *Governor of Illinois Executive Order Number 4.* July, 1981.
6. University of Illinois, College of Agriculture. *Circular 1156.* Urbana.

11 Using LESA in a Purchase of Development Rights Program: The Lancaster County, Pennsylvania, Case

Thomas L. Daniels

The authors of the 1983 land evaluation and site assessment (LESA) handbook envisioned that LESA would be helpful in implementing a purchase of development rights (PDR) program to preserve agricultural land (*3*). The paramount need in administering a PDR program was to identify those farms best suited for preservation and to ration the expenditure of scarce public dollars. PDR programs began in the early 1970s in Suffolk County, New York, and gained momentum through the 1980s. Today, eleven states and a handful of individual counties have PDR programs, and more than 190,000 acres of farmland have been preserved with this technique. Maryland leads the way with more than 94,000 acres preserved (*2*).

In a PDR program, a landowner sells the right to develop the land but retains all other rights and responsibilities. Thus, the landowner receives financial compensation in exchange for keeping the land in farming and open space (*1*).

The Lancaster County Experience with LESA

Lancaster County is the leading agricultural county in Pennsylvania and the entire Northeast, with $841 million in farm products sold in 1990. Located in southeast Pennsylvania, Lancaster County boasts excellent silt loam soils and a mild climate, which have made it the nation's number one non-irrigated county in terms of farm output. Two-thirds of the county's 600,000 acres are in farm use, even though there are 422,000 residents and the county is one of the fastest growing metropolitan areas in Pennsylvania. More than five million tourists visit the county each year. A major draw is one of the largest populations of Amish and Mennonites in the United States, and the cultural ethic of farming is strong in these religious sects.

Since 1984, the county has been operating a PDR program through its Agricultural Preserve Board, and has preserved 128 farms and more than 11,700 acres. County PDR program administrators have used the LESA system to establish a ranking order for development rights sale applications. The actual amount paid for development rights is based on a formal appraisal of the development rights value conducted by a professional appraiser. The LESA ranking determines: first, whether a farm scores high enough to be considered for purchase of development rights; and second, the order in which the farms will be appraised for development rights value. This ranking order is especially important due to the limited amount of public funds available.

The primary advantage of the LESA system is that it provides a quick, consistent, numerically based approach that is easy to understand and defend. The point score for a farm can be determined in a matter of minutes. The LESA system is also flexible, and well-suited for a trial-and-error effort to devise a farmland rating system that reflects the farmland protection strategy of a jurisdiction.

The LESA system provides an evaluation of two general components: land quality for farming (land evaluation) and development pressure (site assessment). These two categories are comprised of several factors that are assigned numerical scores, weights, and total points per factor (*1*). The total points per factor are tallied for each farm to produce an overall score. The score is then compared to a cut-off level to determine whether or not the farm should be accepted for the purchase of development rights program, and, if accepted, the farm is ranked against the point scores of other farms.

The Lancaster County experience with LESA illustrates the flexibility of the numerically based system as well as the trial-and-error attempts to fashion a strategic planning tool. The authors of the LESA handbook recommend that easement applications be ranked according to half of the overall weight on land quality (land evaluation) and half on development pressure (site assessment) (*3*). This emphasis is somewhat different from the recommended weighting of one-third land quality and two-thirds development pressure, which the handbook recommends for judging whether a parcel should be allowed to be developed or remain in farm use. The authors of the handbook in effect advocate a "middle course" strategy of purchasing development rights to properties with good agricultural productivity that are under moderate development pressure. If more weight were given to land quality, this would signal a policy of preserving higher quality farmland under less development pressure. The advantage here is that per acre development rights costs would be relatively low and that public dollars could protect more acres. On the other hand, if more weight were given to development pressure (site assessment) this implies a strategy of preserving farms close to development. Per acre development rights costs would likely be high, and less acreage preserved than under a different strategy.

Lancaster County began using a modified LESA system in 1984 to rank applications for the sale of development rights. The usual method is to deduct points for farms close to urban areas. The modified Lancaster County LESA reverses this method. In addition, the County Agricultural Preserve Board elected to place more weight on development pressure (site assessment) than land quality (land evaluation). The Lancaster LESA weighting of 70 percent development pressure and 30 percent land quality was very similar to the recommended weighting in the LESA handbook for judging whether or not a farm property should be developed. The Lancaster weighting also reflected a particular farmland protection strategy: if the farms fairly close to development could be preserved, this would discourage the extension of sewer and water lines out into good farming areas.

The Lancaster PDR strategy was made possible by two farmland protection techniques: effective agricultural zoning and agricultural districts, locally known as agricultural security areas. About 269,000 acres of the county are zoned for agriculture, generally with the allowance of one building lot per 25 acres. Also, there are 111,000 acres in security areas (which are nearly all zoned for agriculture) where landowners are eligible to apply to sell development rights. Landowners have joined security areas close to development where the development rights have values of anywhere from $2,000 to $6,000 an acre. In addition, a number of large contiguous blocks of farmland, encompassing several hundred acres have been preserved. This helps to create a "critical mass" of farms and farmland that will enable farm support businesses to remain viable well into the future.

Development rights may be purchased for either a 25-year term or in perpetuity. Of the 128 development rights the county holds, only 21 are for 25 years. Since 1987, no 25-year term development rights have been acquired.

The effective agricultural zoning protects the interior farmland from being developed and provides an important backup to the easements that are purchased close to development. The agricultural zoning has enabled the Lancaster program to avoid two problems: first, leap-frog development over preserved farms and out into the good farming areas; and second, the surrounding of preserved farms by residential development. In the latter case, the danger is that preserved farms can act as a magnet for non-farm development because non-farm residents would be assured of a preserved view.

To date, the strategy has worked rather well. The county planning commission has embarked on an attempt to encourage townships and boroughs to create urban growth boundaries, which set a limit on the extension of sewer and water lines for the next 20 years. Through the purchase of development rights, the Agricultural Preserve Board has been able to create some urban growth boundaries (Figures 1 and 2). The 14 easements around the Village of Maytown in Figure 1 cover 1,300 acres and were acquired between 1986 and 1992. The costs ranged from $1,500 to $5,400 an acre, depending on the proximity to public sewer and water. The five easements below the Borough of Strasburg in Figure 2 cover 400 acres and were acquired over the same time period. The easement costs averaged about $3,000 per acre, including $6,100 an acre for a 40-acre parcel adjacent to public sewer and water. Despite these relatively high easement costs, the urban growth boundary strategy is likely to protect much more farmland than just the number of acres placed under conservation easements.

LESA Factors

The Lancaster County LESA system employs several factors under the general categories of likelihood of conversion, land quality, and other factors to generate a total point score. Under likelihood of conversion, the factors include: the extent of non-farm development within one mile, proximity to non-farm zoning and public sewer service, developable road frontage, and an urgency factor of whether a sale of the farm is pending.

The LESA handbook recommends a land quality factor based on soil productivity. The Lancaster land quality factors relate to the viability of the farm: proximity to preserved farms, size of the farm, soils, dollar amount of

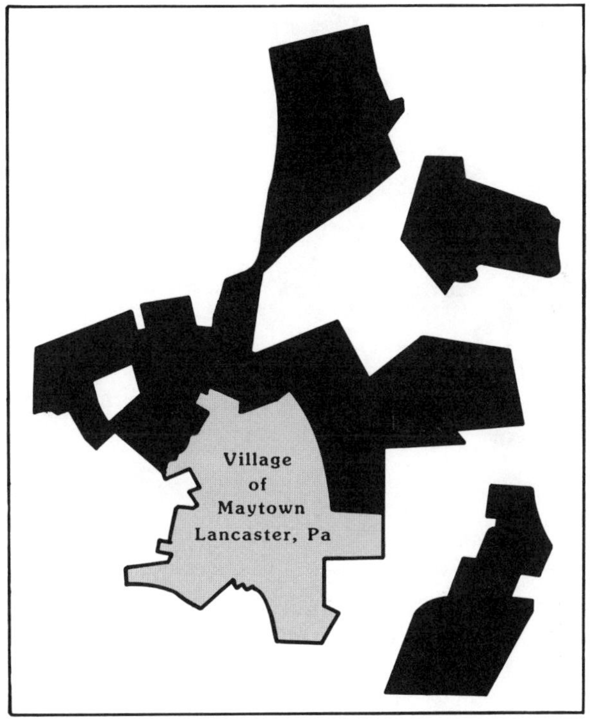

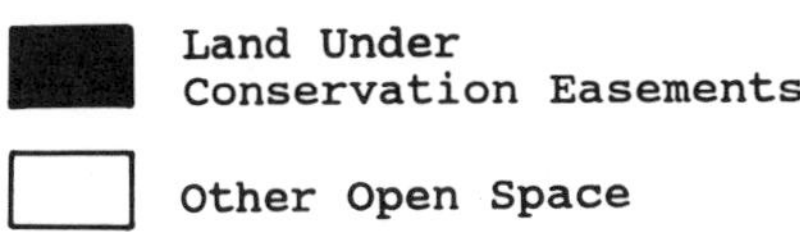

Figure 1. Lancaster County urban growth boundary strategy: The purchase of conservation easements to halt the spread of urban development into the countryside.

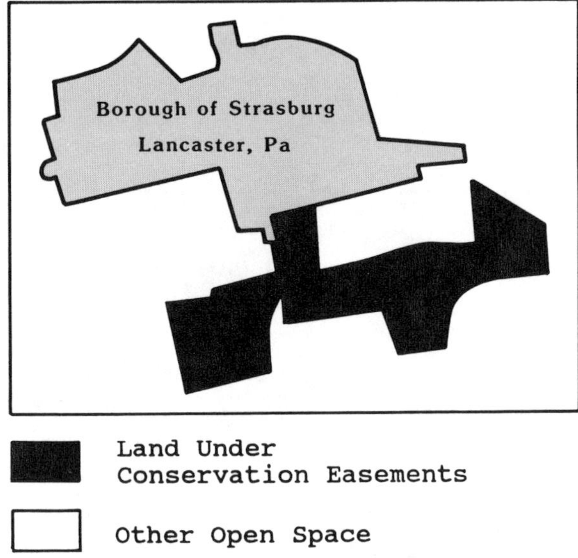

Figure 2. Lancaster County urban growth boundary strategy.

farm product sales, and whether the farm has buildings (*1*). This is quite different from the national LESA system, which places most of these factors in site assessment and emphasizes soils for the land evaluation portion.

Other factors include: whether a Soil Conservation Service conservation plan is being implemented on the farm (all farms that actually sell development rights must have a conservation plan); the historic, scenic, or environmental contribution; the number of times the landowner has applied to sell development rights; and the expected cost of the development rights. If the anticipated cost of the development rights is more than 15 percent of the total annual budget, then the farm receives a lower point score for the cost factor (*1*).

Changes to the Lancaster LESA

In the spring of 1991, the Preserve Board revised its LESA system for ranking applications. Although the county was receiving about $2 million a year under the Pennsylvania purchase of development rights program, county landowners were responding to the PDR program in great numbers. In 1990, 76 applications were received and another 54 applications in the spring of 1991. To ensure that the best quality farms would be accepted and ranked higher, the weighting on the development pressure (site assessment) was reduced from 70 to 60 percent, and the land quality (land evaluation) component was raised from 30 to 40 percent. The change has resulted in higher rankings for larger, more productive farms that are not under so much development pressure, and slightly lower rankings for smaller, less productive farms under heavy development pressure. (See Tables 1 and 2.)

In the likelihood of conversion section (site assessment), the new ranking system deleted points for being on the border of an agricultural security area (agricultural district) because changes in the law resulted in much more acreage being "exposed." The first districts that were created in Lancaster County contained contiguous farmland in blocks of more than 3,000 acres, and farmland had to be enrolled in a district for the landowner to be eligible to apply to sell development rights. In 1988, the district law was amended so that some landowners were allowed to withdraw from existing districts and new districts could be created without contiguous farmland parcels. Thus, far more farmland became located on the edge of the security areas.

The proximity to planned development factor was also dropped because it was felt to be redundant with the proximity to sewer service and non-farm zoning factors. Planned development is accounted for within both the sewer factor and the zoning factor.

Under quality of the land (land evaluation), weightings were increased for the proximity to another preserved farm, farm size, and farm product sales. These changes place greater emphasis on the quality of the farm operation and whether the farm will help create a "critical mass" of preserved farmland, which will help enable farm support businesses to remain in operation.

The Lancaster Old and New LESA Ranking Systems

The following three hypothetical farms were ranked for easement sale using both the original LESA and the revised LESA system. Farm number 1 is 45 acres in size. There is significant residential development within a one-half mile radius. The farm is within one-half mile of a sewer line, but has less than one-quarter mile of road frontage. The farm is carrying a large debt load that could force the sale of the farm for non-farm uses within six months. Farm 1 is adjacent to a farm with a conservation easement. The farm has more than 75 percent prime soils (Class I and II), farm product sales are more than $65,000 a year from two hog houses. The farm has a fully implemented SCS plan. The farmhouse was built in 1790 and was used as a coaching inn. This is the first application and the estimated easement cost is less than 15 percent of the anticipated 1992 budget of $2 million.

Table 1. The original LESA system used to rank applications to sell development rights in Lancaster County, Pennsylvania.

Factors	Maximum Points Per Factor	Weight	Maximum Possible Points	Farm 1 45 Acres	Farm 2 24 Acres	Farm 3 85 Acres
Likelihood of conversion (Site Assessment)						
1. Extent of non-agricultural development in area	10	10	100	80	100	70
2. Proximity to agricultural security area boundary	10	10	100	100	100	50
3. Proximity to planned development	8	8	64	24	64	24
4. Zoning	8	8	64	64	64	0
5. Proximity to sewer service	8	8	64	48	64	24
6. Site development capabilities	10	8	80	40	80	40
7. Urgency	10	3	30	30	0	0
Total points accrued				396	472	208
Total points possible			502			
Total points (adjusted by for 70 points maximum)	.139			55.0	65.6	28.9
Quality of the Farmland (Land Evaluation)						
1. Proximity to a farm with a conservation easement	10	3	30	30	21	0
2. Size of farm	10	3	30	12	0	30
3. Soils	10	10	100	100	80	100
4. Farm product sales	10	2	20	20	0	20
5. Farm buildings	10	2	20	20	10	20
Total points accrued				182	111	170
Total points possible			200			
Total points (adjusted by .125 for 25 points maximum)				22.8	13.9	21.3
Other factors						
1. Stewardship of the land	10	3	30	30	15	15
2. Historic, scenic, environmental qualities	10	10	100	100	60	30
3. Applications	8	1	8	5	5	8
4. Cost	10	10	100	100	100	100
Total points accrued				235	180	153
Total points possible			240			
Total points (adjusted by .021 for 5 points maximum)				4.9	3.8	3.2
Total overall points				82.7	83.3	53.4

Table 2. The revised LESA system used to rank applications to sell development rights in Lancaster County, Pennsylvania.

Factors	Maximum Points per Factor	Maximum Possible Weight	Points	Farm 1	Farm 2	Farm 3
Likelihood of conversion (Site Assessment)						
1. Extent of Non-agricultural development in area	10	10	100	80	100	70
2. Zoning	8	8	64	64	64	0
3. Proximity to sewer service	8	8	64	48	64	24
4. Site development capabilities	10	8	80	40	80	40
5. Urgency	10	3	30	30	0	0
Total points accrued				262	308	134
Total points possible			338			
Total points (adjusted by 0.177 for 60 points maximum)				46.4	54.5	23.7
Quality of land Factors (Land Evaluation)						
1. Proximity to farm with easement or sale application	10	5	50	50	35	0
2. Size of farm	10	5	50	20	0	50
3. Soils	10	10	100	100	80	100
4. Farm product sales	10	5	50	50	0	50
5. Farm buildings	10	2	20	20	10	20
Total points accrued				240	125	220
Total possible points			270			
Total points (adjusted by 0.129 for 35 points maximum)				30.9	16.1	26.9
Other factors						
1. Stewardship of the land	10	3	30	30	15	15
2. Historic, scenic, environmental qualities	3	10	30	100	60	30
3. Applications	8	1	8	5	5	8
4. Cost (if applicable)	10	10	100	100	100	100
Total points accrued				235	180	153
Total maximum points			240			
Total points (adjusted by 0.021 for 5 points maximum)				4.9	3.8	3.2
Total overall points				82.2	74.4	53.8

The 24-acre farm number 2 is adjacent to residential development, sewer service, and residential zoning. There is more than one-quarter mile of road frontage. Farm 2 is within one-half mile of a farm with an easement. The farm has between 50-75 percent prime soils. The farm is a bare land tract that is rented out to a nearby farmer, who grows corn and hay. Farm product sales are below $25,000 a year. There is a stream running through part of the property. This is the first application for easement sale, and the estimated easement cost is less than 15 percent of the anticipated 1992 budget.

Farm number 3 is an 85-acre dairy farm. There is scattered residential development within a one-mile radius. Within a one-half mile radius, the land is zoned for agriculture. Sewer service is within one mile. The farm has hydric soils along much of its road frontage, which limits development possibilities.

Farm 3 is more than one-half mile from a farm under easement. More than 75 percent of the soils are prime. Product sales are over $100,000 a year. Some conservation practices are used, although there is not an SCS plan on the farm. The farm makes a moderate contribution to the local scenery. The landowner rejected the first easement offer and has decided to apply a second time for easement sale. The estimated easement cost is less than 15 percent of the anticipated 1992 budget.

Under the old ranking system, farm 2 ranked highest with 83.3 points, just ahead of farm 1 with 82.7 points, and far ahead of farm 3 with 53.4 points (Table 3). Although farm 2 is the smallest farm, with the least agricultural production, it is under the heaviest development pressure by virtue of its location. Farm 1 is an urgent situation. If an easement is not purchased soon, the farm will most likely be sold for development. The farm is a commercial operation, but not managed as well as farm 3. Farm 3 is surrounded by agricultural zoning. It is a good dairy operation, but is under little development pressure.

Table 3. A comparison of LESA rankings in Lancaster County.

Old LESA Ranking	New LESA Ranking
Farm # 2-83.3 points	Farm # 1-82.2
Farm # 1-82.7 points	Farm # 2-74.4
Farm # 3-53.4 points	Farm # 3-53.8

With the new ranking system, the reduced emphasis on development pressure (site assessment) and greater weighting to land quality (land evaluation), farm 1 tops the list at 82.2 points, farm 2 falls to 74.4 points, and farm 3 rises slightly to 53.8 points. The moderately good farm under moderate development pressure (despite the urgent management situation) is now ranked ahead of the small farm under heavy development pressure. Although farm 3 would be accepted for an appraisal of easement value, the value is likely to be low, probably not more than $1,500 an acre in the case of Lancaster County. Agricultural zoning is probably the best tool to protect farm 3 in the short to medium term. An easement offer on farm 1 will have to be competitive with intensive residential development. An easement offer on farm 2 would have to relieve the debt burden at least to a point where mortgage holders would be willing to allow the landowner to sell an easement, and the landowner would be willing to continue to farm.

LESA in Other Pennsylvania Counties

A ranking system for PDR applications is required for county programs as part of the 1988 Pennsylvania Act 149, which created a $100 million program for purchasing development rights statewide. Since 1989, 26 out of 67 counties have adopted PDR programs that include a LESA system for ranking easement sale applications. Because Lancaster County had already devised a ranking system based on the LESA approach, this model has been used with some modifications by other counties. For example, in southeast Pennsylvania, Berks and Adams counties employ a system that ranks higher those farms under less development pressure. Berks County also has a cap of $2,500 per acre for easement purchases.

Such a ranking system and easement cap are not geared to preserving farms close to development. Rather, the strategy is to preserve farmland in areas of moderate development where a critical mass of farms can be saved. Yet, in both of those counties, there is little if any coordination between land-use planning, zoning, and the purchase of development rights. Such a lack of coordination may cause serious mistakes if a county attempts to devise a LESA system without a clear strategy for purchasing development rights. For example, Montgomery County, Pennsylvania, recently purchased an easement on a 163-acre farm inside a borough (city limits) and zoned for residential use for $2.5 million, or more than $15,000 an acre!

A further problem is that very few Pennsylvania counties have agricultural zoning. The danger is that a LESA ranking system may identify a farm as a desirable candidate for preservation, only to have that farm, once preserved, act as a magnet for development on neighboring properties.

A Closing Observation

Traditional appraisals of the value of development rights are expensive, time-consuming, and ultimately subjective. A logical extension of the LESA system would be to devise a points-based appraisal method to determine the value of development rights, or to reward landowners whose land has qualities that are deemed valuable to preserve. This points-based appraisal is somewhat different from a traditional appraisal of development rights, but it reflects a common problem in PDR programs, namely that good farms are not preserved because the development pressure is not sufficiently high to generate an attractive offer to purchase the development rights. Indeed, if one purpose of a PDR program is to preserve good farmland then this factor should receive strong consideration in the appraisal process. But a traditional appraisal of development rights value is based almost exclusively on development pressure. Such a points-based appraisal method is currently in use in Montgomery County, Maryland, and has been debated in the Pennsylvania Legislature.

References

1. Daniels, T. 1990. *Using the LESA system in a purchase of development rights program.* Journal of Soil and Water Conservation 45(6): 617-621.
2. Daniels, T. L. 1991. *The purchase of development rights: preserving agricultural land and open space.* Journal of the American Planning Association 47(4): 421-431.
3. U.S. Department of Agriculture-Soil Conservation Service. 1983. *National Agricultural Land Evaluation and Site Assessment Handbook.* Washington, D.C.

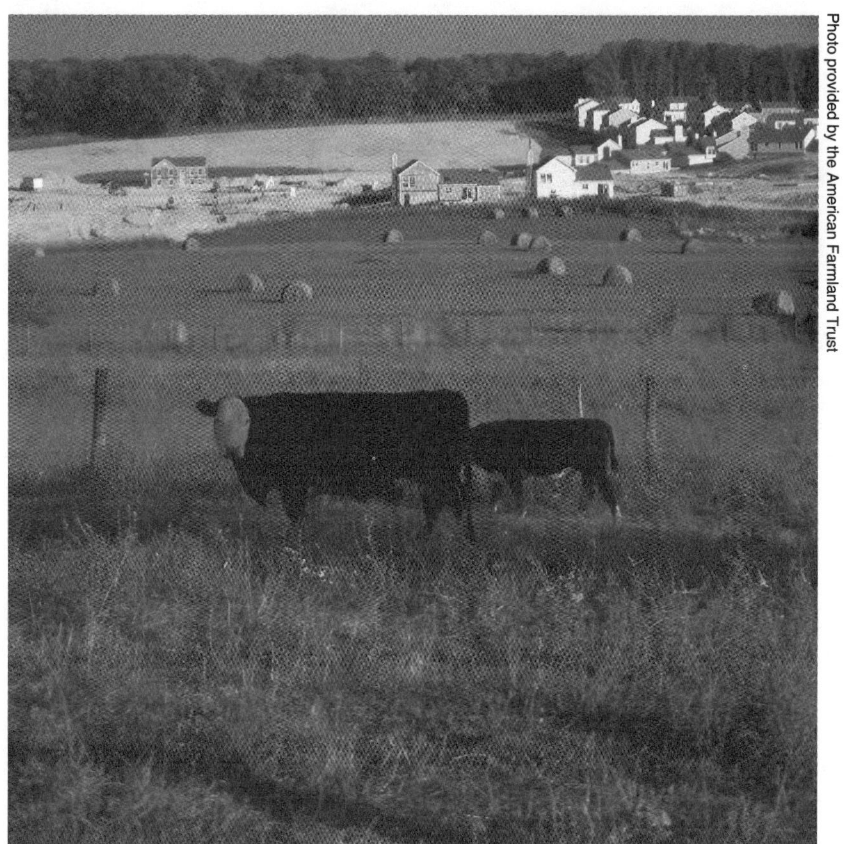

Photo provided by the American Farmland Trust

12 Linking LESA Systems into Local Land-Use Planning

Lee Nellis

At the Idaho state fair this year, I heard these stories: *A man who farms near a westside subdivision can no longer irrigate a strip of his land. Water droplets blow onto subdivision windows and draw complaints.*

A farmer is afraid to run his combines at night because subdivision residents complain he disturbs their sleep. They advise the farmer to confine his activities to normal working hours.

An angry woman fumes that the pasture next to her fashionable home holds bulls as well as cows. The bulls, she protests, mate with cows in full view of her children. She threatens to call the sheriff if such activity doesn't stop.—Patti Sherlock, *Post Register*, Idaho Falls, Idaho, September 30, 1990.

Traditional patterns of land use in the rural United States are being irrevocably altered. The most conservative source estimates that some 740,000 acres are converted from farmland to urban use each year (*6*). While experts debate both the extent and the significance of the decline in farmland acreage (*3*), communities near growing cities and expanding resorts struggle to manage the conflicts that accompany the conversion of rural lands to suburban or exurban use.

The purpose of this chapter is to show how such communities can use a land evaluation and site assessment (LESA) system in their efforts to maintain a rural identity and a viable agricultural economy. Specifically, examples from the recent planning efforts of Bonneville and Fremont counties in eastern Idaho counties are used to:

- explain where development of a LESA system fits into the local land-use planning process;
- show how a LESA system may be used as one basis for the implementation of a local comprehensive plan; and
- suggest that development of a LESA system should be standard practice in planning for any community where agricultural lands are an important economic asset or an essential element in the character of the local landscape.

A major section of this chapter is devoted to each of these tasks. First, however, a brief description of the case study counties will help readers evaluate the relevance of the experience reported here to their own communities.

The Case Study Counties

Bonneville and Fremont counties, Idaho, (Figure 1) offer examples of the changes brought to rural areas by the expansion of cities, commuters' demand for country living, and resort development. As the quotations that introduce this chapter suggest, conflict between agricultural operations and residential subdivisions is a daily reality in Bonneville County. Similar conflicts are anticipated in Fremont County. Open space is still abundant in eastern Idaho, however, and the level of public concern that would lead to progressive farmland protection programs, like the purchase of development rights, is many years away. Any attention given the future of these counties' farmlands at the present time must be reflected in a local land-use planning process that can produce results in a political arena where other priorities predominate.

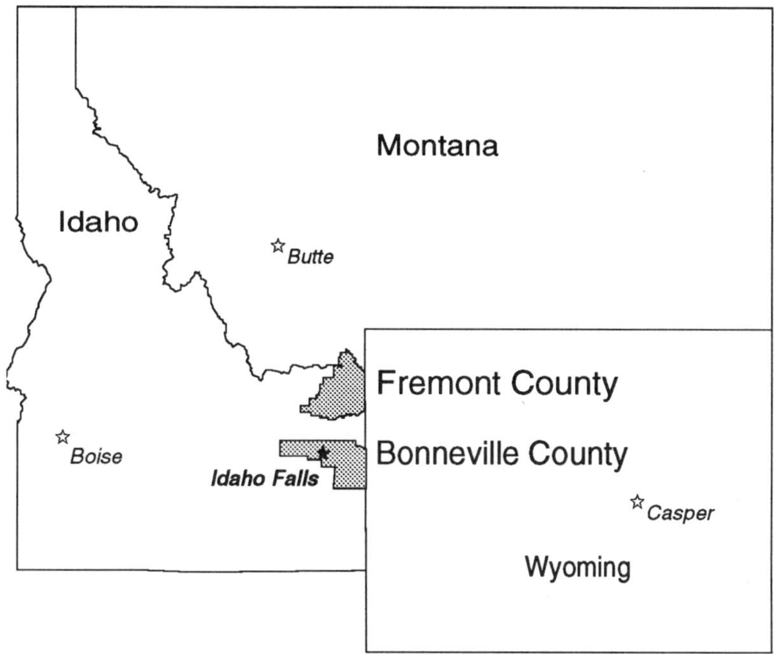

Figure 1. This map shows the location and regional context of Bonneville and Fremont counties, Idaho.

The following paragraphs provide basic demographic, economic, and land-use data on the case study counties. These data are taken from the draft *Bonneville County Comprehensive Plan (2)* and the *Fremont County Comprehensive Plan (5).*

Population. Bonneville County had a 1990 population of 72,207, 9.4 percent more than in 1980. Fremont County barely avoided the rural population decline of the 1980s, gaining only 92 residents during the decade for a 1990 total of 10,937. Its seasonal population is much higher: there are at least 5,700 recreationists and second-home residents in Fremont County on the average summer weekend.

Economy. The Bonneville County economy has three major sectors: agriculture, the Idaho National Engineering Laboratory (a federal energy research facility) and associated enterprises, and service to a 25,000 square-mile trade area. The county seat, Idaho Falls, serves as the principal trade center for a population of about 200,000 in eastern Idaho and western Wyoming. Farming, farm machinery manufacturing, and food processing (local products include fresh-pack and dehydrated potatoes, potato starch, malt, and beef jerky) account for about 40 percent of all local economic activity. Agriculture is also the most important sector in the Idaho Falls trade area, including Fremont County, where it supports more than half of all local economic activity. Fremont County residents also find jobs in government, the wood products industry, and tourism.

Landscape. Bonneville County stretches eastward from the lava fields of the Great Rift Desert to the glaciated peaks of the Snake River Range. Between the lava flows and the mountains are the rolling loess plains and gravelly alluvial flats of the Snake River Plain, where the county's irrigated croplands are found. Dryland grainfields ascend the slopes from the Plain into the foothills. Figure 2 is a typical scene from the interface between irrigated croplands and suburban development in Bonneville County.

Fremont County climbs from the irrigated fields of the Upper Snake River Plain northward, across the western fringe of the Yellowstone Plateau, to the Henrys Lake Mountains, then eastward through an area of lodgepole pine timber and resort development to Yellowstone National Park. The most productive croplands include the sandy, subirrigated soils in the southwestern part of the county and the loess hills east of the Henrys Fork. Figure 3 provides a typical farmland scene from southeastern Fremont County.

Farmlands. Roughly 43 percent of Bonneville County's 1,800 square miles are in private ownership. Some 96 percent of that area is used for agriculture, but there are only about 350,000 ares of cropland. Only 30 percent of Fremont County's 1,900 square miles are in private ownership. Virtually all that private land is used for agriculture, but the cropland base is limited to about 195,000 acres. The most important commodities produced in both counties are potatoes (Fremont is the nation's largest producer of seed potatoes), malting barley, and beef cattle. It should also be noted that the farmlands of these counties produce more than crops and livestock—scenic pastoral landscapes are an essential part of the local quality of life and the area's attraction to tourists.

Land-Use Trends. The density of settlement in the case study counties is declining. In 1960, about 42 percent of Fremont County's people lived outside city limits. That figure grew to nearly 50 percent in 1990. The tendency in Bonneville County is similar. About 21 percent of its residents lived in unincorporated areas in 1960, but that number topped 29 percent in 1990. This trend toward exurban residential development maximizes the potential for conflict between homeowners and agricultural operations. Along with other factors, it also results in the gradual loss of farmland. The acreage in farms in Bonneville County fell from 548,094 in 1959 to 505,173 (7.8 percent) in 1987. Land in farms in Fremont County declined from 411,310 to 383,875 (6.7 percent) acres during the same period.

Local Planning. Both counties recently undertook major planning efforts:

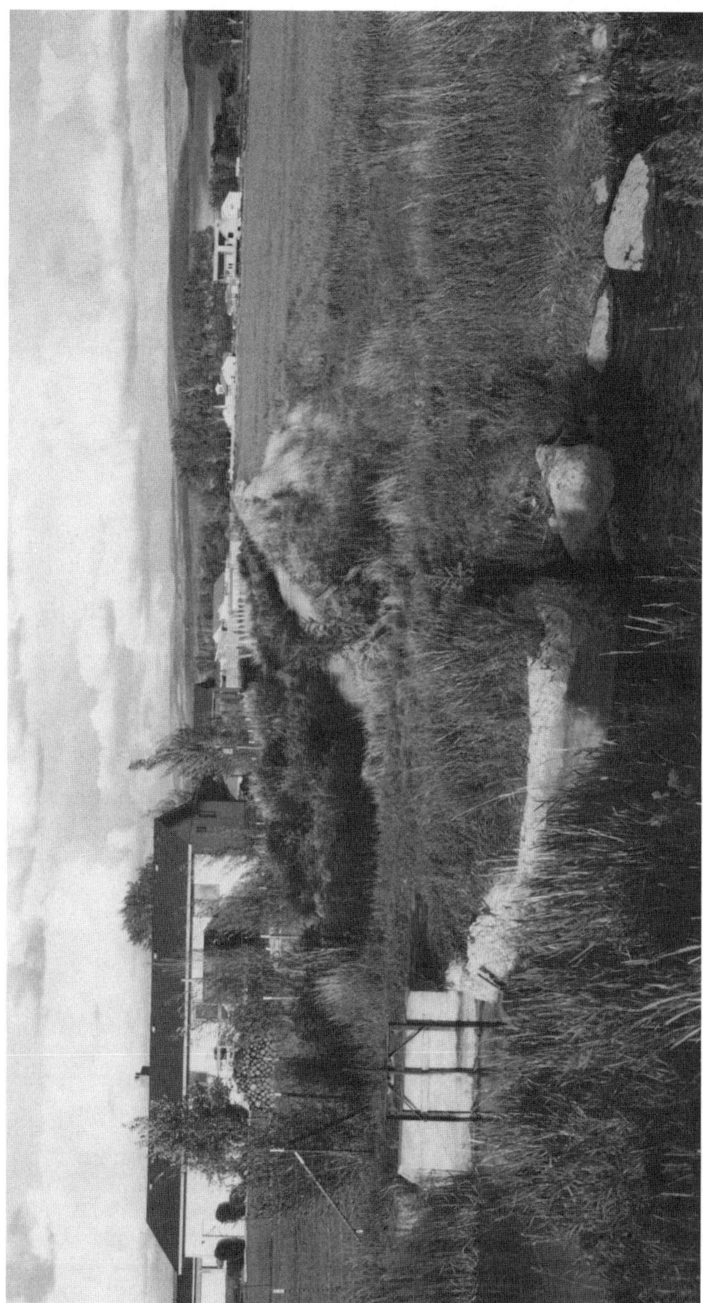

Figure 2. The suburban/cropland interface in Bonneville County. The LESA score of the field to the right of the ditch is 210 (LE = 91, SA = 119) of a possible 305. Discussion continues while the comprehensive plan is in the hearing process, but the score below which the county's proposed cropland protection measures will not apply should be around 240.

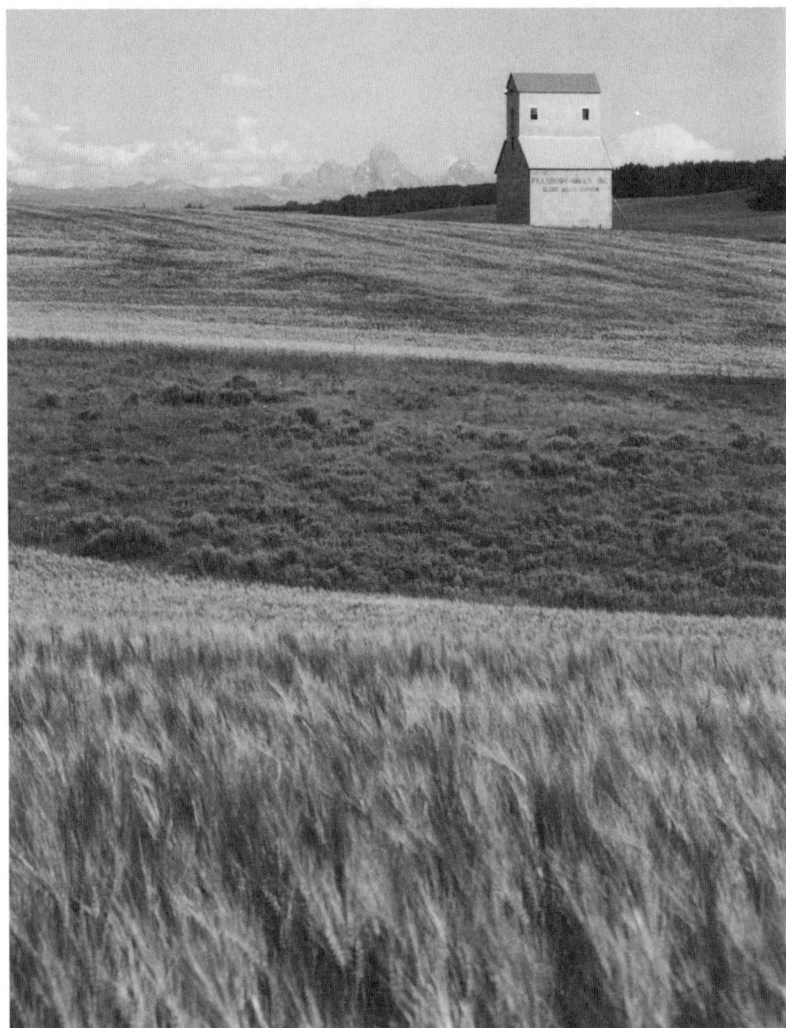

Figure 3. A farmland scene in southern Fremont County, where every barley field has a view of the Tetons. The LESA score of this field is 76 (LE = 53, SA = 23) of a possible 125. Fremont County is planning well in advance of development pressure and decided to allocate only 25 points to site assessment. To be considered "productive," croplands must have a minimum score on both the land evaluation and site assessment. This site scores well on the site assessment, but falls two points short of the minimum land evaluation score. It would be available for development in compliance with the other performance standards of the county's development code.

Bonneville to update its comprehensive plan and a 20-year-old zoning ordinance, Fremont to adopt its first plan. The Bonneville County Planning Commission completed a draft plan late in 1991. It is currently under review by the board of county commissioners. Fremont County renewed planning in 1988, 10 years after the first comprehensive plan proposed for the county was rejected. A four-year process resulted in adoption of a plan and development code early in 1992. The conflict between agriculture and exurban development was a major topic of discussion in both counties, and each planning commission devised a LESA system to help address that issue.

LESA Systems in Plan Development

For the purposes of this chapter, the process of developing a comprehensive plan will be simplified into three elements: analysis, involvement, and implementation. Analysis provides the factual background for planning, involvement brings the public into the process, and implementation puts its results into the form of policies designed to guide local land use decision making. The experience of the case study counties indicates that LESA systems can play a part in all three elements of a local planning process. This section shows how LESA systems fit into the analysis and involvement elements of the Bonneville and Fremont County planning efforts. The next section covers their role in implementation.

Analysis. Planning analysis answers decision makers' questions. When Bonneville or Fremont County planning commission members ask, *"How important is this parcel of cropland in assuring the vitality of our agricultural industry?"* the local LESA system responds. Commission members, or their staff, need only a blank LESA checklist, a legal description of the parcel in question, a soil survey or farmland groups map, and a brief field trip to generate a LESA score. The other background studies included in the counties' comprehensive plans support the LESA systems by answering related questions.

How important is agriculture in the county's economy? A detailed socioeconomic profile helps establish the need for a LESA system by documenting the economic importance of agriculture in each county.

What are the fiscal impacts of rural land development? The fiscal impact analysis included in each county's plan also helps establish the need for a LESA system. These analyses indicate that the average rural dwelling unit fails to generate tax revenues sufficient to cover the costs of the public services it demands. Rural residential development in Bonneville and Fremont counties, as in many other places (*1*), requires tax subsidies from other properties, including farmlands.

What is the current land-use pattern? The site assessment component of a LESA system requires detailed information about the use of land in the vicinity of the parcel being assessed. Land-use data can be collected in the field, but use of the Bonneville County LESA system is greatly facilitated by the detailed land-use maps prepared for that county's comprehensive plan. Those maps also help answer site assessment questions about the proximity of a parcel to sewer lines, city limits, and arterial roads.

Where will development be exposed to natural hazards? Where will it adversely impact wildlife habitat or other sensitive lands? The land evaluation component of a LESA system begins with the same soil survey data that is used, with other resources, in answering these questions. Both counties identified and delineated hazardous and sensitive areas in natural resource inventories. The Bonneville County inventory also produced farmland group maps. Such maps are not essential for the effective use of a LESA system, but do save a step in the land evaluation procedure.

Involvement. The Bonneville and Fremont county LESA systems are products of both professional analysis and public participation in the planning process. The county planning commissions formed LESA advisory committees, as suggested in the national LESA handbook (*10*). Appointments to those committees included agricultural landowners and local representatives of USDA agencies and the University of Idaho Cooperative Extension Service. Committee members contributed their knowledge of crop yields to the land evaluation components and their personal experience with conflicts between agriculture and urban development to the site assessment questions. While the committees were helpful, both counties' experience suggests that sustaining members' interest in technical tasks, like developing the land evaluation component of a LESA system, can be difficult.

Public involvement in the development of the Bonneville and Fremont county LESA systems did not end with the advisory committees. Farmers or their spouses comprise a majority of both planning commissions, and these citizen planners made important contributions to the content of the LESA systems. The Bonneville and Fremont county LESA systems also were presented to the public. The conflict between urban development and agriculture was discussed at community planning workshops sponsored by the Bonneville County Planning Commission, and the use of the LESA system in addressing that conflict was explained. The system also was actively used in meetings with citizens concerned about a proposed highway re-routing and local land developers. The Fremont County LESA system was explained at meetings of the three land-use advisory committees responsible for the initial drafting of the policy elements of the county's comprehensive plan.

Use of the LESA systems in public meetings and planning commission discussions made it clear that they are both products of analysis and involvement, and tools for further analysis and involvement. This observation is illustrated by Figure 4, which shows LESA scores generated during the preparation of the Bonneville County comprehensive plan. The county planning commission asked its consulting planner to generate a score for any specific parcel of land brought to its attention. Those scores helped the commission determine city impact boundaries and evaluate the consequences of alternative land use and density policies. Individual landowners have also requested LESA scores for their properties to help them prepare comments on the draft plan.

The Bonneville and Fremont county LESA systems are designed to provide a consistent answer to one of the most important questions in rural planning: which croplands, if any, merit protection from conversion to other uses? The LESA systems resulted from the analysis and involvement elements of the counties' planning processes. They also contributed to those elements by helping planning commission members and interested citizens understand the issues involved in rural land development, and by providing one basis for the evaluation of different plan implementation policies.

LESA Systems in Plan Implementation

The local LESA systems support the development code that implements the strategies included in the draft Bonneville County plan and the Fremont County comprehensive plan. The case study counties rely on a multi-faceted approach to planning for agricultural areas. That approach has two major elements: right-to-farm strategies and cropland protection strategies. Note that the techniques discussed here have been adopted by Fremont County, but only recommended for adoption in Bonneville County.

Right-To-Farm. The right-to-farm strategies found in the Bonneville and Fremont county comprehensive plans should not be confused with the right-to-farm laws that exist in many states, including Idaho (*7*). Right-to-farm laws react to conflicts between agriculture and other uses by offering farm operators a defense against nuisance actions (*9*). The techniques used by the case study counties, in contrast, proactively seek to prevent, or at least limit, the conflicts that lead to nuisance litigation.

Strict enforcement of an Idaho statute (*8*) regulating the subdivision of irrigated lands is among the most important right-to-farm strategies adopted by Fremont and Bonneville counties, where more than 60 percent of all cropland harvested is irrigated. Both counties supplement state law by requiring developers to demonstrate that their activities will have no adverse impacts on irrigation systems serving other lands.

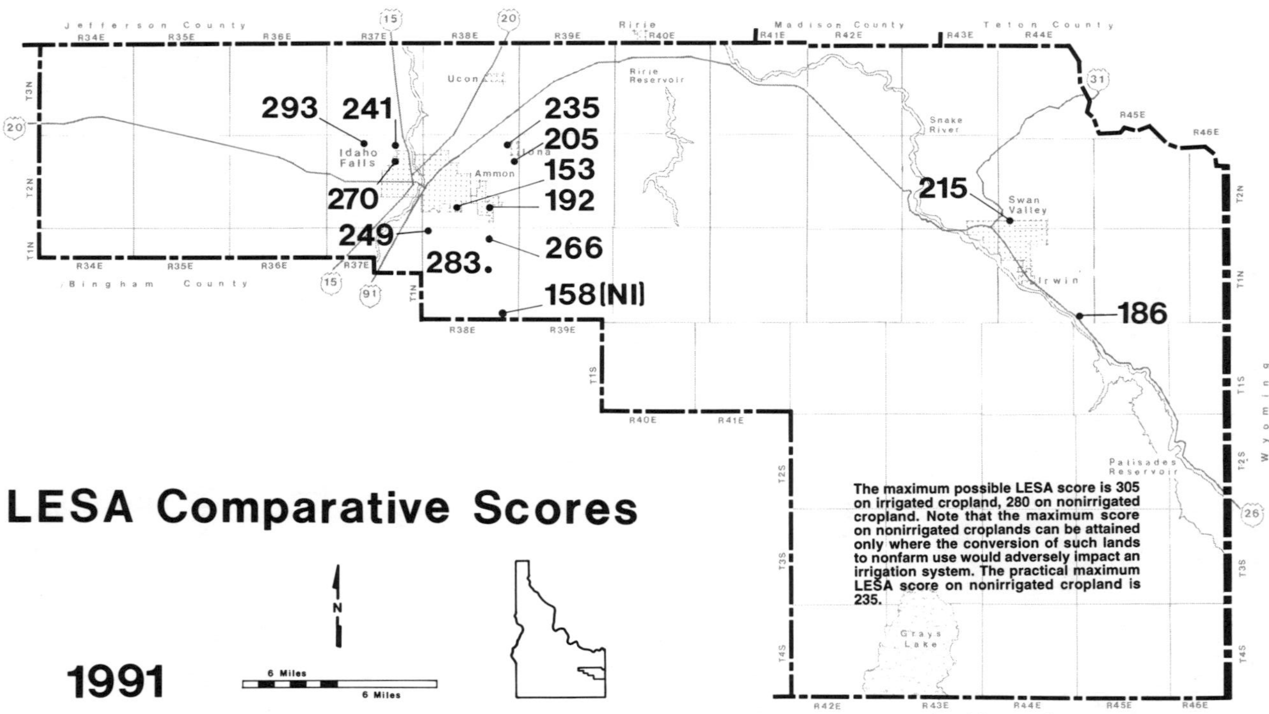

Figure 4. This map shows LESA scores for several locations in Bonneville County. These scores were generated during the development of the draft comprehensive plan, when they were used as a basis for comparing the impacts of different proposed policies.

The case study counties attempt to protect agricultural operations and educate those moving from urban environments into rural areas by requiring resource management easements. Such an easement must be recorded before a building permit is issued for construction of any new residence outside the areas designated for urban growth in the comprehensive plan. The easement formally acknowledges that the proposed home is in an agricultural area, and may be subjected to odors, noise, and other impacts of farming on adjoining lands. The easement is in favor of the continuation of all lawful farm operations on adjoining lands and waives the homeowner's common law rights to object to such operations. Resource management easements also protect other potentially noisome, but necessary rural activities, like gravel mining. They do not grant adjoining landowners access to the residential property.

Other right-to-farm strategies used by Bonneville and Fremont counties include a performance standard requiring control of noxious weeds on non-farm properties and careful definitions, one of which excludes manure and crop residues from the term "solid waste" and the regulations applied to solid waste. The case study counties also encourage home occupations, which often generate important supplemental income for many farm families.

Development of the LESA systems set the stage for adoption of right-to-farm strategies by focusing attention on the conflicts that arise when residential development is permitted in farming areas. **The LESA systems play no direct role in the administration of these strategies, which must be applied uniformly throughout a county's rural areas to be effective.**

Cropland Protection. The local LESA systems are actively used in the administration of the cropland protection strategies adopted by Bonneville and Fremont counties. Those strategies are based on three principles:

- that all landowners are entitled to some development potential;
- that development should be directed away from the most productive croplands; and
- that the rural character of the area, including the opportunity to conduct viable farming operations, should be maintained.

Implementation of the cropland protection strategies requires two basic steps: establishing the amount of development that is compatible with continued agricultural use of adjacent lands (and other planning goals) and identifying sites suitable for development.

Although there are minor differences in their approaches, the Bonneville and Fremont county plans both combine a land use control technique called "fixed area-based allocation" (*4*) with density bonuses to set the balance between development and agriculture. This balance reflects several planning goals, including maintaining viable farm units and the agribusiness enterprises they support, minimizing development of sensitive lands, not overtaxing the limited public facilities available in rural areas, and preserving the character of the local landscape.

The table in Figure 5 is taken from the Fremont County development code. It is the basis for the fixed area-based allocation system that limits development of both productive croplands and naturally hazardous or sensitive sites. The owner of "productive croplands" (which are identified using the local LESA system) may develop one dwelling unit for each 40 acres of such land, but may place that dwelling on as little as one acre, while leaving the remaining 39 acres in production. Development rights are allocated to other land types in accordance with the policies of the comprehensive plan. Density bonuses encourage landowners to transfer the development rights assigned to productive croplands to suitable sites, which are identified, in part, by the LESA system. In Fremont County, the density transferred away from productive croplands may be doubled on a site that is suitable for development. An additional density bonus may result from an overall positive rating of the project's compliance with the performance standards of the county's development code. The difference between the "base density" of one dwelling unit per 2.5 acres assigned to "other lands" and the minimum lot size of one acre allows the owner to maximize the value of the lands best suited for development only by transferring density from productive, hazardous, or sensitive lands to the site.

The local LESA systems are integral parts of the cropland protection

BASE RESIDENTIAL DENSITY ASSIGNMENTS BY LAND TYPE

site characteristics	*base density, one dwelling unit per*
productive croplands	40 acres
wetlands, slopes over 30%	25 acres
stream and lakeshore corridors, slopes of 15-30%	10 acres
other areas	2.5 acres
minimum lot size	1.0 acres

Notes: Where site characteristics overlap, the most restrictive density assignment shall apply. Remember that the base densities are averages, allowing the developer substantial flexibility in the actual arrangement of lots. State health regulations may prevent a development from attaining the average density or minimum lot size permitted by these regulations.

Figure 5. This is one of the density assignment tables adopted in the Fremont County development code. Productive croplands are defined using the Fremont County LESA system.

strategies in both case study counties. LESA scores are used to identify both the productive croplands on which development is discouraged, and, along with other factors, the "other lands" that are suitable for development.

Implementation of Bonneville and Fremont counties' cropland protection strategies should result in a pattern of rural residential "clusters" developed on marginal croplands, or range or timber lands. Ideally, right-to-farm strategies and other performance standards imposed by the counties will ensure that these clusters blend into the surrounding matrix of farmlands with minimal conflict. A useful presentation of the advantages of cluster development in rural areas is found in *Dealing with change in the Connecticut River Valley: A design manual for conservation and development* (*11*). Concrete examples, similar to those given in that manual, are an important aid in explaining cropland protection strategies to local officials and citizens.

It should be understood that the plan implementation strategies described here are not the only way to approach farmland protection. Indeed, it can be argued that other techniques, like exclusive farm-use zoning, are more effective (*3*). That is true, but all farmland protection strategies should be based on a defensible means of delineating the lands to be preserved. The experience reported here makes it clear that the development of a local LESA system is the most effective way to provide that means.

LESA Systems: Essential Rural Planning Tools

This case study has clearly demonstrated the value of LESA systems in rural planning efforts. The experiences of Bonneville and Fremont counties show how LESA systems can accomplish the following:

- complement other planning background studies by providing additional information on farmland resources;
- stimulate public discussion by highlighting the conflicts between continuing agricultural operations and expanding suburban and exurban development;
- provide an effective tool for answering planning commission and public questions about the impacts of alternative land use policies;
- aid in the delineation of broad areas in which farmland protection policies should (or conversely, should not) apply; and
- support plan implementation by specifically identifying the farmlands covered by cropland protection strategies.

Given its ability to offer a useful response to one of the most important questions that will be asked, a LESA system should be among the first products of the planning process in any community where farmlands have economic or social significance.

References

1. American Farmland Trust. 1991. *Making a positive contribution.* American Farmland. Fall: 2.
2. Bonneville County Planning and Zoning Commission. 1991. *Bonneville County comprehensive plan (Draft).* Idaho Falls, Idaho.
3. Bowers Publishing, Inc. 1992. *Study heats up decade-long debate on farmland loss.* Farmland preservation report 2(7):1.
4. Coughlin, R. E., J. C. Keene, J. D. Esseks, W. Toner, and L. Rosenberger. 1981. *The protection of farmland: a reference guidebook for state and local governments.* National Agricultural Lands Study. Washington, D.C.
5. Fremont County Planning and Zoning Commission. 1992. *Fremont County comprehensive plan.* St. Anthony, Idaho.
6. Heimlich, R. E., M. Vesterby, and K. S. Krupa. 1991. *Urbanizing farmland: dynamics of land use change in fast-growth counties.* USDA-Economic Research Service, Agriculture Information Bulletin No. 629, Washington, D.C.
7. Idaho Code §§ 22-4501 et seq.
8. Idaho Code §§ 31-3805 et seq.
9. Thompson, E., Jr. 1982. *Defining and protecting the right to farm.* Zoning and Planning Law Report 5(8):1.
10. U.S. Department of Agriculture-Soil Conservation Service. 1983. *National Agricultural Land Evaluation and Site Assessment Handbook.* Washington, D.C.
11. Yaro, R. D., R. G. Arendt, H. L. Dodson, and E. A. Brabec. 1988. *Dealing with change in the Connecticut River Valley: A design manual for conservation and development.* Lincoln Institute of Land Policy and Environmental Law Foundation, Cambridge, Massachusetts.

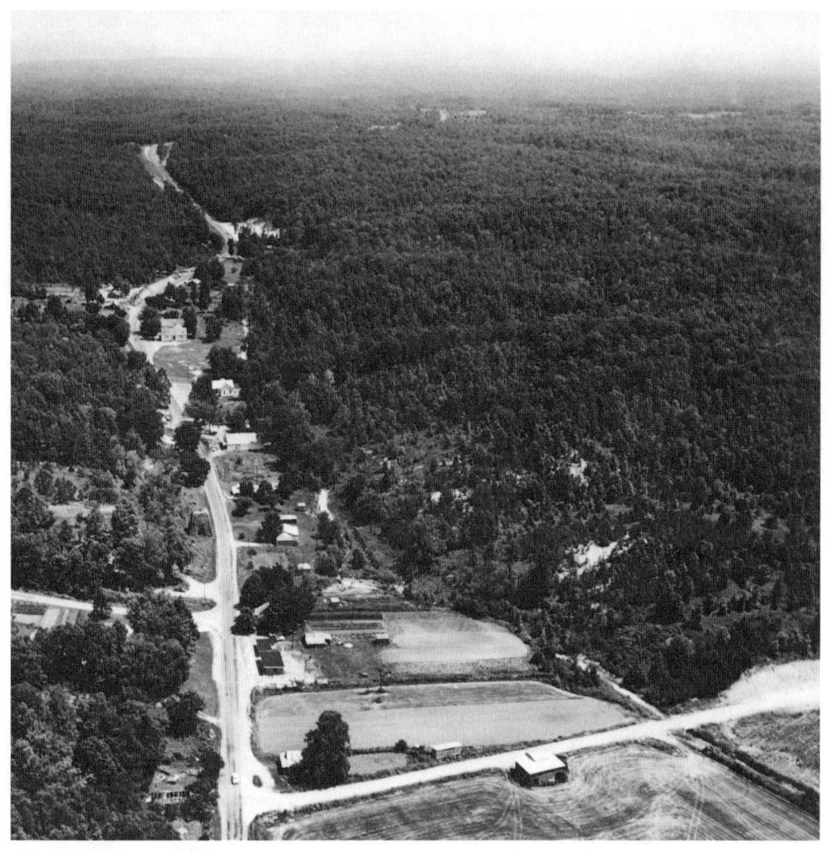

13 Using GIS in a FLESA Study: Observations From the Woods of Vermont

Christopher C. Hamilton

The town of Granby, situated in the rolling hills of northeastern Vermont, has no general store or quaint village center like many Vermont communities. The 36-square-mile town is 98 percent forested, about 10 miles from the nearest store, and has an average income well below the state average. It is not a fancy place. The people, all 74 of them, are hardy souls who make a living working in the woods harvesting trees. To most people, Granby seems like the type of place that time has forgotten. Yet as the price of land in New England soared during the 1980s, the townspeople became concerned that the forest land would be converted to non-forest related uses, such as second homes and private hunting estates.

At a town meeting in 1989, the community formed its first planning commission. As a first step in their land-use planning efforts they wanted to complete a "directed inventory." After looking at different models, they decided on a forest land evaluation and site assessment (FLESA) study that would evaluate the land and find its best use considering its natural resource constraints. The commission intended to use the information collected in the FLESA to complement their town plan and any subsequent land-use regulations. Being a volunteer board, they decided to hire a consulting forester and geographic information system specialist to complete the study. Their FLESA considered four land-use categories: timber, recreation, wildlife, and development potential (*1*).

To evaluate the land and conduct a detailed analysis, the town was divided into 152 tracts. The tracts followed parcel boundaries for those under 100 acres. Parcels in excess of 100 acres were divided following natural boundaries such as watersheds, streams, and elevation. Each tract was scored individually for all four sets of criteria and assigned four separate scores ranging from 0 to 300. The higher the score, the more important the tract in that category. The different category layers (timber, recreation, wildlife, and development) were then placed on top of each other and scores were compared to identify those areas that scored the highest. Of all the evaluation criteria, tract size turned out to be the most influential.

There is no soils information available for the town of Granby. This was a limiting factor when using a traditional LESA evaluation. However, the planning commission believed the model was still useful and conducted the project without the soils data.

The four categories were scored on a variety of attributes, which are listed below.[1]

1. Timber	Score
Parcel size	100
Access	60
Public investment	10
Elevation	10
Forest type	10
Current use	10
Species type	100
	300

2. Recreation	Score
Parcel size	40
Attractions	80
Adjacent use	48
Access	132
	300

[1] Each attribute was broken down into sub-attributes. For complete description of the scoring system, refer to the full report.

3. Wildlife	Score
Parcel size	108
Adjacent use	80
Factors on site	70
Resident areas	42
	300

4. Development Potential (both + and -)			
Access	108	Wetland	-50
Slope	60	Slope <20%	-50
Water present	84	Fragile area	-50
Dist. population	24	Gravel pit	-50
View	6	No access	-50
Electric lines	8		
Open land	10	(Within 500 ft site)	
	300	Wetland	-25
		Gravel pit	-25
		VELCO powerline	-25
			-325

Using a geographic information system (GIS), the tracts were compared to one another to identify trends and areas with the highest and lowest scores. Land-use planning decisions were then drawn from analyzing these trends.

Using A GIS

A GIS (PC Arc-Info) was used to test the software's applicability on a local FLESA project. It was used to create maps, score tracts, and analyze the data. Overall, in this one-town FLESA study, it received mixed reviews when compared to the traditional method of doing the analysis.

The advantages of using a GIS in the Granby FLESA were as follows:

1. The GIS easily allowed the criteria to be changed and different evaluation scenarios to be tried. This type of analysis was tested but not incorporated into the final study.
2. The most time consuming aspect of the GIS work was entering the data. Once the data were entered, however, the GIS saved time when different scenarios were tested.
3. As long as the polygons (i.e. tracts) did not change much, the data and FLESA results could easily be updated as land uses changed.
4. The GIS produced high quality, easy to use, and understandable maps, making the overall project more useful and easy to implement.
5. Once the data were entered, they were available for a variety of uses beyond the FLESA study (e.g. creating planning maps).

In a small rural town like Granby, the GIS had its limitations in the FLESA process, including the following:

1. Since much of the data did not already exist on a GIS, it was extremely time consuming and expensive to digitize the data.

2. Some of the raw data (i.e., soils) did not exist, therefore the complexity of analysis was limited and the real analytical power of the GIS was underused.
3. Since Granby does not have a GIS (or even a computer for that matter), people in general do not understand the technology. It seems too "high-tech" and fancy which politically alienated townspeople.
4. Since the town does not own a GIS, they would need to hire a consultant every time they wanted to manipulate the information. This has limited utility to the townspeople.
5. The GIS macros (the internal computer commands) are specific to the Granby FLESA. Therefore, the Granby FLESA system is not directly applicable to other towns.

The FLESA project, which cost $10,000 and took six months, was completed by a consulting forester and a GIS specialist. The GIS portion of the project took about 125 hours and was spent in the following manner:

60-65 percent database building, digitizing, and acquiring data;
20-30 percent creating macros, developing maps, and scoring parcels; and
10-15 percent administration and project coordination.

Conclusions

In the long-run, using GIS technology in rural land-use planning holds great potential for completing complex projects like the Granby FLESA. However, if much of the basic data (i.e. roads, surface waters, and land uses) needs to be developed, the cost of using a GIS may be prohibitive. Also, even though the GIS produced high quality maps, it was more expensive and sophisticated than what Granby needed for the study itself. The potential exists to do complex data analysis and to experiment with different scenarios, but because the townspeople lacked a good understanding of the analytical power of the GIS, neither of these was accomplished. The long-term benefits of being able to update the data and change the evaluation criteria may be useful in the future. But in the Granby FLESA, a one-town application where a lot of data needed to be developed, the benefits of using GIS technology were marginal at best. The executive summary and full text ($28.00) of the Granby FLESA report is available from the Granby Town Clerk, Granby, VT 05840.

Reference

1. Hegman, W., and R. Carbonetti. 1991. *Granby FLESA Project.* Granby Planning Commission, Granby Town Clerk, Granby, Vermont.

Soil Conservation Service photo

14 Extending the Utility of LESA with GIS

Gene Yagow
and Vernon Shanholtz

The land evaluation and site assessment (LESA) guidelines were developed by the U.S. Department of Agriculture's Soil Conservation Service in the early 1980s. The guidelines are intended for use by local governments in the development of a LESA system for assessing the agricultural productivity and economic viability of land parcels on a parcel-by-parcel basis (*10*). Prior research has pioneered the application of geographic information systems (GIS) for automated evaluation of LESA factors (*7, 9*). The benefits of using GIS for LESA system development include savings of time, the ability to simultaneously analyze all parcels within a county or watershed, and the flexibility to rapidly generate alternative scenarios and plans. Each LESA system consists of a series of factors, selected to reflect local planning objectives, and used to score individual land parcels. The majority of LESA systems are created by local committees consisting of concerned citizens and a combination of local SCS, extension service, county board of supervisors, and Soil and Water Conservation District personnel. Most of these people will have little or no knowledge of GIS. Therefore, if a link between LESA and GIS is to be useful and practical at the local level, a user interface on the computer is essential. The user interface facilitates entering information into the computer through the use of prompts and menus, and guides the user through the interim steps needed to create a local LESA system.

A GIS is a computer-based system used to encode, store, display, analyze, and model geographically referenced data. The Information Support Systems Laboratory (ISSL) at Virginia Polytechnic Institute and State University has developed a PC-based GIS, named PC-VirGIS, which incorporates the major GIS functions needed at the county level for natural resources planning and management (*3*). PC-VirGIS was developed in the MS-DOS environment and currently performs a wide range of spatial analyses with both raster and vector data. Since 1984, ISSL has been involved in the development of an extensive geographically referenced database of the Commonwealth of Virginia that consists of 20 data layers encoded in 1/9 hectare (0.27 acre) raster cells (*5*). This project is commonly referred to as the VirGIS project, which served as the impetus for the development of, and the source of the name for, PC-VirGIS. By October 1993, the database will include 69 counties (about 17 million acres), two-thirds of the entire state.

The existence of PC-VirGIS and the VirGIS database were primary in the decision to develop the GIS link for LESA. Both of these were used in its development, testing, and evaluation. Eleven raster data layers were used in the initial development of the GIS functions for the LESA module. Some of the data layers were from the pre-existing VirGIS database (land use, soils, transportation). Others were pre-existing from another project for Richmond County, Virginia (parcel boundaries, historical sites, floodplains). The agricultural support systems data layer was created from tabular point data, while land evaluation and septic suitability were derived from the soils layer. Buffered data layers were created from the transportation and agricultural support systems layers to simplify the analysis of these factors.

The LESA module is being developed as one component of a larger cooperative project with the People's Republic of China. This project aims to develop a decision support system centered around the LESA module, PC-VirGIS, and a land use change assessment procedure. The DSS will be used to help identify the primary forces responsible for land-use change in specified areas, in addition to serving as a tool for local planners to use for protecting the rapidly eroding agricultural base in urban fringe areas.

The LESA Module

The LESA module automates basic procedures from the SCS LESA handbook (*8*), and consists of a user interface and a series of programmed GIS subroutines or macros, within the modeling component of PC-VirGIS (*4*). The user is required to understand basic GIS techniques for the manipulation and display of GIS data layers within PC-VirGIS. Once inside the LESA module, however, menus guide the user through the procedures needed to develop a LESA system. The user interface further assists the user by defining the options and choices required at each stage of data input. The programmed GIS macros currently support the analysis and evaluation of about 20 site assessment (SA) factors, with future development extending to about 10 additional factors. The LESA module performs three main types of functions: configuration of SA factors, factor value assignment, and parcel scoring. A schematic representation of the functions and components in the LESA module is shown in Figure 1. Each of the main functions are discussed in detail in the following sections.

System Configuration

System configuration involves the selection of SA factors to be used, the definition of scoring criteria, and the assignment of relative weights to each factor. The user will be prompted for all data input needed to configure an individualized LESA system. The first prompt will request the user to choose any number of site assessment (SA) factors from a list adapted from the handbook, for the current LESA configuration. The user has flexibility in assigning individual weights to the land evaluation (LE) and SA components, and to each individual SA factor. The user can either define the number and range of categories needed to establish scoring criteria, or use a default set of categories defined for each SA factor. Once SA factors, weightings, and scoring criteria have been defined, adjusted factor weights are calculated by the program and stored in a configuration file together with the selected SA factors and their respective scoring criteria.

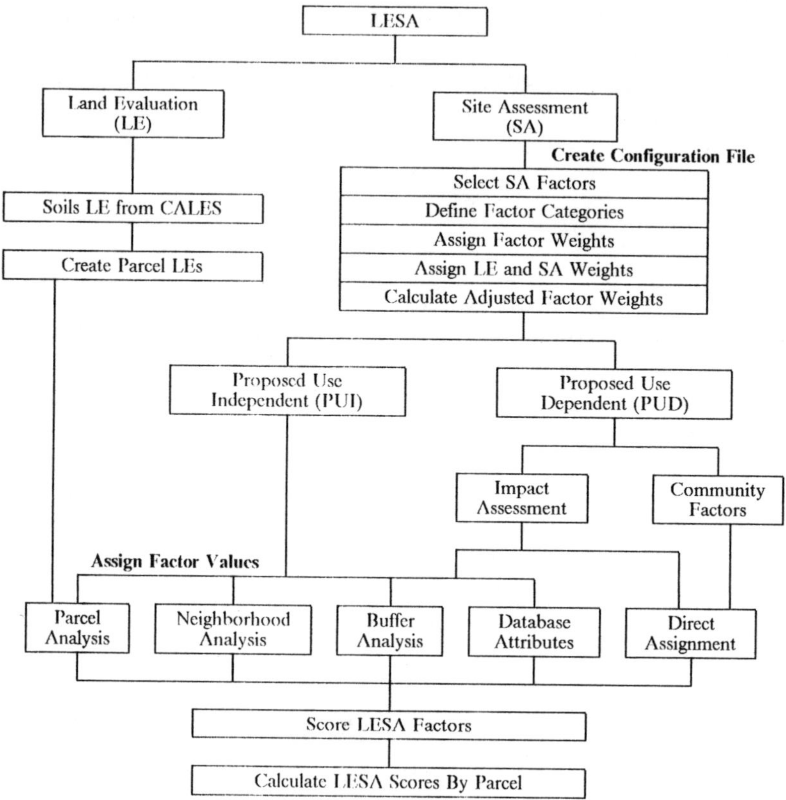

Figure 1. Overview of LESA module.

Factor Value Assignment

Factor value assignment involves determining values for each parcel according to the appropriate procedure for each SA factor, and storing these values by SA factor and parcel in a relational database matrix. The user is guided through this process of individual SA factor analysis by the user interface menus. Depending on the SA factor chosen, the analysis will result in parcel values representing either a maximum, minimum, average, percentage, or count of a specified attribute or attributes from a given data layer. The procedure will consider either the area within the parcel, or the area surrounding the parcel, depending on the SA factor.

Categorizing LESA Factors. For analysis purposes, we divided the SA factors into two categories, designated as proposed use-independent (PUI) and proposed use-dependent (PUD) as shown within a portion of Figure 1. PUI factors are those that are not influenced by a proposed use and tend to be objective in nature, such as the SA factor, “Susceptibility to Flooding.” Regardless of the proposed land use, the assessment of this PUI factor will not change, unless massive earth-moving occurs to change the elevation of the land parcel under consideration. The PUD factors cannot be fully assessed until the specifics of a proposed use are known. For instance, the value of the SA factor, “Environmental Impact,” would vary considerably depending on whether a proposed use was to be a chemical plant, a nursery, an office, or a residence. The module currently provides analysis only of PUI factors.

We defined an additional level of sub-categories under PUD based on the different types of value assignments required for each factor. The categories, their relationships, and examples of factors in each category are shown in Table 1. Once a specific site and proposed use are identified, a number of factors related to impact assessment can be evaluated using GIS and/or expert system functions. Whereas GISs process numerical data, expert systems can assist the user in evaluating information that is not easily quantifiable. The factors included in the sub-category, “Community Factors,” may relate to nonspatial characteristics of land parcels, and may be influenced more by perception than by quantifiable facts. Expert systems are useful in assisting the user to identify and define criteria for evaluating relative values for these factors.

Table 1. Site assessment factors.

Proposed Use-Independent (PUI)
- Percent agriculture in surrounding area
- Susceptibility to flooding
- Distance to services
- Average parcel size in surrounding area

Proposed Use-Dependent (PUD)
- Impact assessment
  - —Environmental impact
  - —Distance to specified services
- Community factors
  - —Compatibility with surrounding land uses
  - —Socio-economic importance
  - —Site suitability

Factor Assignment Procedures. We identified five different types of procedures that can be used to assign values to parcels for any of the LESA factors currently included in the module. Three of these procedures rely on GIS spatial analysis functions: neighborhood analysis, buffer analysis, and parcel analysis. The last two procedures for LESA factor assignment are relational database related. The fourth procedure allows for direct value assignment by parcel from a relational database and the fifth procedure allows for direct input to a relational database by the user.

- Neighborhood analysis looks at the percentage of an attribute in a specified data layer within a user-defined radius of each parcel, e.g., "Percentage of Agricultural Land in the Surrounding Area." For this assignment procedure, the menu prompts the user for the numerical attributes to be classified as agriculture, while being shown a legend of the land-use data layer. The user also is given a limited choice of radii (one-fourth mile, one-half mile, one mile, one and one-half miles, and two miles) with which to define "surrounding area" for this SA factor.
- Buffer analysis calculates the percentage of a specified attribute in a one cell (33 meters) buffer around each parcel. An example of a factor requiring buffer analysis would be "Percentage of Adjacent Land Zoned Agriculture."
- Parcel analysis concerns the calculation of several different statistics for each parcel, depending on the LESA factor being evaluated. The SA factor, "Average Parcel Size in the Surrounding Area," is calculated as a weighted average value for each parcel. The SA factor, "Agricultural Support Systems," is assigned the number of systems found within a three-mile radius. When evaluating "Septic Limitations," the program calculates the percentage of land with severe septic limitations. For many of the urban SA factors, this procedure calculates the minimum distance to a given feature. Other factors, such as "Unique Features," evaluate the occurrence or count of specified attributes within each parcel.
- The fourth procedure retrieves and assigns parcel attributes from a relational database. SA factors using this procedure include "On Site Investment," and "Conservation Plan Status."
- The fifth procedure, direct assignment, is not currently implemented. It will allow users to directly enter values for "Community Factors" into a relational database, on a parcel-by-parcel basis.

One procedure is not included in the preceding scheme for value assignment. A detailed evaluation procedure for the assessment of the land evaluation (LE) portion of LESA already exists in the Computer Aided Land Evaluation System (CALES), jointly developed by USDA-SCS and the U.S. Army Corps of Engineers' Construction Engineering Research Laboratory (*6*). This system accesses the SOILS-6 database maintained by USDA-SCS at the Statistical Laboratory at Iowa State University, which is updated every six months at the rate of about 4,000 changes per month. The SOILS-6 database is the most up-to-date source of soils information available and is accessible through county and state offices of USDA-SCS. For this LESA application, we used CALES as the source of LE values by soil type. We manually transferred the LE scores from a CALES generated printout to a relational database file by corresponding soil type. GIS routines were then used to generate a land evaluation data layer by relabeling the soils map, overlaying with the parcel boundary layer, and calculating the weighted average LE score for each parcel.

Parcel Scoring

The parcel scoring function compares each parcel-factor value with its associated criteria, or ranking categories, defined during system configuration, and assigns it a factor score. For example, the SA factor "Percentage of Adjacent Land in Agriculture" for a given parcel has a value of 82 percent. Let us assume the following scoring categories:

Value Categories	Score
91-100 percent	10
75-90 percent	8
50-74 percent	5
30-49 percent	3
0-29 percent	0

Our parcel with a value of 82 percent, would have a score of 8. The program then multiplies each factor score by its associated weight, and sums these values over all factors for a LESA score for each parcel. The parcel LESA scores are stored as columns in a relational database file corresponding to the parcel numbers. These results can either be printed out as a summary report, or used to create a map.

Extending the Utility of LESA

The proposed LESA module increases the flexibility of a locally designed LESA system in at least two ways. First, it allows the user to perform partial LESA calculations at any point in the development process, so that, prior to having developed values for all factors, the user can discern the impact of the factors assessed up to that point. And second, the system allows the user to easily create alternate LESA configurations (SA factor lists, the LE:SA ratio, individual SA factor weights, and scoring criteria). After the parcel-factor value table is created for one scenario, only the attributes changed in future configuration files will need to be generated. This makes it easier and faster to generate alternate plans, or to evaluate the impact of an individual factor or scoring criterion on the system. Within the GIS environment, this evaluation takes place during the development stage of the system, not after implementation, where changes will be relatively more difficult.

The current LESA module is in its initial stage of development. While programming of GIS functions are complete for most factors, proposed development will extend the module's utility even further through enhancement of the user interface. Linkage to an expert system will be explored to define user-specified SA factors not currently in the system. Many of the SA factors suggested in the SCS handbook are closely related to others, and selection of some combinations of factors may unintentionally bias the parcel scoring procedure. DeMers (*1, 2*) proposes using the Delphi technique and the Kane Simulation Model both to reduce the impact of such SA factor interactions and to incorporate the knowledge and opinions of all LESA committee members in determining factor weights (see also chapters 6, 8, and 9). Future revisions will consider ways to minimize SA factor interaction based on DeMers' research. Possibly the greatest extensions will be in the realm of the proposed use dependent (PUD) factors. The PUD factors can be evaluated in several different ways for LESA. One such factor listed in the SCS handbook, but not currently modeled, is "Impact on the Environment," which now relies on qualitative evaluations. The fully developed PUD component can help to quantify this factor by incorporating spatially modeled results from models within PC-VirGIS for one or more environmental parameters, e.g. surface water sediment or nitrogen loads.

A GIS-based LESA system also presents a unique opportunity for use as a proactive tool for use by land-use planners. Most communities do not necessarily want to stop growth. They do, however, want to control and direct it. The availability of GIS can help local planners work together with developers prior to their investment in specific land parcels. Instead of having to debate and defend the merits of a previously purchased parcel for a proposed use, the GIS can be used by planners working cooperatively with developers and new businesses to identify a number of sites that would both meet the client's needs and be consistent with the locality's growth management plan. While this capability exists with any GIS, the real benefits will occur when these analysis functions are available through the user interface.

Some of the PUD factors cannot be modeled, as they are totally subjective, depending primarily on the disposition of the community. These community factors include such things as "Socio-Economic Benefits," "Quality of Life," and "Compatibility with the Existing Neighborhood." These and other factors may require the use of expert systems to help elicit information that could be used as a basis for evaluation. We plan to explore the use of expert systems for defining the vague terminology that surrounds some of the SA factors identified by SCS or that may be identified by a given locality, such as "Alternative Sites," "Socio-Economic Benefits," and "Scenic Quality."

Summary

LESA procedures have been computerized using menu-driven data input screens combined with GIS spatial analysis functions. The resulting LESA module builds a configuration file containing selected SA factors, individual factor weights, and their scoring criteria. This module is designed to calculate adjusted factor weights, to generate and evaluate individual LE and SA factors, and to calculate LESA scores on a parcel basis over county-wide areas. County-wide assessment provides for greater consistency in land-use decisions and for compatibility with, or as a basis for, comprehensive plans. The LESA module is functional, but still in the developmental phase since not all factors can presently be evaluated. Even at this stage, though, the module shows advantages over the conventional manual approach to LESA and takes advantage of the increasing amounts of digital data and computing power available to local governments. The user interface, once complete, will reduce the need for extensive familiarity with GIS to perform county-wide LESA assessments. In the future, the user interface will be expanded to incorporate environmental modeling results, to allow user specification of additional SA factors, and to develop a procedure for proactive site selection assistance to developers and builders. Eventually, the LESA module will be incorporated as part of a decision support system for application.

References

1. DeMers, M. N. 1986. *A knowledge base acquisition strategy for expert geographic information system development.* In: B.K. Opitz (ed.), Geographic Information Systems in Government. A. Deepak, Hampton, Virginia. pp.837-850.
2. DeMers, M. N. 1989. *Knowledge acquisition for GIS automation of the SCS LESA model: An empirical study.* AI Applications 3(4):12-22.
3. Desai, C. J., and V. O. Shanholtz. 1990. *Application of GIS technology in natural resources: System functionality.* Paper No. 90-3031. 1990 International Winter Meeting. American Society of Agricultural Engineers, St. Joseph, Michigan.
4. Information Support Systems Laboratory. 1992. *ISSL User Manual.* ISSL PC-VirGIS Version 2.0, Geographic Information System. Department of Agricultural Engineering, Blacksburg, Virginia.
5. Shanholtz, V. O., J. M. Flagg, C. Desai, E. Garland, E. Fox, B. Jadeja, E. Schrading, and K. Koehler. 1991. *Agricultural pollution potential database for Southside (Charlotte County) Soil and Water Conservation District.* Interim Report ISSL 91-6. Prepared for the Department of Conservation and Recreation, Information Support Systems Laboratory, Virginia Tech, Blacksburg, Virginia.
6. Thompson, P. J., K. Young, W. D. Goran, and A. Moy. 1987. *An interactive soils information system user's manual.* USA-CERL Technical Report N-87/18. U. S. Army Corps of Engineers, Construction Engineering Research Laboratory, Champaign, Illinois.
7. Thum, P. G., S. R. Pickett, B. J. Niemann Jr., and S. J. Ventura. 1990. *LIS/GIS: Integrating nonpoint pollution assessment with land development planning.* In: Wisconsin Land Information Newsletter. University of Wisconsin-Madison Vol. 5, No. 2.
8. U.S. Department of Agriculture-Soil Conservation Service. 1983. *National Agricultural Land Evaluation and Site Assessment Handbook.* Washington, D.C.
9. Williams, T. H. Lee. 1985. *Implementing LESA on a geographic information system—a case study.* Photogrammetric Engineering and Remote Sensing 51(12):1923-1932.
10. Wright, L. E., W. Zitzmann, K. Young, and R. Googins. 1983. *LESA-agricultural land evaluation and site assessment.* Journal of Soil and Water Conservation 38(2):82-86.

Photo by Philip Maechling

15 Requirements Analysis for GIS LESA Modeling

Michael N. DeMers

The attractiveness of using geographic information systems (GIS) to automate the land evaluation and site assessment (LESA) model conceals the difficulties of implementation. A structured requirements analysis is recommended, especially one performed simultaneously with the development of the LESA model itself. The analysis should achieve the following tasks: (1) make all factors and factor description definitions both explicit and precise; (2) determine all data layers necessary for modeling factors having an explicit spatial character; (3) establish the appropriate selection of spatial surrogates for aspatial factors; (4) evaluate availability of factor maps; (5) determine analytical techniques needed to construct the individual LESA factors and to combine them into a complete model; (6) determine whether raster, vector, or a combination of data structures is needed to perform these operations; (7) select appropriate grid cell size (raster) or scale (vector); (8) choose the appropriate grid and map projection; (9) flowchart the model; and (10) prototype the model using a small, well-known study area as a test case. Such an analysis will speed the process of LESA modeling inside a GIS and will have the added benefit of demonstrating limitations, pitfalls, and logical inconsistencies in the implementation of LESA with a specific set of factors and criteria.

A fundamental limitation of the Soil Conservation Service land evaluation and site assessment system has been, and continues to be, the necessity to evaluate each site on a parcel-by-parcel basis. This approach, although functional, requires that LESA practitioners or researchers spend time on each site to determine the land evaluation value, to establish the degree of adherence for each site assessment factor at each locale, and finally to compile the weights and ratings into a LESA score. In political units where few sites threatened by conversion of farmland to alternative uses this procedure is quite adequate as long as the appropriate data are available for the region. However, for regions with rapidly growing urban areas, this would require enormous, possibly prohibitive levels of staff time. This is especially true if factors are changing constantly, and are in need of frequent updating. These regions could benefit greatly from a spatial model of the LESA system using modern raster- or vector-based GIS.

The earliest published record of an attempt to automate LESA with a GIS was by T.H. Lee Williams for Douglas County, Kansas, in 1985 (*18*). This academic exercise showed the great promise of using inexpensive raster-based software for GIS implementation of LESA. It also demonstrated many of the steps necessary to develop such a system. More specifically, it showed the tremendous opportunities to access LESA values quickly and easily for any location in the database, to update the degree of location-specific adherence to individual factors, to modify the weights assigned to factors as conditions change, and even to assist in the initial formulation of factors, especially where neighborhood attributes and spatial dimensions contribute to them. In short, the success of the LESA GIS experiment has shown that GIS is not only an effective tool for use with the LESA model, but is a particularly attractive one.

The potential for using GIS for county-level resource evaluation was recognized by the Medina County, Ohio, (Figure 1) Planning Commission, which contracted with the Ohio Capability Analysis Program (OCAP) of the Ohio Department of Natural Resources (ODNR) to produce computerized

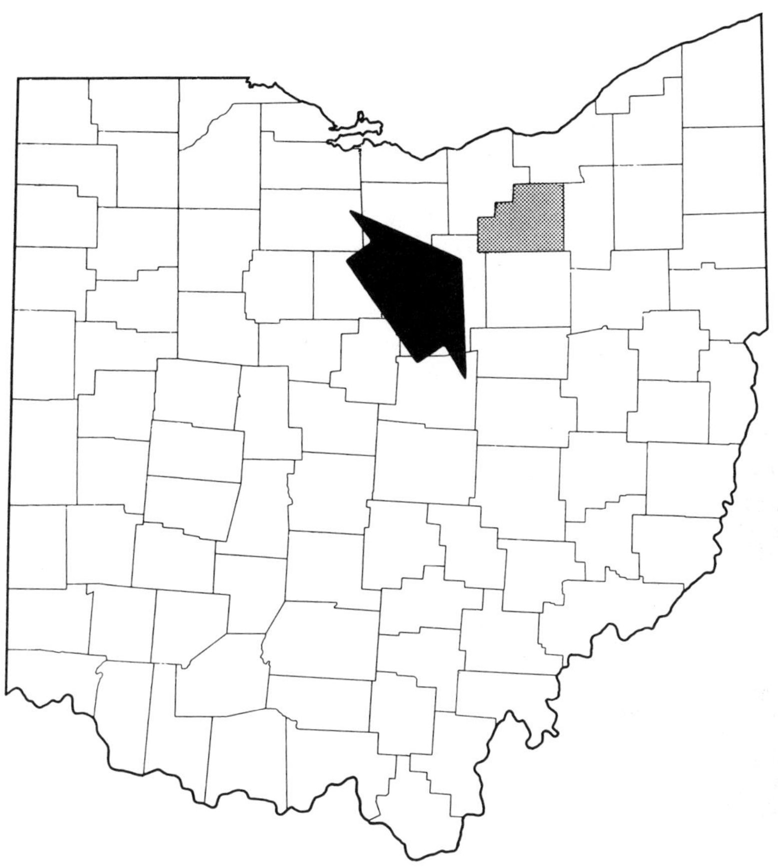

Figure 1. Medina County, Ohio.

map data files for their county within the OCAP raster-based GIS. Their database currently includes land use, groundwater availability, till suitability, sand and gravel resource, sludge application suitability, erosion loss, political boundary, flooding potential, watersheds, census tracts, and soils map data layers. Separately, a LESA system was developed for the county by a committee composed of the Medina County Soil and Water Conservation District and the Medina County Planning Commission in cooperation with the Soil Conservation Service, the Medina County Board of Commissioners, and the Medina County Engineer. With the existence of the county GIS database and the completed LESA system, and because the county is experiencing rapid expansion, especially near the city of Medina (Figure 2), it should have proven to be an excellent opportunity to develop a GIS LESA model. For example, with the data available in the GIS database, it was a simple matter for OCAP to produce a map of LE values (Figure 3), but the site assessment values were never fully integrated into the GIS database for compilation of a complete spatial LESA model. Although it was never attempted, there are indications that GIS modeling of SA factors might not be entirely straightforward (personal communication with Wayne Channell at the ODNR).

The Medina County example is only one case that shows that the apparent simplicity of GIS LESA modeling can be misleading. Even the simplest LESA model can be difficult to implement with a GIS (*11*). There are factors, for example, that do not possess explicit spatial dimension requiring aspatial surrogates to be used instead (*10*). Selection of grid cell size in raster-based GIS may place limitations on the accuracy of distance and areal measures (*7*). Raster coding methods also impose a map structure that might differ significantly from reality (*1*) and may result in large-scale measurement errors, particularly where many data layers are integrated. Placing small-scale maps together with large-scale maps in the vector domain adds to the errors found when comparing areal units between maps. Other elements such as methods of factor selection, accounting for factor interaction, factor weight determination, and group decision making, although primarily LESA problems rather than GIS problems, all play a role in complicating GIS implementation of the LESA model (*4, 5, 6*).

A primary limitation of the Williams' prototype that was not addressed, was that it was restricted to the LESA system parameters then in place for Douglas County, Kansas (*18*). That LESA system was surprisingly similar to the original design (*16*), but was limited in scope, and prohibitively expensive to extend because of its locational specificity and regional identity. Any general plan for GIS LESA automation must take into account a broader range of factors, factor weights and interactions, data availability, the aspatial nature of some LESA factors, regional uniqueness, different map scales, necessary GIS operations, computer graphics data structures, grid cell size, coding methods, and map error, before it is useful. This chapter presents a first cut at a more general operational plan for GIS implementation of LESA, based on experiences with Douglas County, Kansas, but with considerations both for differences in LESA models from region to region and for disparate data availability as well. It further clarifies some of the more general requirements for implementation and provides a logical, two-fold structure within which to approach LESA GIS development. In essence, it is a modified, application specific example of the feasibility study module of structured GIS design proposed by Marble and Wilcox (*12, 13*), but with the emphasis on technical issues rather than legal, institutional, and organizational ones.

Figure 2. Aerial photograph of central Medina County, Ohio. The city of Medina, on the left side of the photograph is expanding eastward rapidly, putting increasing development pressure on the agricultural base in the region. Photograph courtesy of the Ohio Department of Natural Resources, Remote Sensing Program.

Figure 3. Raster-based GIS map showing LE scores for approximately the same portion of Medina County, Ohio, illustrated in Figure 2. The map was produced by Terry Wells at the Ohio Department of Natural Resources, OCAP program.

The Structured GIS Development Model

The suggested structured GIS development model is in two parts: A preprocessing subsystem, and an implementation and testing subsystem (Figure 4). In the preprocessing subsystem the model is flowcharted, data needs are defined, spatial surrogates delineated for aspatial factors, map layers selected, factor weights chosen, and analytical techniques determined for modeling. The implementation and testing subsystem allows for the choice between raster- and vector-based GIS, selection of grid cell size in raster, determination of projection, scale, and coding methods, accounting for error, prototyping, and testing and implementing the model. All of these will be discussed in detail below.

Preprocessing Subsystem

The first of the two subsystems of this structured LESA GIS development model, the preprocessing subsystem, includes most of the functions that must be performed prior to database encoding and modeling. As a first step, the developers flowchart the LESA model with mapped data elements as the focus. It is generally considered easiest to proceed deductively, focusing on what the necessary GIS data layers are for the LESA model. This begins with dividing LESA into its two basic component parts, land evaluation and site assessment.

Focusing on land evaluation, it is obvious that this layer (and its attendant weights) can be derived from a soil survey map of the county or other level of local government. This fact places an initial constraint on the remaining data layers because it is the only source of land evaluation and because it has a known scale. The problems associated with scale are addressed later. To complete this portion of the model the land evaluation was derived from the soils tables and flowcharted to see how this would be accomplished using our automated soil map. Generally this is a very straightforward task requiring only renumbering of soil class cells in the raster domain or re-coding them using the database management system portion of a traditional vector-based GIS.

Having finished flowcharting and defining modeling needs for the land evaluation subsystem, attention was turned to the more difficult task of flowcharting and defining modeling needs for the site assessment subsystem. Williams (*18*) clearly outlined 21 site assessment factors and the source maps from which they were obtained. His source maps included land use, which was used, either in total or in part, for creating three of the 21 factors. A zoning map was also used to create four of the factor maps. Other maps

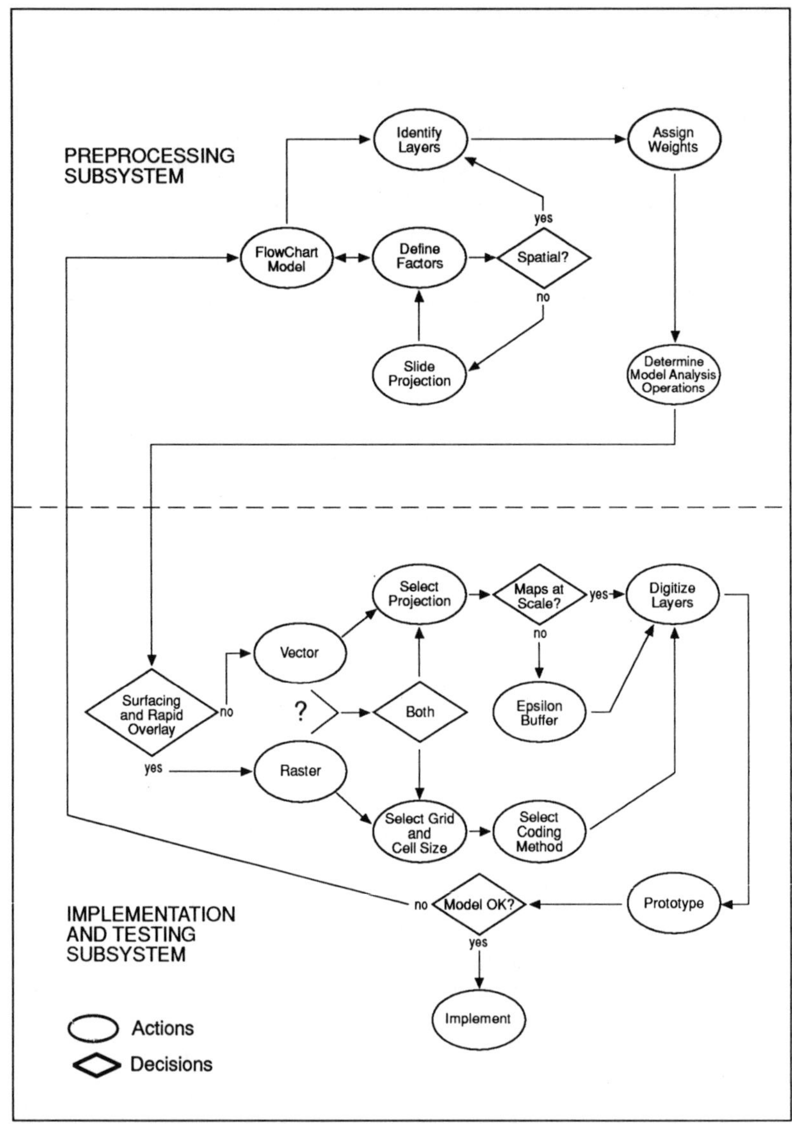

Figure 4. Flowchart of the structured LESA GIS development model. The top half shows the preprocessing subsystem and the bottom half shows the implementation and testing subsystem.

used for the site assessment factors include those showing parcel size, soils, city limit, unique areas, surface hydrology, master plan, growth areas (derived from the master, comprehensive, or general plan), transportation, water, and sewer lines.

All of these maps were readily available for computer encoding into the GIS. It is unlikely that these same maps will be available for all areas attempting to implement a GIS LESA model.

Williams (*18*) indicated that data access was a potential problem due to "... availability, cost or rate of change of the data." In addition, Williams (*18*) encountered two factors that could not be placed in the database, not because of unavailability, or cost, or rate of change of the data, but because the factors were inherently aspatial. The agricultural investment factor (on-site investments in barns and conservation measures), as well as the agricultural support systems factor (seed suppliers, equipment suppliers, and tire service) did not exhibit a readily mappable set of criteria.

As indicated in Figure 4, the lack of mappability is considered in the structured LESA GIS development model by using a decision block immediately following the task blocks for model flowcharting, factors definition, and layers identification. The question is whether or not the factors are inherently spatial. If they are, the final identification of layers can proceed. If not, surrogates must be found and the factors re-defined so that they have a spatial character. Once the latter is accomplished, the layers for these now spatial factors can be chosen.

At first look, the assigning of spatial surrogates for aspatial factors seems trivial, but it is not. If, as in the Douglas County, Kansas, example concerning agricultural investment, the factor is more economic than spatial, it must somehow be related to some spatial character. To do this may require a parcel-by-parcel enumeration of new construction as a method of determining the spatial extent of each type of agricultural investment, for example. This is no easy task, and may be impossible because of the possible invasion of privacy needed to obtain this information from those whose land may not be in the process of conversion.

It might be easier to consider providing a spatial dimension to something like agricultural support systems. Certainly distance factors, road conditions, and the availability of certain services within specified reasonable distances could be encoded in a GIS. This may lead to questions about the legitimacy of using distance to available agricultural support services as a measure. Yet it does have a spatial surrogate that could at least be included in the model. It is interesting to note here that this factor was considered easily mappable for the Hawaii LESA system (*9, 10*) (see also chapter 9).

A site assessment factor from the LESA system in Medina County, Ohio, indicates how even factors that are inherently spatial, but with a strong temporal dimension, become difficult to integrate into a spatial database. The site assessment factor used is "percentage of site under consideration utilized for agricultural land uses in three of the last five years." At first it seems that a land use-map should satisfy the mapping of this factor quite nicely. However, to define a map explicitly for this factor in a raster-based GIS requires that a land-use map for each year be included in the database. In fact, at least five of these maps must be included because maps of the previous five years are required to develop a map showing those sites that were in agriculture for three of the last five years. In a vector-based GIS a single parcel map could be used, while attributes for each year could be stored in a relational database. All of this presupposes that land-use maps for successive years are available, which is usually not the case.

Although many communities possess comprehensive plans for the development of their urban areas, many even in map form, these maps are not at all useful for defining site assessment factors that require aspatial judgement. For example, in the Medina County, Ohio, LESA, one factor is the economic/social importance of the proposed use to the community. To encode this requires first that the LESA system both rank and assign a weight to possible non-agricultural land uses. These weights may also be modified based on the nearness to land uses that might be either positively or negatively affected.

Once the data layers and their weights have been identified, it is necessary to determine the necessary operations to create individual maps and to combine them into a model. Most factors used in LESA models lend themselves to simple "reclassification" routines, which either assign a different class name or assign a numeric value. Factors that are categorized based on the presence or absence of a given attribute at a selected site, such as designated growth areas, flood zones, zoning category, locations suitable for waste disposal, or unique locations, are all reclassified based on the weight assigned by the LESA system and the degree to which each cell exhibits the attribute. For most of these, a proposed development site either exhibits or does not exhibit the necessary or prohibitive attributes, and is, therefore, either assigned a score of 10 or 0. The final score is multiplied by the relative weight to create a weighted data layer for incorporation into the final LESA model.

Other factors will also require reclassification operations, but exhibit a wider range of values. The LE scores, for example, are calculated by reclassifying the soils polygons based on the productivity ratings, and producing a number of scores. In other cases, one is required to reclassify portions of a map based on its measured distance, for example when measuring the distance from city limits, transportation, central water, or sewage lines for their SA factor scores. Similarly, measurement of adjacency can easily be performed in a GIS to accommodate factors such as whether a proposed site is next to agricultural land or alternative sites. Other measurement operations include the determination of the size of land units related either to the proposed site or the area farms. The map polygons can easily be reclassified based on all of these measurements and their combinations.

Finally, the selection of which techniques will be used for a given set of LESA factors depends on the nature of those factors. Williams (*18*) provides an excellent set of example operations and their solution within a GIS setting. A careful study of the techniques used for his LESA GIS model for Lawrence, Kansas, will provide a basic blueprint for most of the factors typical of LESA models. Factors not found within Williams (*18*) prototype can usually be suggested by their similarity to others that have been automated.

Implementation and Testing Subsystem

Having identified the appropriate data layers and their weights and having at least a working knowledge of the kinds of data analysis techniques necessary to build the GIS-based LESA model, the question of whether to build a raster- or a vector-based GIS must next be answered (Figure 4). The general rule of thumb is if one is planning to use operations that require the use of explicit cartographic surfaces or needs rapid response to overlay operations, a raster-based GIS is considered best (*2*). This rule of thumb, however, is misleading and may, in fact, be a moot question considering the more advanced nature of today's GIS technology. It is misleading because, although rapid overlay is certainly a strength of raster-based GIS software, the lack of resolution from the raster map output of such operations may be both visually unappealing to the user and notably in error spatially. This, of course, can be minimized by selecting a very small cell size. Given the possibility of litigation, it is highly desirable that either a very small cell size be selected in a raster-based GIS, or a vector-based GIS be used.

The argument for raster-based GIS for rapid overlay also assumes that there is a relatively small number of data layers to overlay. This may not be true in the case of a large number of possible scenarios involving, for example, the ranked economic/social impact of all possible alternative land uses, each weighted based on its potential spatial association with numerous possible existing land uses. In fact, such a large list of possibilities may immediately suggest the use of a relational database management system capable of intermixing these scenarios based on formula. This precludes the necessity of creating a voluminous spatial database, requiring frequent updating and error checking, and making data layer selection nearly impossible. Considerable storage space can be saved by using a vector-based GIS over a raster-based GIS, especially where multiple attributes are associated with a single set of points, lines, and polygons. DeMers (*8*), for example, has shown that, because of the large number of possible combinations and permutations of attributes associated with a single map, a raster-based GIS is not practical in such circumstances.

Raster systems are well designed for modeling surfaces, and their use may very well be highly desirable for GIS LESA modeling. It is well known that many functions requiring cost surface estimation, shortest path determination, and other non-network modeling techniques are easier to perform on a raster system. Indeed many of the maps used in the Douglas County, Kansas, GIS LESA prototype required heavy use of these surface modeling techniques.

In any case, many of the common GIS systems available today have both raster and vector capabilities. As such, the analytical operations required to model LESA in a GIS are all available in such a mixed system. If such a system is available, the typical approach is to code all maps in the vector mode through digitizing and then create a raster database from the necessary layers when needed. Regardless of whether or not a combined raster-vector system is available, the questions of projection, raster, and raster cell size must be addressed (Figure 4).

The selection of the appropriate map projection is determined primarily by the intended use or proposed analytical techniques for which the maps are produced. No single projection can preserve both size and shape. As such, techniques that require measurement of area (as in the percent area within one mile of a site) of necessity require equal area projections, while calculation of distance within the same projection may not produce the correct results. An even more disturbing problem arises when two maps, each input under a different projection, are overlaid in the GIS. Although most modern vector-based GIS software has projection conversion capabilities, there are still likely to be registration errors between the two maps because of computer processing errors. As disturbing as this is, the problems of selecting the best projection can be minimized by selecting a relatively small study area within which to model LESA.

Many prefer to avoid the problem entirely by choosing to use a raster-based GIS, which assumes that the area is flat. Although this produces some measurement inconsistencies, the simplicity of working with raster cells especially when comparing maps within the same database is frequently preferred by non-GIS specialists.

Selection of the raster-based GIS, however, requires the answers to other questions. The most notable of these is the determination of raster cell size. In general, the smaller the raster cell size, the more detail is obtainable. Too small a raster size will, however, quickly overwhelm smaller computer systems, especially if large numbers of maps must be stored. A general rule might be to select a raster cell size that is less than half the size of the smallest feature you are trying to measure. For LESA this would generally indicate a cell size of about one acre (*7*).

Once the projection question has been answered for vector-based systems, or the raster-cell size question for a raster system, the next question concerns the selection of the raster itself. This is important for both vector and raster because all data layers must be in the same coordinate system and because the data may be more amenable to one system or another. For example, available land ownership maps may be in the United States Public Land Survey System (USPLS) or township and range system. If this system is most familiar to the users it might be the best raster system choice for GIS implementation. Alternatively, the universal transverse Mercator system (UTM) is more universally accepted and might prove to be a good choice if the GIS-based LESA model is to be extended to other areas, or implemented on large portions of land (*14*). Alternatively, if one is not concerned with inter-state applications, the state plane coordinate system provides very accurate renditions of irregularly shaped areas. Here again, the choice is determined by the use for which the LESA model is to be developed and the regional setting.

A necessary final choice, if a raster-based GIS is being used, is the method of encoding map polygons. According to Berry and Tomlin (*1*), there are four general methods of encoding raster data in a raster GIS. The first method, called presence/absence, assigns a value to each raster cell based entirely on whether or not the feature occurs in the cell. This approach is best for point and line features that will not show up at all using some of the alternative methods. A second method of raster encoding, called dominant type, assigns a single value to each raster cell based on which factor takes up the most area of the cell. The centroid of cell method, the third method, codes only those factors that have some portion occurring at the center of each raster cell. Both of these latter two methods are useful for coding areas rather than points and lines but the maps produced from each will not be alike.

A final method, called percent occurrence, deserves special attention. This method, again best for areas rather than points or lines, assigns a factor and a measure of how much area of each raster cell is occupied by each category. Percent occurrence coding is very useful if detail is required. The length of time necessary for data input, however, and the necessity for storing all of the additional data, frequently precludes its use in real-world applications.

In a raster-based GIS, the selection of raster-coding method is the last step prior to actual data coding or digitizing. For a vector band system, however, a final detail must be examined, stemming from the large variety of maps that are normally put together in a complete GIS database. Because these maps will typically come in different scales, the GIS modeler must be aware of the potential errors associated with mixing data from variously scaled source maps. In the raster domain it is relatively easy to enlarge a map before encoding, but, because the accuracy of the spatial database is somewhat sacrificed in the use of the raster cell itself, accuracy changes resulting from scale change are generally considered relatively unimportant as long as the scale differences are not extreme.

In vector, however, because the GIS software can represent the map at any desired scale, it is often incorrectly assumed that small-scale maps (maps covering large areas) can easily be converted to larger scale and that these enlarged maps somehow contain the same accuracy as maps that were originally digitized at these larger scales. This assumption is primarily an artifact of the graphic impact and "truth value" of maps wherein we frequently forget that lines drawn on a map are themselves generalizations. Lines drawn on a map enlarged by xerography would become fatter in direct proportion to the scale change rather than staying the same thickness.

The lines drawn on the map should be thought of as areas of uncertainty or zones between regions. These zones were first noted by Perkal (*15*) and were termed epsilon bands. Although there are complex models of how epsilon bands work, for pragmatic reasons it is best to assume that as the map scale changes, so does the zone of uncertainty. For example, a change of scale from 1:100,000 to 1:25,000 is a four power increase in scale. As such, a line drawn at .05 centimeters in diameter on the 1:100,000 scale map should be represented by a line .20 centimeters in diameter on the 1:25,000 scale map, rather than being represented by the same diameter line.

If one were to use multiple maps at different scales, especially if these scales are magnitudes of difference apart, one should then create a zone around each boundary line equal to the scale change. The generally accepted procedure for this is to digitize the lines as if they were all at the same scale, but to note the actual scale of map input. Once digitized, the lines on the smaller scaled maps are converted to polygons of uncertainty with width corresponding to the scale of the largest scaled map in the database by using a common GIS function called buffering. This procedure measures out a prescribed distance from points, lines, or areas and creates polygons of uniform thickness. The zones of uncertainty or epsilon bands can be used to indicate those regions for which the data were of insufficient quality to evaluate the final LESA scores. Whether one uses a raster-based or a vector-based GIS, questions of data quality must be at least acknowledged to assure against possible litigation as a result of decisions made from the GIS manipulation.

Of paramount importance to the user, beyond data accuracy, is the degree to which the GIS LESA model reflects the real world. For this reason it is suggested that the next step in the structured LESA GIS development model is the application prototype. Unlike remote sensing, the model results cannot be checked by simply going into the field and ground-truthing its validity as one might a color aerial photograph. The results of the model, assuming that the input data are relatively error free, should be tested at two levels: (1) Are the data manipulated in a manner consistent with the established LESA procedures and therefore give results identical to those which would be achieved through manual LESA modeling? and (2) Do the results of such manipulation conform to LESA's intended purpose? A suggested method for testing the GIS LESA model is to use a subset of the study area that is generally representative and allows for the greatest possible range of LESA values. After generating a LESA map from the GIS, a stratified random sample of land parcels (cells in raster or polygons in vector) should be selected from the database. For each of these samples, all intermediate scores and a final LESA score should be calculated by hand and checked against its GIS counterpart. Inconsistencies should be tracked at each step in the model to determine their source. Some errors may result from improper model flowcharting, incorrect data input, or the inability of surrogates to be found for spatial factors. If errors are detected, one should return to the beginning of the preprocessing subsystem (Figure 4). Once the model operates correctly for all possible LESA values in the study area it can be implemented with a complete set of data.

Determination of the degree to which the GIS model conforms to LESA's stated purpose is much less straightforward. Yet because of the powerful impact maps have on decision making it is especially important that it be evaluated. One method of determining such validity is to ask experts whether selected sites should be allowed to be converted from agriculture (see also chapters 6, 7, and 8). Such a technique will also allow for adjustment of the relationship between the LESA score and decision making. A second method suggested by Luckey and DeMers (11) is to implement LESA using data for sites where conversion decisions have already been made as a basis for determining the likelihood of such conversion under the LESA model. Neither this nor any other method of model validation will be foolproof. However, some attempt at a documented validation of the LESA model, whether implemented in a GIS or not, will prove useful for achieving long term acceptability.

Final Considerations

There are two aspects of this method of GIS LESA modeling that deserve special attention. First, all aspects of the GIS implementation should be undertaken simultaneously with the selection of factors, weights, and methods of LESA modeling itself. Although it is possible to perform a GIS implementation of a LESA system a posteriori, such an approach will lead to technical difficulties as aspatial surrogates are selected without input by the LESA committee, and implementation difficulties as they are eliminated from the process. If the LESA committee participates in the GIS development, their conviction about the validity of their model and their commitment to its implementation will be greatly enhanced (*3*).

The second aspect is the utility of using the GIS itself during LESA development. The LESA system requires an interaction between factors favoring development and those favoring agricultural preservation. These two competing aspects of LESA are most apparent by the two-fold nature of LESA (i.e., land evaluation and site assessment). During LESA development within a GIS, separate land evaluation and site assessment maps can be produced. If one considered each, or selected subsets of each of these maps, and then compared the maps as competing aspects of the system using a simple overlay function, the LESA developers might easily see the immediate impact of changes in these opposing factors. As a simple example, regions known to have very high LE scores could easily be compared to areas with low SA scores to illustrate the relationships between highly productive soils and locations that are known to be good for development based on non-soils factors. Intermediate values of LE and SA could be compared this way as well. With this knowledge, the weights of certain factors could be adjusted to accommodate competing demands. As a result, the GIS LESA could act as a tool for conflict resolution as suggested by Tomlin's (*17*) Orpheus project.

References

1. Berry, J.K., and C.D. Tomlin. 1980. *Map analysis package GIS mini-workshop.* Yale School of Forestry, New Haven, Connecticut.
2. Burrough, P.A. 1990. *Geographic Information Systems for Natural Resources Management.* Oxford University Press, New York, New York.
3. DeMers, M.N. 1988. *Policy implications of LESA factor and weight determination in Douglas County, Kansas.* Land Use Policy 5(4):408-418.
4. DeMers, M.N. 1989a. *The importance of site assessment in land use planning: A re-examination of the SCS LESA model.* Applied Geography 9:287-303.
5. DeMers, M.N. 1989b. *Knowledge acquisition for GIS automation of the SCS LESA model: An empirical study.* AI Applications in Natural Resource Management 3(4):12-22.
6. DeMers, M.N. 1990. *Adding robustness to linear planning models through simulation.* Technological Forecasting and Social Change 37(4):139-158.
7. DeMers, M.N. 1991. *Classification and purpose in automated vegetation maps.* Geographical Review 81(3):267-280.
8. DeMers, M.N. 1992. *Resolution tolerance in an automated forest land evaluation model.* Computers, Environment and Urban Systems 16(5):389-401.
9. Ferguson, C.A., R.L. Bowen, and M.A. Khan. 1991. *A statewide LESA system for Hawaii.* Journal of Soil and Water Conservation 46(4):263-267.
10. Ferguson, C.A., R.L. Bowen, M.A. Khan, and T. Liang. 1990. *An appraisal of the Hawaii land evaluation and site assessment (LESA) system.* University of Hawaii, College of Tropical Agriculture and Human Resources, Information Text Series, No. 035.
11. Luckey, D., and M.N. DeMers. 1986-87. *A comparative analysis of land evaluation systems for Douglas County.* Journal of Environmental Systems 16(4):259-277.
12. Marble, D.F., and D.L. Wilcox. 1991a. *Measure twice—cut once: A structured approach to successful GIS design and implementation.* Proceedings, 11th Annual Environmental Systems Research Institute User Conference, 585-596.
13. Marble, D.F., and D.L. Wilcox. 1991b. *The Marble-Wilcox model: A structured approach to effective geographic information systems design.* Proceedings, III Conferencia Latinoamericano Sobre Sistemas de Informacion Geografico. San Jose, Costa Rica.
14. Muehrcke, P.C. 1992. *Map use: Reading, analysis and interpretation.* 3rd ed. JP Publications, Madison, Wisconsin.
15. Perkal, J. 1965. Translated by W. Jackowski. *An attempt at objective generalization.* Michigan Inter-University Community of Mathematical Geographers. Discussion Paper 9.
16. U.S. Department of Agriculture-Soil Conservation Service. 1983. *National Agricultural Land Evaluation and Site Assessment Handbook.* Washington, D.C.
17. Tomlin, C.D. 1990. *The Orpheus land use allocation model.* Journal for Cross-disciplinary Exchange of Knowledge in the Geo-Sciences 3:10-13.
18. Williams, T.H. Lee. 1985. *Implementing LESA on a geographic information system—A case study.* Photogrammetric Engineering and Remote Sensing 51(12): 1923-1932.

Thanks are due to Wayne Channell, David Crecelius, and Gary Schall of the Ohio Department of Natural Resources for assistance and advice, and to Terry Wells, of the Ohio Department of Natural Resources, for producing the land evaluation map for Medina County. I also thank the reviewers for their many helpful suggestions.

SECTION IV

Conclusion: The Need for Improvement

Photo by Philip Maechling

Soil Conservation Service photo

16 LESA: The Next Decade

Nancy Bushwick Malloy
and Joyce Ann Pressley

very tradesperson, professional, and manager has a tool box for carrying out work. Which tools are used, how often they are used, and how effective they are in doing a job depends upon certain essentials. First, potential users must know that the tool exists and what it can do. This involves training. In order that the tool be applied regularly, users must have confidence in the tool, and a belief that it is a good instrument to use. This requires development of technical competence and political acceptance. Lastly, the effectiveness of the tool depends upon experience. Users must practice using the tool and evaluate the results.

LESA, a decision-making tool only slightly more than 10 years young, is no exception. The future of LESA in the next decade depends upon training, political acceptance, technical competence, and practice in using it.

Training: Knowledge about LESA

Many potential users of LESA do not even know that this decision-making tool exists. The federal Farmland Protection Policy Act (FPPA) of 1981 (*2*) gives the Soil Conservation Service (SCS) lead responsibility for assisting federal agencies in using LESA to carry out the intent of the act. However, the initiative to approach SCS (as interpreted by the Reagan and Bush administrations) is placed on federal units of government. Neither the SCS organization nor federal agency officials have been systematically briefed about the FPPA requirements and statutory requirement to use LESA nor trained in the LESA system. It was not until March 1992 that a small group of SCS officials were trained in LESA, which occurred at a workshop directly preceding the "First National LESA Conference" (hereafter referred to as the LESA conference).

More than 10 years ago, in February 1983, SCS made initial attempts to inform people about LESA by developing a LESA handbook (*5*) and circulating copies to its state offices and national technical centers. State offices were to distribute copies to area and field offices and to state and regional government officials and organizations. Field offices were authorized to distribute copies to other local offices of U.S. Department of Agriculture (USDA) agencies, soil and water conservation district officials, county planners, local government officials, and other potential members of local LESA committees. Obviously, this authorization was not acted upon, considering that a survey in 1987 determined that there were 20 local LESA systems in Illinois and only 26 local LESA systems in 18 other states. The SCS never sent a directive down its bureaucratic lines of command to implement the FPPA or LESA. Thus, a basic requirement for the wider use of LESA is for SCS to make the FPPA a priority policy.

SCS Support of the Revised LESA Handbook: A Training Guide. A first step in the effort to make LESA a priority is for SCS to vigorously support the distribution of the LESA handbook now under revision. To start that process, participants at the LESA conference made recommendations to SCS for revising the land evaluation (LE) and site assessment (SA) portions of the handbook (*5*). Table 1 summarizes their priority recommendations. All of the recommendations, in addition to experience with LESA over the last 10

Table 1. Summary of priority recommendations for the LESA handbook developed by participants of the LESA conference, March 28, 1992.

Land Evaluation Portion of the Handbook:

1. Policy Directions
   - Counties should be used as a target unit.
   - Land evaluation should be flexible for local conditions.
   - Multiple indicator crops and multiple land evaluation systems should be explored by individual units of government.
   - Local goals should be used for land evaluation.
2. Redundancy of Factors
   - Soil potential index and ratings may be sufficient for land evaluation ratings.
   - Factors used in land evaluation should be evaluated for intercorrelation.
3. Delivery - Technical Assistance
   - Different clients of LESA need different land evaluation formulations.
   - National clearinghouse is necessary as required by FPPA.
   - Data sources and consultants should be listed in the handbook.

Site Assessment Portion of the Handbook:

1. Things to Keep in the Handbook
   - Emphasis on local committee involvement.
   - Make site assessment flexible for a) needs, b) audiences, c) factors, and d) scoring.
   - Use a step-by-step approach to analysis.
   - Keep it simple.
   - Keep the focus to agriculture.
   - Adopt an implementing rule in order to put some teeth into FPPA and make the handbook more meaningful.
2. Things to Change in the Handbook
   - Provide better instruction for defining factors and scoring.
   - Make criteria clear, simple, and flexible.
   - Keep agricultural factors separate from development suitability factors.
   - Reduce the number of factors, and discuss the problems of intercorrelation.
   - Discuss the need for thorough field checks and benchmarking of scores.
   - Revise the packaging of the handbook to make it more user-friendly and the design more attractive.
   - Clarify the primary purpose of the system, and discuss flexibility of non-agricultural uses of the system.

years, are being considered in the revisions of the handbook. The handbook can function as an educational reference at training sessions and later as a "how-to" guide for local and state LESA committees.

As a second step, SCS should continue to push for the adoption of the final rule that implements the 1985 amendments to the FPPA (see Table 1). Once published in the *Federal Register*, the rule would legitimize LESA for other federal agencies. In order to ensure appropriate LESA training, leadership must come from the U.S. secretary of agriculture and the SCS chief.

SCS Leadership for Training. Several groups of people need to be trained: (1) SCS personnel who are responsible for implementing the federal Farmland Protection Policy Act; (2) federal agency personnel who are required by the FPPA to assess the impacts of their projects on the conversion of farmland to non-agricultural uses, defined in the act as prime, unique, or state or locally important; and, (3) groups who will be developing and applying LESA systems at the state and local levels.

SCS Training. SCS's top training priority should be to train its own field directors who will actually complete the LE portion of Form AD-1006 when requested by federal agencies, and who will help state and local governments design their own LESA systems. Because of budget restrictions, training should be targeted. There are several ways to decide who gets priority.

One option would be to evaluate readily available data that show the fastest growing counties and states, the counties that are economically dominated by agriculture, and the states and localities that have farmland protection policies in place. An overlay of such data can quickly reveal the locations of greatest need for LESA implementation, given high probabilities of farmland conversion and local support for decision-making tools.

For example, California and Florida are among the fastest growing states and both have farmland protection policies in place. According to the American Farmland Trust (*1*), Florida is losing more farm ground than any other state—150,000 acres a year, with about 800 new residents moving to the state each day. Nine of its metropolitan areas are ranked among the nation's 12 fastest growing. In California, AFT estimates that 100,000 acres of farmland go out of production every year. Nevertheless, according to the recent national survey of LESA systems (see chapter 4; hereafter referred to as the LESA survey), there are no LESA systems in California and only two in use in Florida and one under development. These two states are obvious targets for SCS training.

According to Ken Trott, the program administrator for California's farmland protection policy—the Williamson Act—no counties have developed local LESA systems for farmland protection, although two counties employ LESA-like models that use points and thresholds, and two counties (Stanislaus and Colusa) have proposed similar models. Tulare County is using a LESA-like system for local, rural valley planning. Santa Barbara County uses a system of points and thresholds for preparing impact statements under the California Environmental Quality Act. The California Department of Conservation has worked through the state SCS office in submitting a proposal to the national SCS office for developing five or six regional LESA systems that could be demonstrated locally (*3*). Thus, California is an ideal state for targeting training, since there is already state agency interest for introducing LESA to selected local communities. In addition, the California Department of Conservation has worked with the state legislature to recognize LESA as a system to be used under the California Environmental Quality Act for identifying sub-impacts on the environment, including on farmland. In this 1993 legislation is a provision that would set LESA as a model that state and local agencies could use (not mandatory) in determining environmental significance. The bill also authorizes the Department of Conservation to develop a state LESA model and to work with local agencies in providing assistance to develop local LESA models. Funding for this activity would depend on SCS allocations from the Resources Conservation Recovery Act.

Once SCS targets training to priority states and localities, it will become clear where to hold training workshops. Workshop sites could be planned according to the geographical concentration of need, or if more appropriate, one training workshop could be held in each of the four U.S. regions.

Federal Agency Training. The record of federal agency compliance with the FPPA thus far is very uneven (see chapter 3). SCS's data from FPPA annual reports (*6*) on the federal agencies requesting SCS assistance between fiscal years 1986 and 1991 showed that the Federal Highway Administration and the Farmers Home Administration made up 73 percent of the requests. Seven other agencies made up the next 20 percent, with an assortment of other federal agencies making up the final seven percent of requests. The annual average number of requests during this period was 2,051 but that number was heavily weighted by thirteen states. For perspective, only one state submitted more than 200 forms in fiscal year 1991 (Mississippi submitted 493 forms); five states (Louisiana, Minnesota, Missouri, Ohio, and Utah) submitted 100-199 forms, and seven states (Alabama, Arkansas, California, Iowa, North Carolina, South Carolina, and Virginia) submitted 51-99 forms. Half of the fifty states submitted 20 or fewer forms. Moreover, there is no evaluation of how many of the requests for land evaluation assistance made it to the next stage of site assessment, and to the final stage of consideration of mitigating action.

The targeting of training to federal officials serving at the state level could be expedited through a joint effort between SCS and the Rural Development Administration (RDA) of USDA, focusing on the priority states. RDA participates in multi-departmental support of state rural development councils, which convene federal agencies and other rural development interests to develop and implement strategies that efficiently and effectively use public and private resources for development in each state. A council is composed of state and regional executives from federal agencies along with local government leaders, state agency executives, private sector representatives, and officers of regional and local development organizations. Thus, the councils are an ideal forum for introducing LESA and the FPPA requirements to federal officials and for identifying follow-up needs for in-depth LESA training.

Training for LESA Committees. The third user group of LESA are persons involved in developing and applying LESA systems at the state and local levels. This group includes district conservationists, cooperative extension service staff, soil and water conservation district directors, farmers, planners, local agricultural officials, and other people concerned with land use, including the building industry, recreational users, and public interest and environmental groups. SCS could target information and training to the non-federal groups by simply arranging to offer a LESA workshop in conjunction with the annual meetings of professional groups such as, the National Association of Conservation Districts, the American Farm Bureau Federation, the American Planning Association, the American Society of Landscape Architects, and the Soil and Water Conservation Society.

Development of Technical Know-How and Political Acceptance: Confidence with the Tool and a Belief that it is a Good Instrument to Use

Like any apprentices, once people learn about a tool, they will regularly employ it if they develop technical competence and believe it is a good instrument for getting the job done. They will believe it is a good tool first if the master of the craft or profession believes it is. SCS, in the case of LESA, plays this role.

Because of the FPPA, SCS is in the official position for promoting the use of LESA. Publishing the FPPA final rule and placing a line-item in the SCS budget for training are first steps to increase LESA usage. Yet, for state SCS officials and other federal agency officials to accept LESA fully as a valid decision-making tool, the secretary of agriculture will need to send them a clear message emphasizing that LESA is a priority and a valuable tool for implementing the FPPA and the USDA land-use policy embodied in the Departmental Executive Order 9500-3.

LESA's future depends largely upon such USDA political leadership to bring about utilization of LESA by federal officials in fulfilling FPPA requirements. Others can also play this legitimizing role, for example the SCS district conservationists and state and local LESA committee members who have found LESA to be an effective tool. In fact, the LESA conference participants suggested that the new handbook include names, addresses, and telephone numbers of jurisdictions that have used LESA (see Table 1). This is a very good idea because these contacts are now LESA "masters" and can become a valuable source of information and expertise for people beginning to use LESA. SCS should consider them as potential training partners, providing LESA information and training in-state or to neighboring states.

An even greater challenge than developing political credibility of LESA systems at the national level is developing political acceptance of a specific LESA system by the public and officials at the state and local level. Most respondents to the LESA survey indicated that local LESA committees designed the SA portion of the LESA system. In designing a LESA system for use on a regular basis, local committees must become technically competent in (1) selecting site assessment factors, (2) clearly defining them, (3) determining the criteria for measuring and weighting the factors, and (4) applying the measurements and weights consistently in the field among alternate sites.

Issues of Redundancy in Developing Technical Competence. As shown in Table 1, participants at the LESA conference recommended as priorities in a revised handbook: (1) changes needed in the definitions and criteria of the SA factors, and (2) the need to reduce redundancy (see chapters 6, 8, and 9 for detailed discussion of redundancy). They recommended a reduction in the number of SA factors in the LESA to help eliminate redundancy if they are intercorrelated. However, a reduction in the number of SA factors may impinge upon two features of the system that they highly valued: flexibility in factor specification to adjust to local needs and the diversity of the SA factors.

LESA was designed to be applied consistently among sites within a community and flexibly by many communities. The SA portion gives LESA its flexibility. Through the construction of the SA portion, the LESA committee can incorporate the community's values concerning land use. Thus, the LESA tool does more than evaluate land use on a particular site and in relationship to surrounding land uses. It also reflects local values.

Since local public policy already reflects local values, the LESA committee should select and weight SA factors in accordance with those policies. For example, if proximity to open space is an important goal, that attribute could be selected as an SA factor and weighted heavily in relative importance to other values expressed in the farmland protection policy or other land-use policies. Localities with comprehensive or general plans should use the plans in designing the LESA. For areas without plans, LESA can be used to assist in designating land uses in the comprehensive or general plans.

The desire of LESA committees to emphasize local issues is a natural course of group dynamics in decision making, but can be a source of redundancy. If a LESA committee wants to emphasize certain goals or attributes in the LESA system, it is more efficient and effective to assign that goal or attribute as a single factor with a high weight or ranking rather than to use multiple factors that possibly measure the same aspect. Full or partial repetition of measurements—either within the SA portion or between the SA and LE portions—does not provide new information and is wasteful of staff time.

To illustrate this point, consider the 36 criteria grouped as seven factors in section 602.3(e) of the LESA handbook, which many local LESA committees have used in designing their systems (*5*). Factor 2 is "agricultural economic viability." Suggested criteria to measure this factor include the agricultural support system (infrastructure) and on-site investments (barns, storage, conservation measures, etc.). If data to measure both criteria are used in the scoring of factor 2, redundancy will occur unless the definition of infrastructure is explicitly restricted to agricultural infrastructure located in the community and excludes on-site infrastructure. The fixed capital components of on-site investments are often included in definitions of agricultural infrastructure (*7*).

For factor 4, "impacts of proposed use," suggested criteria include impact on historical areas, impact on cultural features, and impact on recreation and open spaces. For many communities, separate measurements of these criteria will prove redundant.

Thus, there are two sources of possible redundancy. The first is the tendency of LESA committees to use multiple factors to measure a local value. The other source of redundancy is the inclusion of criteria that use different data sources to measure essentially the same factor. It is essential that criteria be clearly defined and can be consistently measured in the field in order to foster acceptance of the tool by the implementing agency. This is of particular importance in those communities that view the application of a federal LESA system under a federal agency mandate as an intrusion into local land-use regulation.

It is highly recommended that the pilot phase of testing a local LESA system include investigation of redundancy problems. One method is to take the results and run a standard statistical test for intercorrelation. The results should be presented to the local committee for their consideration of revising relevant factors and changing the data used to measure them. The risks of basing revisions to a LESA system on an intercorrelation test are reduced community involvement in developing a LESA system and lack of public understanding about the technical basis for resultant decisions. However, the guidance that the test can provide to the LESA committee for creating a more effective system—and one that can be consistently applied—far outweigh such risks.

Evaluating LESA's Effectiveness: Summary and Conclusion

The first decade of LESA has provided opportunity for some evaluation of its effectiveness as a decision-making tool to help protect prime, unique, or locally important farmland. At minimum, 212 local and state jurisdictions in 31 states are former, current, or future agricultural LESA users. While most jurisdictions found LESA to be an effective tool for decision making to protect the best agricultural land from conversion, some localities did not (see chapter 4).

Ten years of experience has raised several issues pertaining to LESA's effectiveness that need to be addressed in the next decade. They are: (1) resolving issues of redundancy, flexibility, and local values in the development of LESA systems; (2) use of LESA for a variety of land-use planning and decision-making purposes; and (3) automation.

As discussed in chapters 6, 7, 8, 9, and above, experience with LESA has shown that there are methods available to resolve issues of redundancy, flexibility, and local values when designing and applying a LESA system. To prevent reduced effectiveness or use of LESA, future LESA training should address how to solve these issues.

LESA systems have been developed for evaluating impacts on the best farmland; for local, rural land-use planning (see chapter 12); and for forestry planning (see chapter 13). The LESA survey found these decision-making uses of LESA—for environmental impact assessments (60 jurisdictions), lending to property owners by a federal agency (40 jurisdictions), acquisition of land by a federal agency (27 jurisdictions), and zoning permit decisions (83 jurisdictions). Future users have two issues to consider.

One issue pertains to creating efficiencies in using LESA systems to protect the best farmland from conversion to other uses. Usually, a state or locality will employ several methods to implement its farmland protection policy. LESA systems have been shown to be an effective tool for implementing an individual method (for example zoning, land acquisition, purchase of development rights, designation of agriculture districts, impact assessment, etc.). As examples, the LESA survey found that 71 jurisdictions used their LESA systems for implementing purchase of development rights programs (see chapter 11), and that 41 jurisdictions used their LESA systems for designating agricultural districts. One future challenge may be to determine whether a single LESA system can serve as an effective tool for implementing a farmland protection policy that is based on various protection methods. Alternatively, the challenge to jurisdictions using multiple farmland protection methods may be to assure that multiple LESA systems (one system used for each farmland protection method) are consistent with one another in implementing the farmland protection policy.

The other issue concerns the use of non-agricultural factors in agricultural LESA systems. The LESA conference participants cautioned in their recommendations to revise the LESA handbook (see Table 1) so that a LESA system must have its primary purpose on agricultural productivity, and that agricultural criteria must be kept separate from development suitability criteria in the LESA rating system.

In regard to automation of LESA, SCS has developed a computer program for the LE portion, which is being run at Champaign, Illinois. The incorporation of LESA into geographical information systems (GIS) is more difficult but also holds promise (see chapters 13, 14, and 15). Much more work in automation and GIS incorporation is needed in order to realize the potential to make use of LESA systems more effective, efficient, and accurate.

In conclusion, the next decade of LESA may bring much more widespread use of this decision-making tool if adequate training is provided to potential users and if LESA systems gain greater political credibility and acceptance by potential users. The application of LESA systems may be enhanced by greater technical competence of those developing the systems and by technical progress made to automate LESA data and to incorporate LESA into geographical information systems.

References

1. American Farmland Trust Northeastern Office. 1992. *Northeastern Farmland Update* 4(2):6. Northampton, Massachusetts.
2. Office of the Federal Register, National Archives and Records Administration. 1990. *The Farmland Protection Policy Act,* part 658. Code of Federal Regulations-Agriculture, Parts 400 to 699, January 1, 1990. Washington, D.C.
3. Trott, K. 1992. Personal interview. California Department of Conservation, Sacramento, California.
4. Trott, K. 1993. Personal interview. California Department of Conservation, Sacramento, California.
5. U.S. Department of Agriculture-Soil Conservation Service. 1983. *National Land Evaluation and Site Assessment Handbook.* Washington, D.C.
6. U.S. Department of Agriculture-Soil Conservation Service, Conservation Planning Division. Unpublished. *FPPA Reports to Congress 1986-1991.* Washington, D.C.
7. Wharton, C. R. 1967. *The Infrastructure for Agricultural Growth.* In: Southworth, H. M., and B. F. Johnston (eds.) *Agricultural Development and Economic Growth.* Cornell University Press, Ithaca, NY. pp. 107-146.

Bibliography

Aradas, Steve, Ron Darden, Sue Pfluger, Lloyd Wright, and Warren Zitzmann. 1982. *Farmland Protection: Knowing What To Protect.* Planning Advisory Service Memo, American Planning Association, Chicago.

Bartelli, L.J., A.A. Hingebiel, J.V. Baird, and M.R. Huddleston. 1966. *Soil Surveys and Land Use Planning.* Soil Science Society of America, Madison, Wisconsin.

Beek, K.J. 1978. *Land Evaluation for Agricultural Development* (Publication 23). International Institute for Land Reclamation and Improvement, Wageningen, Netherlands.

Bouma, J. 1989. *Using Soil Survey Data for Quantitative Land Evaluation.* Advances in Soil Sciences 9: 177-213.

Bowen, Richard, Carol Ferguson, and Akram M. Khan. 1990. *Developing a Statewide Land Evaluation and Site Assessment (LESA) System for Hawaii Using GIS.* College of Tropical Agriculture and Human Resources, University of Hawaii at Manoa, Honolulu, Hawaii.

Breimer, R.F. 1986. *Guidelines for Soil Survey and Land Evaluation in Ecological Research.* UNESCO, Paris.

Coughlin, Robert E. 1991. *Formulating and Evaluating Agricultural Zoning Programs.* Journal of the American Planning Association 57(2): 183-192.

Coughlin, Robert E. 1992. *The Adoption and Stability of Agricultural Zoning in Lancaster County, Pennsylvania.* Research Report Series: No.15. Department of City and Regional Planning, University of Pennsylvania, Philadelphia.

Coughlin, Robert E., John C. Keene, J. Dixon Esseks, William Toner, and Lisa Rosenberger. 1980. *The Protection of Farmland: A Reference Guidebook for State and Local Government* (National Agricultural Lands Study Report). U.S. Government Printing Office, Washington, D.C.

Daniels, Thomas. 1990. *Using LESA in a Purchase of Development Rights Program.* Journal of Soil and Water Conservation 45(6): 617-621.

Daniels, Thomas L. 1991. *The Purchase of Development Rights: Preserving Agricultural Land and Open Space.* Journal of the American Planning Association 57 (4):421-431.

Davidson, Donald A., [ed.] 1986. *Land Evaluation.* Van Nostrand Reinhoid Co., New York.

DeMers, Michael N. 1988. *Policy Implications of LESA Factor and Weight Determinations in Douglas County, Kansas.* Land Use Policy 5(4): 408-418.

DeMers, Michael N. 1989. *Knowledge Acquisition for GIS Automation of the SCS LISA Model: An Empirical Study.* AI Applications in Natural Resource Management 3(4): 12-22.

DeMers, Michael N. 1992. *Resolution Tolerance in an Automated Forest Land Evaluation Model.* Computers, Environment, and Urban Systems 16:389-401.

Dent, David, and Anthony Young. 1981. *Soil Survey and Land Evaluation.* Allen and Unwin, London and Boston.

Dosdall, Nancy. 1985. *The Extent and Use of the Agricultural Land Evaluation and Site Assessment (LESA) System.* A master's thesis, Program in Environmental Science and Regional Planning, Washington State University, Pullman.

Dunford, Richard W. 1984. *Feds Drag Their Feet on Three-Year-Old Farmland Conversion Law.* Planning 50(12): 24-25.

Dunford, Richard W. 1984. *The Development and Current Status of Federal Farmland Retention Policy.* (Library of Congress Report No.85-21 ENR.) Congressional Research Service, Washington, D.C.

Dunford, Richard W., R.D. Roe, Frederick Steiner, W.R. Wagner, and Lloyd E. Wright. 1983. *Implementation of LESA in Whitman County, Washington.* Journal of Soil and Water Conservation 38(2): 87-89.

Ferguson, Carol A., Richard L. Bowen, and M. Akram Khan. 1991. *A Statewide LESA System, for Hawaii.* Journal of Soil and Water Conservation 46 (4): 263-267.

Ferguson, Carol A., and M. Akram Khan. 1992. *Protecting Farm Land Near Cities, Trade-offs with Affordable Housing in Hawaii.* Land Use Policy 9(4): 259-271.

Food and Agriculture Organization of the United Nations.1977. *A Framework for Land Evaluation* (Publication 22). International Institute for Land Reclamation and Improvement, Wageningen, Netherlands.

Freiberg, Nancy. 1991. *Forest Alert.* Planning 57 (9): 22-23.

Gordon, Steven I. and Gaybrielle E. Gordon. 1981. *The Accuracy of Soil Survey Information for Urban Land-Use Planning.* Journal of the American Planning Association 47(3): 301-312.

Harvey, L.R., A.E. House, K.K. Cybulski, and D.R. Walker. 1987. *Agricultural Land Values and Assessments in Selected Michigan Counties.* Agricultural Ecoromics Report. Michigan State University, Department of Agricultural Economics (503): 196.

Heimlich, Ralph E., [ed.] 1989. *Land Use Transition in Urbanizing Areas: Research and Information Needs.* Proceedings of a workshop sponsored by the Economic Research Service, U.S. Department of Agriculture, and The Farm Foundation. Washington, D.C. June 6-7,1988.

Hogan, Phil. 1993. *Agricultural Land Evaluation and Site Assessment: Status of California's County Programs.* USDA Soil Conservation Service, Dixon, California.

Hiemstra, Hal, and Nancy Bushwick, [eds.] 1989. *Plowing the Urban Fringe: An Assessment of Alternative Approaches to Farmland Preservation.* Florida Atlantic University, Florida International University, Joint Center for Environmental and Urban Problems, Monograph No.88-2. Fort Lauderdale, Florida.

Huddleston, J. Herbert, James R. Pease, William G. Forrest, Hugh J. Hickerson, and Russell W. Langridge. 1987. *Use of Agricultural Land Evaluation and Site Assessment in Linn County, Oregon, USA.* Environmental Management 11(3): 389-405.

Lee, Linda K. 1984. *Land Use and Soil Loss: A 1982 Update.* Journal of Soil and Water Conservation 37(3):133-136.

Lower Chattahoochee River Soil and Water Conservation District. 1984. *Agricultural Land Evaluation and Site Assessment (LESA) System.* Leesburg, Georgia.

Markert, Kenneth. 1984. *Application of the Land Evaluation and Site Assessment (LESA) System in Virginia.* A master's thesis, Department of Urban and Regional Planning, Virginia Polytechnic Institute and State University, Blacksburg.

McRae, Stuart G., and C.P. Burnham. 1981. *Land Evaluation.* Clarendon Press, Oxford, England; Oxford University Press, New York.

Miller, Fred P. 1978. *Soil Survey Under Pressure: The Maryland Experience.* Journal of Soil and Water Conservation 33(3):104-111.

Monroe County, New York. 1984. *Monroe County LESA. Land Evaluation Site Assessment System.* Rochester, New York.

Nellis, Lee, and John Nicholson. 1985. *Utah's Learning Approach to Farmland Protection.* Journal of Soil and Water Conservation 40(3):271.

Nellis, Lee, John K. Nicholson, Bruce Chesler, Kevin Krough, Brooks Robinson, and Kirsten Whetstone. 1984. *Utah Cropland Evaluation System: User's Guide.* Utah Department of Agriculture.

Pease, James R. 1990. *Land Use Designation in Rural Areas: An Oregon Case Study.* Journal of Soil and Water Conservation 45(5):524-528.

Pease, James R. 1991. *Farm Size and Land Use Policy: An Oregon Case Study.* Environmental Management 15(3):337-348.

Peters, James E. 1990. *Saving Farmland: How Well Have We Done?* Planning 56(9): 12-17.

Reganold, John P. and Michael J. Singer. 1978. *Defining Prime Agricultural Land in California* (Environmental Quality Series No.29). University of California, Institute of Government Affairs, Davis.

Reganold, John P. and Michael J. Singer. 1979. *Defining Prime Farmland by Three Land Classification Systems.* Journal of Soil and Water Conservation 34(4):172-176.

Singer, Michael J. 1986. *The USDA Land Capability Classification and Storie Index Rating: A Comparison.* Land Evaluation. D.A. Davidson, [ed.] Van Nostrand Reinhold Co., New York. pp 280-284.

Soil Conservation Service. 1975. *National Soils Handbook.* U.S. Department of Agriculture.

Stamm, Todd, Ron Gill, and Kari Page. 1987. *Agricultural Land Evaluation and Site Assessment in Latah County, Idaho, U.S.A.* Environmental Management 11(3):379-388.

Steiner, Frederick R. 1987. *Agricultural Land Evaluation and Site Assessment: An Introduction.* Environmental Management 11(3): 375-377.

Steiner, Frederick, J.H.Huddleston, James R. Pease, Todd Stamm, and Melanie Tyler. 1984. *Adapting the Land Evaluation and Site Assessment (LESA) System in the Pacific Northwest* (WRDC 26). Western Rural Development Center, Corvallis, Oregon.

Steiner, Frederick, Richard Dunford, and Nancy Dosdall. 1987. *The Use of the Agricultural Land Evaluation and Site Assessment System in the United States.* Landscape and Urban Planning 14:183-199.

Steiner, Frederick, James R. Pease, Robert E. Coughlin, John C. Leach, Joyce Anne Pressley, Adam P. Sussman, and Christine Shaw. 1991. *Agricultural Land Evaluation and Site Assessment: Status of State and Local Programs.* Herberger Center, College of Architecture and Environmental Design, Arizona State University, Tempe.

Tyler, Melanie, Frederick Steiner, Dennis Roe, and Liese Hunter. 1987. *The Use of the Agricultural Land Evaluation and Site Assessment System in Whitman County, Washington.* Environmental Management 11(3):407-412.

U.S. Department of Agriculture-Soil Conservation Service. 1983. *National Agricultural Land Evaluation and Site Assessment Handbook.* Washington, D.C.

U.S. Department of Agriculture-Soil Conservation Service. 1984. *Farmland Protection Policy, Final Rule.* Federal Register 49 (130): 27716-27727.

Van Horn, T.G., G.C. Steinhardt, and J.E. Yahner.1989. *Evaluating the Consistency of Results for the Agricultural Land Evaluation and Site Assessment (LESA) System.* Journal of Soil and Water Conservation 44(6): 615-620.

Ward, Robert M. 1991. *The U.S. Farmland Protection Policy Act, Another Case of Benign Neglect.* Land Use Policy 8 (1): 63-68.

Williams, T.H. Lee.1985. *Implementing LESA on a Geographic Information System—A Case Study.* Photogrammetric Engineering and Remote Sensing 51(12): 1923-1932.

Wright, Lloyd E. 1983. *LESA Shows Which Lands Should Stay in Farms (Clarke County, Virginia, and McHenry County, Illinois, as examples).* Yearbook of Agriculture. U.S. Department of Agriculture, Washington D.C., pp. 508-516.

Wright, Lloyd E. 1984. *Agricultural Land Evaluation and Site Assessment (LESA): A New Agricultural Land Protection Tool in the U.S.A.* Soil Survey and Land Evaluation 4(2).

Wright, Lloyd E., Warren Zitzmann, Keith Young, and Richard Googins. 1983. *LESA—Agricultural Land Evaluation and Site Assessment.* Journal of Soil and Water Conservation 38(2):82-86.

Contributors

Richard L. Bowen is professor and chair of the Department of Agricultural and Resource Economics at the University of Hawaii. He received a B.S. in economics from Nebraska Wesleyan University, a M.A. in economics from Syracuse University, and his Ph.D. in economics from Colorado State University. He teaches and conducts research and extension programs on agricultural and natural resource policy issues. He has helped prepare legislation and testified before the Hawaii legislature on LESA and has coauthored several publications on Hawaii's LESA system.

Galen Bridge is retired from the U.S. Department of Agriculture, Soil Conservation Service. He has held numerous positions in the USDA in Washington, D.C., including acting chief of SCS, deputy chief for programs, and deputy chief for administration. In addition, he worked as a state conservationist with the Soil Conservation Service in Spokane, Washington; Denver, Colorado; Portland, Oregon; and as an agricultural engineer in Orono, Maine. He is a native of Maine, and received a B.S. in agricultural engineering from the University of Maine, and a Master of Public Administration from the University of Virginia.

Robert E. Coughlin is senior fellow with the Department of City and Regional Planning, University of Pennsylvania, Philadelphia, and a partner in the planning and consulting firm of Coughlin, Keene, and Associates. He is the principal author of *The Protection of Farmland: A Reference Guidebook for State and Local Governments* (National Agricultural Lands Study, 1981), and *Guiding Growth: A Planning and Growth Management Handbook for Pennsylvania Municipalities* (Pennsylvania Environmental Council, 1991). He received his Ph.D. from the University of Pennsylvania, Master of City Planning from the Massachusetts Institute of Technology, and his A.B. from Harvard College.

Thomas L. Daniels is director of the Lancaster County Agricultural Preserve Board in Pennsylvania. Previously, he taught at Kansas State University and Iowa State University. Dr. Daniels is the coauthor of *Rural Planning and Development in the United States* (Guilford Press, 1989), and *The Small Town Handbook* (Planners Press, 1988). He received his Ph.D. in agricultural economics from Oregon State University, a M.S. from Newcastle-Upon-Tyne, and an B.A. from Harvard College.

Michael N. DeMers is an assistant professor of geography at New Mexico State University. Previously, he was on the faculty of Ohio State University. He received his bachelor's and master's degrees from the University of North Dakota and his Ph.D. from the University of Kansas. His dissertation involved the development of knowledge acquisition strategies for expert geographic information system development of the LESA model. His current research efforts involve the development of GIS models for range, forest, and agricultural land evaluation strategies; ecosystems and habitat assessment and modeling; and floral and faunal mapping. He is also participating in a multidisciplinary research project involving the experimentation and prototyping of GIS databases and analysis techniques to examine spatio-temporal land cover change in central Ohio landscapes and the impacts of these changes on plant and animal species.

Carol A. Ferguson is associate professor in the Department of Agricultural and Resource Economics at the University of Hawaii. She teaches and conducts research on agricultural and natural resource policy issues. Her research on LESA systems includes analyses of Hawaii's GIS data and simulation of agricultural land protection policies. She received a B.A. in economics from Stanford University and a M.S. and Ph.D. in agricultural economics from Cornell University.

Ralph Grossi has served as the president of American Farmland Trust since 1985. AFT is a national nonprofit organization whose mission is to stop the loss of productive farmland and to promote farming practices that lead to a healthy environment. Former President George Bush presented AFT with the 1991 President's Environment and Conservation Challenge Award. Mr. Grossi, a third generation Marin County, California, farmer, graduated from California Polytechnic State University and has been managing partner of Marindale Ranch, a family partnership of registered Holstein dairy cattle and Black Angus specialty beef. Mr. Grossi was a founder and chairman of the Marin Agricultural Land Trust, which protects Marin County agricultural land by acquisition of conservation easements. From 1977 to 1979 he was a member of the California Agricultural Water Problems Advisory Committee; 1979 to 1981, president of Marin County Farm Bureau; and from 1989 until he became president, a member of the board of directors of American Farmland Trust.

Christopher C. Hamilton is the director of planning at the Northeastern Vermont Development Association, the regional planning commission for the Northeast Kingdom of Vermont. He has worked at the local level with several LESA studies and was the project manager for the Granby FLESA. Mr. Hamilton assists local municipalities write land-use plans and complete implementation strategies. He earned a master's degree in natural resources management, planning, and policy from the University of Michigan.

J. Herbert Huddleston is a professor of soil science and extension soils specialist, Department of Crop and Soil Science, Oregon State University. He has conducted research and worked with local and state governments on LESA and other farmland projects since 1980. He has published several articles on soil productivity ratings, LESA, and other related topics. He received his B.S. and M.S. from Cornell University and his Ph.D. from Iowa State University.

John C. Leach received his Master of Environmental Planning from Arizona State University (ASU) in December 1992 and now works as an environmental planner for Rumpke Waste Systems in Cincinnati. From 1975 to 1990, he was a journalist with the *Cincinnati Enquirer*, the *Cincinnati Post*, and other newspapers. With the *Enquirer*, he supervised ten copy editors as they edited stories and wrote headlines for five daily editions of the newspaper. In addition to serving as a research assistant at ASU, he has worked for the City of Phoenix Planning Department. He earned his bachelor's degree in political science from Miami University.

Patrick Leahy is a U.S. Senator representing Vermont. He is chairman of the Senate Agriculture, Nutrition, and Forestry Committee. He also serves on the Appropriations and Judiciary Committees. He has a B.A. from St. Michael's College and a J.D. from Georgetown University.

Nancy Bushwick Malloy is associate for leadership development at the National Center for Food and Agricultural Policy in Washington D.C. Formerly, she was director of the Farmland Project at the National Association of State Department of Agriculture Research Foundation, where she monitored policy developments of farmland protection including LESA and soil and water conservation at the federal, state, local, and international levels. From 1978 to 1980, she was a policy analyst at the Council on Environmental Quality, Executive Office of the President, and was detailed as the public participation coordinator of the National Agricultural Lands Study. She is co-editor of *Plowing the Urban Fringe: An Assessment of Alternative Approaches to Farmland Preservation* (Florida Atlantic University-Florida International University, Joint Center for Environmental and Urban Problems, 1989). Ms. Bushwick Malloy received her M.S. in land resources and her B.S. in human ecology from the University of Wisconsin, Madison.

Lee Nellis is currently a consulting planner in Pocatello, Idaho. Mr. Nellis earned a B.A. from the University of Wyoming and an M.A. from the University of Wisconsin, Madison. In addition to consulting with rural communities throughout the West, he has experience as a staff planner with rural Wyoming counties and an assistant professor at Utah State University and Eastern Washington University. He was named Planner of the Year by Western Planning Resources in 1990.

Lyssa Papazian is senior historic preservation specialist at the Office of New Jersey Heritage. She has been assistant manager of a dairy farm and has taught dairy science at the Putney School in Vermont. She earned her M.S. in historic preservation at the University of Pennsylvania and her B.A. at Brown University.

James R. Pease is professor of resource geography and extension land resource management specialist, Department of Geosciences, Oregon State University. He has been involved in farmland protection since the early 1970s and has published numerous papers and reports on land use and agriculture. He has worked on several LESA and other land-use projects with local and state government in Oregon as well as on federal projects. He received his M.S. and Ph.D. in resource planning from the School of Natural Resources, University of Massachusetts.

Joyce Ann Pressley joined the University of Illinois faculty as a lecturer in 1991, and is completing her Ph.D. dissertation in city and regional planning at the University of Pennsylvania. She holds two Master of Arts, one in planning theory and the other in South Asia regional studies, and her Bachelor of Arts in a double major of economics and South Asia regional studies from the University of Pennsylvania. Her work on LESA at that institution was on a national inventory. Under the direction of Robert Coughlin, she organized the collection of LESA information from 17 eastern states. In addition to teaching, Ms. Pressley has over the past fifteen years worked for private planning research groups, an international development planning firm, and on several publications.

James D. Riggle is a research fellow with the Institute of Public Policy, George Mason University. He was director of field operations for American Farmland Trust from 1983 to 1993. Prior to joining AFT, Mr. Riggle worked as a management operations analyst for the Illinois Department of Agriculture from 1980 through 1983, responsible for developing and implementing Illinois' farmland protection program. During 1979 and 1980, Mr. Riggle was a researcher, author, and editor for the National Agricultural Lands Study, which documented the nationwide extent and effects of farmland conversion. Mr. Riggle's education includes a B.A. in political science and a Master of Public Administration, both with honors, from Northern Illinois University, DeKalb. He is currently a candidate for a Ph.D. in Public Policy at George Mason University.

Vernon Shanholtz is an associate professor with the Department of Agricultural Engineering at Virginia Polytechnic Institute and State University, Blacksburg. He received his B.S. and his M.S. in agricultural engineering from West Virginia University and a Ph.D. in civil engineering from Virginia Tech. Dr. Shanholtz has more than 30 years experience in small watershed hydrology, hydrologic monitoring, computer-based modeling, and information support systems. Since 1985 he has been the project director for the Virginia Geographic Information System (VirGIS), which was initiated to create a digital geographic database for Virginia's Chesapeake Bay drainage basin, and to develop procedures for identifying and ranking agricultural land areas based on their non-point source pollution potential. A spin-off from the VirGIS project has been the development of the highly functional PC-based GIS package—PC-VirGIS. He is also director of the Information Support Systems Laboratory, which was organized in 1985 to conduct research on the use of geoprocessing techniques, modeling/simulation in the planning and/or management of natural resources, and additional applications of the existing database.

Frederick R. Steiner is professor and director of the School of Planning and Landscape Architecture, Arizona State University, Tempe. He has cooperated with the U.S. Soil Conservation Service with the development and analysis of LESA since 1981. He is the author of *The Living Landscape* (McGraw-Hill, 1991) and *Soil Conservation in the United States* (Johns Hopkins, 1990). Professor Steiner received his Ph.D., M.A., and Master of Regional Planning degrees from the University of Pennsylvania and Master of Community Planning and B.S. degrees from the University of Cincinnati.

Adam P. Sussman received his M.S. degree in resource geography, Department of Geosciences, Oregon State University, in June 1992. He worked as a graduate research assistant on several phases of the USDA SCS funded LESA project. He is currently employed as a water resources planner, Department of Water Resources, State of Oregon.

Gene Yagow is a research associate working in the Information Support Systems Laboratory, Department of Agricultural Engineering, at Virginia Polytechnic Institute and State University. He received a B.S. in agriculture and a B.S. in agricultural engineering from the University of Illinois in 1969 and an M.S. in agricultural engineering from Virginia Tech in 1983. Prior to his work at Virginia Tech, he served with the Virginia Division of Soil and Water Conservation as a technical advisor and project officer for agricultural non-point source pollution control programs. Throughout his employment at the university and in state government, he has been involved with the development and modeling applications of geographic information systems for agricultural non-point source pollution targeting and land-use planning. He is currently working with the Institute of Remote Sensing Application in China to develop a knowledge-based agricultural land-use planning tool, the Land Resource Decision Support System.

Lloyd E. Wright is the director of the Basin and Area Planning Division in the U.S. Department of Agriculture, Soil Conservation Service, Conservation Planning Division. He is the principal author and designer of the LESA system. Prior to moving to his present position, he completed an assignment with the State of New York, Department of Agriculture and Markets, where he developed a land evaluation system that is now being used for agricultural tax assessment in New York. Other positions with SCS include state resource conservationist, and area, district, and soil conservationist. He has a B.S. degree in agronomy from Virginia State University and a M.S. degree in human resource management from the State University of New York at Binghamton.

Index